DATE DUE

JY 00			

DEMCO 38-296

The Horn of Africa

INTERNATIONAL LIBRARY OF AFRICAN STUDIES

The Horn of Africa:
State politics and international relations

PETER WOODWARD

Tauris Academic Studies
I.B.Tauris Publishers
LONDON · NEW YORK

Published in 1996 by Tauris Academic Studies
an imprint of I.B.Tauris & Co Ltd
45 Bloomsbury Square, London WC1A 2HY
175 Fifth Avenue, New York NY 10010

In the United States of America and in Canada
distributed by St Martin's Press
175 Fifth Avenue, New York NY 10010

A full CIP record for this book is available from the British
Library

A full CIP record for this book is available from the Library of
Congress

ISBN 1 85043 741 6

Library of Congress catalog card number 94–60176

Set in Monotype Ehrhardt by Ewan Smith, London
Printed and bound in Great Britain by WBC Ltd,
Bridgend, Mid Glamorgan

Contents

Acknowledgements

My thanks to Lester Crook of I.B.Tauris for encouraging the writing of this introduction to the politics and international relations of the Horn of Africa: he showed great patience as it dragged on beyond its initial timetable. Thanks as well to the many friends and colleagues with whom I have been involved in seminars, conferences and discussions about the Horn. I deeply regret the premature death in 1995 of two old friends who taught me much about the region, Ahmed Karadawi and Khalid el-Kid. Special thanks are due to the Rockefeller Foundation for the invitation to spend a most memorable and valuable period at the Bellagio Center, Italy. Ann Cade and Marjorie McNamara helped with my incompetence on the word processor; and my wife Carol showed her customary forbearance.

Peter Woodward
Reading, 1995

Abbreviations

CARE	CARE International
CART	Combined Agency Relief Team
COPWE	Commission for Organizing the Party of the Working People of Ethiopia
DFSS	Democratic Front for the Salvation of Somalia
DUP	Democratic Unionist Party
ECOWAS	Economic Community of West African States
ELF	Eritrean Liberation Front
ELF-PLF	Eritrean Liberation Front-People's Liberation Forces
EPLF	Eritrean People's Liberation Front
EPRDF	Ethiopian People's Revolutionary Democratic Front
EPRP	Ethiopian People's Revolutionary Party
ERA	Eritrean Relief Association
FAO	Food and Agriculture Organization
FLN	Front de Libération National
FRUD	Front pour la Restauration de l'Unité et la Démocratie
GONGO	government-organized non-governmental organization
GUNT	Government of National Unity
ICRC	International Committee of the Red Cross
IFAD	International Fund for Agricultural Development
IGADD	Inter-Governmental Authority on Drought and Development
IMF	International Monetary Fund
MEISON	All Ethiopia Socialist Movement
NDA	National Democratic Alliance
NFD	Northern Frontier District
NGO	non-governmental organization
NIF	National Islamic Front
NUP	National Union Party
OAU	Organization of African Unity
OLF	Oromo Liberation Front
OLS	Operation Lifeline Sudan
ONLF	Ogaden National Liberation Front
OPEC	Organization of Petroleum Exporting Countries
PA	Peasant Association

PDF	People's Defence Force
PDO	People's Democratic Organization
PDP	People's Democratic Party
PDRY	People's Democratic Republic of Yemen
PFDJ	People's Front for Democracy and Justice
PLO	Palestine Liberation Organization
PMAC	Provisional Military Administrative Council (Dergue)
POMOA	Provisional Office of Mass Organization
RCC	Revolutionary Command Council
REST	Relief Society of Tigre
RRC	Relief and Rehabilitation Commission
SALT	Strategic Arms Limitation Talks
SACDNU	Sudan African Closed District National Union
SANU	Sudan African National Union
SCF	Save the Children Fund
SDA	Somali Democratic Alliance
SDM	Somali Democratic Movement
SNM	Somali National Movement
SPLA/SPLM	Sudan People's Liberation Army/Movement
SPM	Somali Patriotic Movement
SRC	Supreme Revolutionary Council
SRRA	Sudan Relief and Rehabilitation Association
SRSP	Somali Revolutionary Socialist Party
SSDF	Somali Salvation Democratic Front
SSU	Sudan Socialist Union
SYL	Somali Youth League
TGE	Transitional Government of Ethiopia
TMC	Transitional Military Council
TPLF	Tigrean People's Liberation Front
UN	United Nations
UNHCR	United Nations High Commissioner for Refugees
Unicef	United Nations (International) Children's (Emergency) Fund
UNITAF	United Nations Task Force
UNOSOM	United Nations Operation in Somalia
UNSERO	United Nations Sudan Emergency Relief Office
USC	United Somali Congress
USF	United Somali Front
WFP	World Food Programme
WPE	Workers' Party of Ethiopia
WSLF	Western Somali Liberation Front

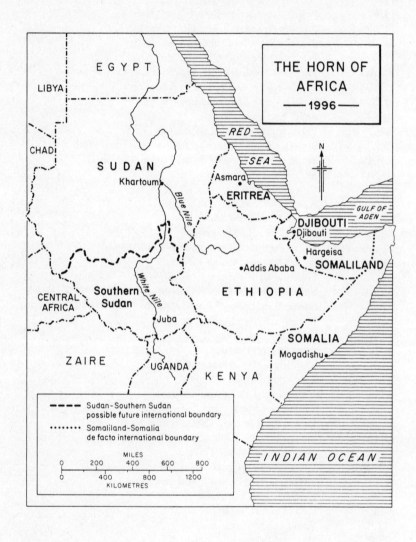

THE HORN OF
AFRICA
— 1996 —

EGYPT

LIBYA

CHAD

RED

SEA

SUDAN

Khartoum

Asmara

ERITREA

N

GULF OF
ADEN

DJIBOUTI

Djibouti

Hargeisa

SOMALILAND

Blue Nile

CENTRAL
AFRICA

Southern
Sudan

White Nile

Addis Ababa

ETHIOPIA

Juba

ZAIRE

UGANDA

KENYA

SOMALIA

Mogadishu

- - - - Sudan-Southern Sudan
possible future international boundary
· · · · Somaliland-Somalia
de facto international boundary

MILES
0   200   400   600   800
0   400   800   1200
KILOMETRES

INDIAN OCEAN

Introduction

In recent years there has been a spate of books on the Horn of Africa, as well as numerous papers, articles and conferences. These have been not only historical in character but have also sought to offer solutions to the problems of the Horn.[1] Yet at the time of completing this book in 1995 the 'problems' of the Horn seem as complex and 'unresolved' as ever, despite the independence of Eritrea and greater peace in Ethiopia.

The 'Horn of Africa' is not an indigenous term; it springs from a glance at a map rather than any perception of inhabitants of that area of north-east Africa. Indeed, there is no agreement on exactly what it is; the concept of the Horn has grown from an early concern about Somalia's relations with Ethiopia, to take in all of the latter's problems, and then increasingly to include Sudan as well. The reason for this expansion lies primarily in the perception that there seems to be a history of common problems in the region: disputes over borders both between states and within them; widespread and prolonged civil war threatening not only governments but the survival of states themselves; economic regression that appears to owe something at least to domestic policy failure, as well as the vagaries of the world economy and environmental decay; in addition to the famines that seemed to grow in scale and regularity. (Indeed, in assessing food shortages and environmental degradation in Africa the term 'greater Horn' has been used to include neighbouring East African states threatened with food deficits as well.)

In addition to the list of inflictions experienced by the peoples of the three adjacent countries – Somalia, Ethiopia and Sudan – there is a sense that there are connections between their plights, and that these connections are not just confined to the Horn but reflect both regional and wider international influences that have in various ways contributed to the situation. As Otto Hintze remarked at the start of the century, in examining the politics of states one must also consider 'The external ordering of states – their position relative to one another, and their overall position in the world'.[2] Much of Africa has been experiencing major problems, politically, economically and socially, but few other regions of the continent appear as devastated as these three adjacent countries, and it appears to be more than coincidence. In the last decade certain states in southern Africa have been similarly blighted by violence and famine in which over and beyond the indigenous seeds of conflict have lain regional issues, especially the attempted defence of racist rule in South Africa, as well as superpower rivalry. The combination of indigenous conflicts, ambitions of a regional character and superpower rivalry has proved a particularly lethal cocktail in Africa, and one that has left a complex and bitter aftermath in the context of the post-Cold War world.

The connections between intra-state, regional and wider international issues themselves are not simply of any one particular character, but they do appear to have multiplied with the passing of time. The first 'problem of the Horn' as a region concerned the international boundaries bequeathed by the departing imperial powers, especially with regard to Somalia's irredentist claim to Ethiopia. That was a dispute between two states over the legitimate border between them and was taken up vociferously by Somalia from its independence in 1960, leading on eventually to a major war in 1977–78 as Somalia's troops attacked Ethiopia. While that was the only major international dispute among the states of the Horn it came to be perceived as part of a wider question of borders and societies. Somalia's actions arose from its claim that the disputed territories are inhabited by Somali peoples; elsewhere in the Horn other peoples disputed the legitimacy of the states and governments that ruled them. At approximately the same time as the Somalis were first making their claim, civil war was breaking out in the area of Eritrea in northern Ethiopia. The war there was to grow in the 1970s, particularly following the overthrow of the Emperor Haile Selassie, and was to be accompanied by other conflicts within Ethiopia, most notably in Tigre. At the same time as civil war was starting in Eritrea in the 1960s, another conflict was opening in the southern Sudan, and though it ended by negotiation in 1972, a new and more virulent war broke out in the same region eleven years later in 1983. Somalia was spared outright civil war until much later but by the 1980s it too was experiencing rising conflict, and from 1988 it intensified to the point at which insurgents eventually overthrew the longstanding president, Mohamed Siad Barre, in 1991. The civil wars of the three countries not only put them into a similar category, thus contributing to the perception of an unstable region, it also appeared that there were links between them. Partly on a tit-for-tat basis, it appeared that Ethiopia and Sudan were at least acquiescing in, and sometimes abetting, cross-border activities of the respective guerrilla forces their governments were facing; and in the 1980s a similar situation developed with Ethiopia and Somalia.

The Horn also began to distinguish itself as a region of famine. Behind famine lay not only civil war, but deep economic problems and issues. However, it was inevitably the identification of the phenomenon of famine, and especially its visual images of apparent passive helplessness in suffering, that gripped the headlines. Televized images of famine in northern Ethiopia first flashed around the world in 1973. In 1984–85 famine in northern Ethiopia and northern Sudan once more hit the headlines, and the world responded to Bob Geldof's dramatic invitation to run to raise money. Disasters of no lesser scale followed in subsequent years, though international perception and response was not again to be so dramatic until the intervention in Somalia in 1992. Famine was both a contributor to political instability and a reflection of it: it helped bring down Haile Selassie in Ethiopia in 1974; it contributed similarly to the overthrow of Ga'afar el-Nimeiri in Sudan in 1985; and it was intensified by the struggle to overthrow Siad Barre in Somalia in 1991. Together with civil war it also generated flows of refugees from one country into another, sometimes in opposite directions at the same time: people from Eritrea and Tigre sought refuge in eastern Sudan, while further south on the same border southern Sudanese were fleeing from war and famine into Ethiopia. In the short term famine turned into a race against time and the elements to mobilize international donors and relief agencies to staunch the mounting death tolls. In the long term it presented challenges not only to improve famine predictions and relief, but also to the whole character of domestic and international politics and economics in which such disasters were possible.

While donor governments, primarily from the West, sought to appear as rescuers of benighted Africa, an awareness of a further dimension of regional consciousness was also growing. The Horn was an area of significant international rivalry. It all started quietly enough with American interest in the strategic position of Ethiopia, but later escalated into a broader rivalry along the south-eastern flank of the oil-producing Middle East, as well as a major international waterway, the Red Sea. The Soviet Union was welcomed in Sudan in 1969, only to be hurriedly ejected two years later, but then appeared to dig in much more firmly in Somalia in the 1970s. Following the Ethiopian revolution of 1974 there unfolded a dramatic tango of the superpowers, as a result of the catalyst of the Somali–Ethiopian war of 1977–78. The outcome was a change of partners that saw Ethiopia embrace the Soviet Union, while United States involvement in Somalia and Sudan rose significantly. At the same time there was a realization that the various civil wars in particular were also involving a number of Middle East countries, conservative and 'radical', and including Israel. The question behind all these outside interventions was the contribution they were making to the cycle of insurgent guerrillas and repressive governments which itself was contributing to the economic decay and ultimate human degradation of famine. (Of course the 'Middle East' was not just an 'external' dimension of the Horn: Sudan was much shaped by the coming of Arabs and Islam into the north, while Islam was a major theme in the history of Ethiopia (with Coptic Christianity) and Somalia. It suggested in all a kind of Afro-Middle Eastern sub-region.) By the late twentieth century the Horn was becoming a sub-region defined not only by its historical position, but by the scale and intensity of its problems; not just coincidentally located in neighbouring countries but in various ways inter-connected. Conversely, moves to improve the situation would also require the tackling of problems at a regional as well as a state level.

While the problems briefly outlined above constitute the broad agenda for this book there are still issues of outline and approach. Though it is common to see Africa's problems as largely contemporary, few writers would doubt that there is an historical legacy.[3] Independence in the cases of Sudan in 1956 and Somalia in 1960, or the revolution that brought down Haile Selassie in 1974, were not wholly new starts. It has been common to refer back to the period of imperialism, but while that had a great impact, the preceding history of the region requires review as well. Largely for reasons of geography the Horn has had an important and relatively well-charted history, and in particular state formation and decay partly reflect ancient patterns and processes of change. Thus the opening chapter reviews salient background including pre-imperial history as well as the impact of Western imperialism on the Horn.

At the same time as deep roots to some of the problems of the Horn, the recent experiences of political instability, conflict and civil war, and even state collapse, have also to be assessed in their own contemporary terms. The immediate origins lie within the individual states as recognized by the international community, and thus the contemporary developments need to be assessed individually. However, as already indicated, the positions of the three countries with regard to each other are a significant dimension of the conflicts within each of the individual states, and thus a chapter is devoted to consideration of the character and importance of neighbour-state relations and cross-border movements. Neighbour relations, however, are only one dimension of international politics. The strategic position of the Horn with regard to the Red Sea, the Arabian Sea, the Indian Ocean and the

Gulf has long meant that the waters surrounding it have been less a barrier than a link: less an isolating factor than a communications route both into and out of the Horn. The international actors with an interest in the Horn have been both regional powers and superpowers. Superpowers are the more obvious and more recorded of these foreign influences, but regional powers also have their own motives for involvement, as well as sometimes acting as proxies for superpowers.

Popular attention to the Horn has been galvanized by the worst of all disasters, famine, and while the experiences underlying famine vary from country to country, there also seem to be two themes in common – war and drought. Thus while the former is covered mainly within the political consideration of each country, the latter will be discussed as a regional phenomenon, together with the relief efforts and longer-term development policies attempted.

This book does not attempt to offer an overall theory of the problems of the Horn, an ambitious exercise that has already been attempted. John Markakis' pioneering comparative study focused upon the domestic socio-political causes of conflict in the three states centring on class analysis. He emphasized in particular the growth of conflicts between new Westernized ruling classes and exploited or neglected pastoralists, with the former retreating into forms of 'garrison socialism' against which the oppressed peoples responded with growing civil wars.[4] Instead, the approach attempted here is to present the three states as having significantly different rather than similar historical experiences and political structures. But there are comparisons to be made that will help to illuminate both the similarities and contrasts in their political and military conflicts, as well as state decay, while their own interaction, coupled with the growing regionalism within which the international political community has set the Horn, has also impinged significantly on developments.

State collapse has risen as a theme in the study of a number of states in Africa in particular. As a theme it has grown under a variety of labels. Early functionalist views of political development brought the corollary from some more cautious writers of possible dysfunctional tendencies.[5] Later, where civil war in particular broke out, came the suggestion of 'broken-backed states'. While in the 1980s the distinction was drawn in the African context, above all between the 'juridical' state, recognized internationally, and the 'empirical' reality which fell well short of it.[6] The latter point has clear links to Migdal's later discussion of strong and weak states in the Third World, identifying the former as states capable of controlling societies, and the latter with the effective resistance of numerous 'weblike' social organizations.[7] (Migdal also stresses the significance of the international environment in the rise of the phenomenon of states in various regions of the world.) By the 1990s state collapse was looking increasingly like the obverse of state-building of the kind associated so particularly with the rise of the nation-state in Western Europe in the nineteenth century and transmitted by various means internationally as a modern independent state. Such a state enjoys sovereignty over its recognized territory. It is able to control its borders, regulating movements of peoples and goods across them. Within its borders it has a virtual monopoly of coercive powers, and with growing legitimacy. It is able to make policy and implement it through the machinery of the state. It has the capacity to extract the resources to perpetuate the functioning of the state, and at the same time promotes the necessary economic capacity in society to ensure the symbiotic continuation of both state and society. The latter goal is facilitated by opportunities for popular accountability of the state and participation therein by the populace, most commonly through some form of representative government, frequently liberal democracy. The liberal element is in turn strengthened by the recognition and promotion of civil society, broadly understood as social organizations that link and represent the people to the state, but which do not in themselves seek to acquire direct political power. Finally, states exist by dint of their international recognition and relations with other states and international organizations. State collapse, then, has focused increasingly on the partial or total failure of one or more of these characteristics of the model state.[8]

Yet collapse, to whatever extent and for whatever reasons, may be a reminder of the artificiality and newness of a virtually worldwide set of state structures, related to each other in a dynamic system of international relations. While there have been states of various kinds for millennia, the division of the whole of the occupied territory of the globe into an internationally recognized world of states is very new. Empires, states and stateless societies had existed for a long time in partial or total ignorance of each other; nor, until the Peace of Westphalia in 1648, could one really speak of 'international relations'. It has taken the two world wars of the twentieth century and their aftermath to bring us to a complete world of states in the inhabited continents, but one in which many are new and of imperial delineation and initial shaping rather than a product of indigenous societies themselves. State collapse in such new and artificial states raises issues about the stability of a particular pattern of states, and even about the survival of any state in some areas. Yet can the modern world return to areas of 'statelessness': for all the states acknowledged capacity to damage society, especially through violence and exploitation, does it not yet remain in some shape or degree also a necessity for development? Thus, as well as reviewing aspects of decay, there will be an attempt to consider some of the political issues, both domestic and international, raised in trying to think of resolving problems of states in the Horn. With the ending of the Cold War and the collapse of the Marxist-Leninist alternative state model, attention has focused on democratization in particular. This may indeed be the main issue where the state itself has been maintained. It may also be an important part of the discussion of countries in which there has been partial or total state collapse, but in such cases it will clearly not be a sufficient discussion, for the other aspects of the state referred to above will also be an essential undertaking. Nor is it necessarily the case that state collapse will give rise to a consideration of the rebuilding of the same state: in Africa, as in the former USSR, the possibility of a new state structure may also arise.

The political map of the Horn has already changed with the independence of Eritrea; and other issues of new statehood have been raised most notably in the former British Somaliland in northern Somalia, and in southern Sudan. Constitutional issues have resurfaced, but go well beyond any simple proclamation of 'democracy', especially in fields such as the incorporation of ethnicity, decentralization and federalism. As well as constitutional issues, as already indicated, state collapse has raised issues of the rebuilding of basic institutions, such as police, and systems of administration and justice. Recovery involves social and economic as much as political issues. Relations between the neighbouring states of the Horn, as well as broader regional relations, will be as relevant to recovery as they have been to decay. And finally, the changed international environment with the end of the Cold War has already had a very different impact, albeit one that has been deeply ambiguous, and is unlikely to be the final act in international involvement in this troubled region.

PART ONE

The Making of the Horn

I

The Historic Horn

The pre-modern era

The Horn's geography has been central to its political, social and economic development for centuries. Within the Horn this includes its major river system, the Nile; and while the Nile is seen as having its source in Lake Victoria, the majority of the water that flows down to Egypt starts from the rains on the Ethiopian highlands, and especially drainage into Lake Tana. The Ethiopian highlands have themselves constituted an obstacle to external penetration which has contributed to the emergence of a distinct civilization in that part of Africa. Away from the Nile and the highlands, the major feature of the region has been its plains, ranging from the rain-watered central belt of *bilad as-sudan* (the land of the blacks) to the arid lands of the Somalis in the tip of the Horn and the deserts of the Sahara to the north. In contrast to the riverain and highland settled agriculture of Sudan and Ethiopia respectively, the plains have encouraged the evolution of nomadic and semi-nomadic pastoral communities.

The region's wider geography has also been significant. The Nile, the Red Sea, the Gulf of Aden and the Indian Ocean have all exposed the region to outside influences. The ancient world of the Egyptians, Greeks and Romans had an impact, as the medieval world of Islam did later. The degree of penetration and control varied. Sometimes it amounted to influence, at others to conquest, but above all it reflected the Horn's position on the periphery of wider world developments that contributed to, rather than determined, the course of events within the Horn. And at the same time as influences impinged from outside the region, so it was also an area of human evolution for millennia. The first large-scale society to develop was the civilization of Meroe centred north of the junction of the Blue and White Niles. Emerging in the third century BC it was itself an offshoot of declining pharaonic Egypt (which had in turn drawn extensively on its African hinterland), though it became a distinct civilization. Though Meroe declined, its long-term significance was its contribution to the tradition of state formation. The skills of mining and metallurgy, coupled later with the introduction of the horse, gave rise to the formation of conquest states ruling over pre-existing agricultural societies which spread south into central Africa, and west across the Sahel. In the Sahel in particular, these states were associated with trade, including trans-Saharan trade involving slaves and commodities.

Meroe was to last for several centuries, but an aspect of its decline was the rise of its rival Axum, a trading empire based in the northern highlands of Ethiopia in the present-day province of Tigre. Axum rose in the second and third centuries AD, becoming a Christian kingdom in the process, and its influence spread not only on the African side of the Red Sea but into Arabia as well, especially the most fertile and populated part of the peninsula, generally known as 'Arabia felix' as Pliny dubbed it. Axum was to become the first step in a long history of statehood in the Ethiopian highlands. A succession of wars and counter-wars were to have at their core the expansion southwards of what had become by the fourth century AD the Christian, semitic state dominated by Tigreans and Amharas. Successive monarchs had the capacity to raise military forces and operate a basic administration, with the spiritual backing of the Coptic Christian church. This state formation was made possible by the existence of a settled society based on arable agriculture which encouraged a regionalized identity under local lords rather than the existence of a more shifting local or 'tribal' community. Though the parallels are far from exact, it is understandable that to European observers Ethiopia has often conjured up images of a 'feudal' society, which was very distinct from the land tenure systems found in most of the rest of pre-colonial Africa. And as in other 'feudal' societies, the degree of state formation was intermittently questioned by regionally based instability. Ethiopia rose to create the glories of the city of Gondar in the seventeenth century, but later the power of the monarchy declined. The country descended into a period of turbulent struggles among local notables, a time often referred to as the 'age of the princes', until in the mid-nineteenth century awareness of growing external threats contributed to the attempted unification, undertaken from the Emperor Tewodros onwards.

This general picture had been interrupted by a challenge in the sixteenth century from the pastoral Cushitic people of the south-east, the Galla (now known as Oromo), who swept into the highlands and occupied large areas. This was swiftly followed by a short-lived conquest by a Muslim from the Somali coast, Imam Ahmed Gran (the left-handed). Though eventually driven back, it served to reinforce the relationship between the Ethiopian state and the Coptic Christian church on the one hand, and its rivalry with the Muslim communities on the other. These included the highlands (the Oromo) and the Somalis to the east: as early as the thirteenth century a series of Muslim sultanates encircled the medieval Ethiopian empire to the south and south-east; and in the nineteenth century Muslim sultanates and kingdoms developed among the Somalis and Oromos respectively. In addition, there was the increasingly Muslim northern Sudan and Red Sea coast where, after being checked by the medieval Coptic Christian states of Nubia that had succeeded Meroe, Islam expanded southwards from the fourteenth century, including into the lowlands of what is now Eritrea.

The history of the Horn of Africa has thus long involved the rise and fall of states, with the Ethiopian state sustaining the greatest longevity overall. As well as temporal change there has also been lateral movement. The Ethiopian state has moved its centre southwards, while in Sudan successive states rose and fell in different latitudes of the Nile, from Meroe north into Nubia, and later, from the sixteenth century, to the Funj kingdom based at Sennar on the Blue Nile. Probably founded by people from the south, possibly Shilluk, the Funj became the first Islamic state in Sudan and spread its power widely in what is now central Sudan.

Mobility has been a feature not only of state-building but of the stateless societies as well. Nomadic and semi-nomadic pastoralism, largely beyond the confines of indigenous state formation, has also been a marked feature of the region. The Somali peoples in the tip of the Horn are the most obvious example. The arid lowland areas were home to a Cushitic-speaking Muslim people who, away from the few small coastal trading cities, lived a pastoral life. While sharing in the perception of a common ancestor, as well as religion, culture and language, the Somali people were also highly divided by clan, sub-clan and family, in their harsh environment. Similarly segmented were the pastoralists of Upper Nile. Lying south of the penetration of the successive states on the Nile and of Islam, the Dinka and Nuer peoples in particular were to come to be regarded as classic acephalous, or stateless, societies.

Naturally, this mobility was in no way to correspond to the later borders drawn by colonial powers for these were to reflect European rivalries rather than the ethnographic character of Africa. Probably, the classic disparity in the region was to be the case of the Somalis, who were to find borders imposed which left many of them outside independent Somalia in Ethiopia, Djibouti and Kenya. But that is to jump ahead. For the moment it is the variety of the Horn which is to be emphasized. From historic states to acephalous societies, from settled agriculturalists to nomads, from trade to self-subsistence, from the competing 'religions of the book' to African traditions and customs, all have contributed to the makings of the modern conflicts. And while these conflicts have deep indigenous roots, so too they have regional and wider international dimensions for which there are long historical precedents. But before considering those parallels between pre-colonial and contemporary events, the important phase of Western imperialism in the region must be reviewed.

The imperial era

The rise of 'world systems' had been significant down the centuries in influencing developments in the Horn, albeit in a peripheral way. The ancient pharaonic, Greek, Roman and Byzantine systems flowed continuously from one to the next. There was something of a space, with major indigenous development, including Nubia and Axum, before the subsequent emergence of a new system, that of the Islamic world. The third major 'world system', the rise of the West, had already had an impact in the form of the Portuguese in Ethiopia and elsewhere on the coast from the end of the fifteenth century, but it was the nineteenth century that brought the competition for territory that was to create the map of Africa. First on the scene was a curious imperial hybrid, the Egyptian khedivate of the Ottoman empire. Mohamed Ali, the Ottoman soldier of Albanian origin who seized power in Egypt following the vacuum created by the brief occupation of Napoleon I's French forces from 1798–1801, was acting on his own rather than in the sultan's interest when he sought to build a Turco-Egyptian empire; and was inspired not just by oriental despotism, but by the example of European modernization, the economic aspects of which he sought, unsuccessfully, to replicate in Egypt. His dream of an east African empire fell well short of fulfilment but did lead to the conquest of Sudan in 1820, which successive khedivates ruled until the revolt of Ahmed el-Mahdi from 1881 to 1885, ending in the downfall of Khartoum and the death of Britain's and Egypt's agent, General Gordon. In addition to Sudan, Egypt controlled a string of posts on the Red Sea coast.

The concern of Europe, especially France and Britain, for the Ottoman empire and for Egypt in the second half of the nineteenth century was one important factor leading to increased intervention. Another was the enormous strategic significance attached to Egypt and the Red Sea once the Suez Canal had been built in 1869 by a Frenchman, Ferdinand de Lessops, and then bought by Britain; in 1882 Britain also seized control of Egypt (though still nominally a part of the Ottoman empire). This strategic rivalry for Egypt has been seen as the spring from which the European scramble for Africa flowed; but it has also been suggested that it was fear of economic protectionism by other European powers as nineteenth-century industrialization spilled out of Europe to all corners of the world that encouraged the formal acquisition of territory to replace the informal activities from trading ports, such as those around the coasts of Africa.

The three European powers most involved in the Horn were Britain, France and Italy. It was Italy that first acquired territory, developing what was to become the colony of Eritrea from 1869. The French moved into French Somaliland, the area around the port of Djibouti in 1885. Britain took a slice of Somali-occupied land, British Somaliland in 1887 (Britain already had nearby Aden and looked to Somaliland for meat supplies). The Italians moved to the more southerly territories from 1888. But the rivalry became more intense in the hinterland. From the position in Eritrea, Italy's eyes were on Ethiopia, where, from the mid-nineteenth century, the latter had been undergoing one of its periodic experiences of centralization. The Emperor Tewodros had reasserted control over warring local *ras* (lords), and though he was later defeated by a British expeditionary force in 1868, his successor but one, Menelik II, extended his policy of centralization and began a new era of modern Ethiopian history. At that stage relations between Italy and Ethiopia were amicable (Menelik having been armed by the Italians to move against his predecessor Yohannes), with the Treaty of Wuchale being signed in 1889. But interpretation of it was to vary, especially over Italy's apparent belief that it was the establishment of a protectorate. Menelik skilfully built up his armoury, with purchases from France and Russia in particular, and by the time relations with Italy had deteriorated to the point of war his forces were well prepared. The rout of the Italian troops at Adowa in 1896, which so shocked Europe, was a not unreasonable outcome when the size of the two forces and their weaponry is compared. Yet for all its apparent confirmation of Ethiopia's success in repelling invaders, which had been one of the two main themes of the nineteenth century (the other being centralization), Italy was still in control of Eritrea, thus denying successive Ethiopian rulers their ambition of a coastline of their own. Menelik had also been extending imperial territory by conquest in the west, south and south-east, and the carve up of Somali-inhabited lands by 1897 included the incorporation of the Haud and Ogaden regions into Ethiopia. Ethiopia under Menelik was proving as much of an imperial power in the Horn as the Europeans, and indeed, but for them might have achieved his hopes of reaching the Somali coast.

Meanwhile the rivalry of France and Britain had also been intensifying. Frustrated in Egypt, France turned its attention to West and Equatorial Africa, though with west–east ambitions. A young Frenchman, Captain Marchand, had marched from the equatorial coast to plant the tricoleur on the Upper Nile at Fashoda in 1898. But at the same time as he had been marching east, an Anglo-Egyptian army had been proceeding up the Nile to defeat the forces of the Khalifa Abdullahi at the Battle of Omdurman, also in 1898; and as soon as its commander, General Kitchener, heard the news from Fashoda, he proceeded there with a larger force to confront the small band of Frenchmen. Matters were not settled at Fashoda: rather the Fashoda crisis briefly threatened war in Europe between Britain and France, the result of which was a climb-down by the latter power leaving the whole of Sudan under British control, though nominally an Anglo-Egyptian condominium.

Anglo-French animosity was rapidly reversed in the light of growing German power in Europe. It was followed by the entente cordiale of 1902, which led to an Italian, French and British Tripartite Convention on the Horn in 1906 that appeared to establish spheres of influence threatening Ethiopia's independence once more. However, by a combination of strength at home and skilful diplomacy abroad, Menelik was able to resist this threat and keep Ethiopia as one of the two states in Africa (the other being Liberia) that did not come under European imperial control as a result of the scramble for Africa.

With hindsight, it was the drawing of the map of the Horn that was to be as important in the post-independence period as what actually transpired under imperial rule. Certainly, in looking at later anti-imperial charges from numerous individuals and groups, it is to the consequences of the division of the Horn as much as to developments within individual territories that they point.

In terms of international politics, the ructions involved in the scramble for Africa, which in the Horn included major battles between indigenous armies and imperial invaders at Adowa and Omdurman, were followed by a quieter period. Britain was firmly established as the major power in the north-east as well as East Africa, especially after the First World War and the transfer of Tanganyika to Britain from Germany. But all three European powers in the Horn were on the same side and the war had only a limited direct impact on the region, a point underlined by the short reign (1913–16) of the uncrowned emperor of Ethiopia, Lij Yasu, with his apparent pro-German and pro-Turkish sympathies. The European powers established a new role in the Middle East as well, for the collapse of the Ottoman empire, including in Arabia, was followed by British and French dominance which ensured that international rivalry in that crucial area would be contained in the years after the war.

Instead, as in the late nineteenth century, it was to be seeds of confrontation in Europe that were to provoke conflict in the Horn. The rise of fascism under Mussolini in Italy was to lead to a new burst of imperialism in that country, this time ostensibly evoking Roman grandeur rather than simply following other modern European imperialists. Activity was to centre on Libya in north Africa and on Ethiopia, with revenge for the defeat of the Italians at Adowa. Mussolini's plotting against Ethiopia began in 1930, though it was not until 1935 that his troops finally began a brutal conquest of the country which was completed in the following year. The international community was embarrassed by the appeal of Emperor Haile Selassie at the League of Nations, but only wrung its hands. Nothing was done and the opportunistic international advancement of both Italian and German fascism proceeded until the outbreak of the Second World War in 1939. Since the three imperial powers in the Horn were now divided, with Italy and Britain on opposite sides and France having capitulated, war came to the Horn as well. (Ethiopia, understandably regards 1935 as being the start of the war.) Forces of the British empire staged a pincer invasion of Ethiopia from East Africa and Sudan and with the aid of Ethiopian partisans defeated the Italians in 1941, reinstalling Emperor Haile Selassie.

In the short term the outcome of the war was to re-establish the international dominance of Britain. Britain had restored Ethiopian independence and taken over the administration of Eritrea on behalf of the United Nations; and though Italy was permitted to return to administer her former Somali territory as trustee from 1950, she posed no threat. But Britain, though a war victor, was much weakened by the conflict, while politically it and other western European powers were fading stars in the international community. Much as the British right wing resented it, Britain's role in the world was rapidly being overtaken by the rise of two superpowers, the USA and the USSR, and their rivalry was to be at the core of the developing Cold War. Though centred on the iron curtain dividing Europe, the Cold War was to spill over into various other regions of the world, and as a first step contributed to the weakening of the old European empires.

At the same time as the international environment was changing, so to some degree was the situation within the Horn. Though set in a dynamic international context, a feature of imperial boundary-drawing had been the relative isolation from one another of events within the different territories. Instead of indigenous states interacting directly with each other, as they had as late as 1889 when Emperor Yohannes had been killed in a battle with Mahdist forces in the Ethiopian–Sudanese marches, indigenous political developments were largely confined by the new borders for much of the first half of the twentieth century. It thus becomes necessary to look at developments within each of the major states in the period of imperialism.

Sudan

The exception to the general regional isolation encouraged by imperialism was Sudan, but its involvement was not with the Horn, so much as with Egypt. Sudan's long history as an area of Nile-centred state development acting as a conduit between the Middle East and Africa was being maintained, essentially by an imperial ambiguity, the so-called Anglo-Egyptian condominium in Sudan. It was a deliberate ambiguity designed by Britain's effective ruler of Egypt, Lord Cromer, and its purpose was to avoid causing unnecessary political difficulties in Egypt by totally annexing to Britain Egypt's re-conquered former territories in Sudan. The condominium solution was workable as long as Britain remained in control of Egypt, but the virulent nationalist struggle at the end of the First World War brought Britain's declaration of Egyptian independence, though with reserved points to protect British interests. These comprised: the maintenance of British military bases and the overseeing of Egypt's defences; the protection of imperial communications, notably the Suez Canal; the protection of foreign interests in Egypt; and Britain's continuing domination of the condominium in Sudan. This 'semi-independence' from 1922 was an understandable anomaly to Egypt, and it repeatedly sought negotiations on the reserved points, all of which broke down over its claim to Sudan, which it regarded as its possession both by right of conquest (the invasions of 1820 and by the Anglo-Egyptian force in 1898) and because of the vital importance to Egypt of the Nile waters, control of the flow of which lay largely in Sudan. It was only the growing threat of Italy, and especially the invasion of Ethiopia in 1935, that led in 1936 to an Anglo-Egyptian treaty involving some concessions to Egypt in Sudan. From the end of the Second World War these concessions were no longer sufficient and further rounds of Anglo-Egyptian negotiations once more foundered on Sudan. The failure to resolve Anglo-Egyptian questions, and thus, as it saw it, Egypt's full independence, contributed to the making of the Free Officers' coup of 1952, led by Colonel Nasser, which was to demolish the upper levels of the power structure in Egypt and transform Anglo-Egyptian relations.

The contribution of Anglo-Egyptian failure to the major upheaval in domestic politics in Egypt was an indication that Anglo-Egyptian relations were not just about 'high politics' but had deep implications for the state in Egypt. The same was true for Sudan, though in rather

different ways. Sudan's British rulers governed a vast country with a
history of revolt against imperialism, yet although extremely sensitive
to the dangers of another Mahdist uprising, administratively they built
on both the Turco-Egyptian state and its Mahdist successor. Both had
mixed coercion and repression with elements of political management
to sustain themselves. The Turco-Egyptians had converted indigenous
ethnic communities into tribal administration, while a commodity-
seeking economic drive had encouraged indigenous traders (*jallaba*),
especially from the riverain north of the country, notably Nubia, to
spread south and west as an emerging trading class (including for
many years taking slaves from the Nuba mountains and the south).
Meanwhile, there was a relaxed acceptance of the Muslim *sufi tariqas*
(religious orders) that had grown since the eighteenth century. The
Mahdist state altered rather than destroyed its predecessor, but economically it fared badly. Severe famine was but one disaster, and it fell
back increasingly on coercion based on western pastoralists, the Ta'isha
Baqqara, of whom the ruling Khalifa Abdullahi was one. Thus the
Mahdist state has been seen as reflecting Sudanese state traditions of
core–periphery relations albeit with the state 'captured' by a people
from the periphery.

Confronted by a vast poor country with an immediate history of
Mahdist-inspired independent statehood and with only a small administration and British garrison, Sudan's British rulers employed
careful political management once the initial phase of conquest at the
Battle of Omdurman and beyond had been completed (though 'pacifi-
cation' in the south still proved necessary as late as 1928). Particular
fear existed in officials' minds of the possibility of a new Mahdist
revolt and numerous early outbursts were swiftly suppressed; but the
need to counter the appeal of the Ottoman sultan as caliph of Islam
during the First World War led to the need to rehabilitate Mahdism as
an anti-'Turkish' movement. This was done through the promotion of
the Mahdi's posthumous son, Abd el-Rahman el-Mahdi. As his neo-
Mahdist movement continued to grow in the inter-war years, funded
by his agricultural and commercial activities, the only counter the
Sudan government could devise was the promotion of the rival
Khatmiyya *tariqa* led by Ali el-Mirghani. The centrality of rival Islamic
groups to the evolution of Sudanese politics was thus a product of
state policies judged necessary not only for reasons of domestic politics
but also for Sudan's position in the wider Islamic world. This was to
be magnified after the Second World War when party mobilization in
Sudan centred around the two major Islamic sects, while the rival co-
domini, Britain and Egypt, each became informally allied with the
Mahdists and the Khatmiyya respectively.

While the politics of Islam was the most dramatic manifestation of the state's need to seek clients or collaborators from Sudanese society, as in most parts of Africa the British rulers' most formal ties were with ethnic communities through the promotion of native administration. Pre-colonial ethnicity in Sudan had been relatively fluid and flexible, and of greater significance in the outlying regions away from the Nile than in riverain areas. The experiences of the nineteenth century had both reduced the 'primordial' significance of ethnicity and enhanced its state-related role. British rule in Sudan involved sustained efforts to promote native administration by identifying indigenous communities as separate tribes, and recognizing, and ascribing designated powers to, tribal leaders. Native administration was to have only partial success – it was especially difficult to establish hierarchical administration among the acephalous peoples of the south – but it did serve to emphasize the importance of ethnic identity in local politics, the arena of greatest significance to the majority of the population.

Simultaneously, British imperialism was involving Sudan in the international economy. The financial backbone of the state was the Gezira scheme. Established in the 1920s, it was the largest cotton growing scheme in the world and soon produced Sudan's major export, far ahead of gum arabic. However, its unusual tenant-based production system was to leave the Gezira as a social organization relatively detached from the evolution of national politics. Much more important for that was the development of trade within the country, facilitated by the long period of peace and improved communications. The scale and range of trade varied widely, including oil seed, sorghum and livestock, and it was frequently organized by extended family-based trading networks. Some of the bigger companies involved foreigners similar to those in other parts of Africa – British commercial houses (and banks) in Khartoum, as well as Greek and Syrian merchants – but many of the smaller enterprizes were Sudanese-owned, especially by traders of the riverain Northern Region. The hub of this commercial network was Omdurman and it extended out to the remotest rural areas, taking northern traders deep into the south. The impact of this diaspora of northern traders – partly a continuation of similar developments in the nineteenth century – cannot be exaggerated. It reflected not only the making of a national economy (with some international links), but had a major impact locally, especially through the *shail* system by which traders provided credit facilities to small farmers which have been criticized frequently as exploitative. Socially, the traders were also the transmitters of an evolving Sudanese identity, based on the customs of the riverain north as well as Arabic and Islam (the impact of these traders was such that in the south in the 1930s there was a policy of seeking to restrict if not eliminate them).

The religious, tribal and commercial networks were interrelated in complex ways. The *sufi tariqa* centres in Sudan had long combined public asceticism with commercial activities, and the expanding merchant networks extended their influence. At the same time, the response of local communities to the Mahdiyya (both positive and negative) also influenced identification with political evolution in the twentieth century. The enhancement of local elitism by native administration also encouraged the development of links between the traders and tribal chiefs, sometimes involving marriage arrangements. This was not the making of a simple homogeneous elite, but rather a more fragmentary stratification, containing elements of commerce, religious affiliation and ethnicity.

However, Sudan's was a fundamentally uneven development geographically, with social and economic development focused around the centre of the country. Islam and Arabization had not extended into the south before the Turco-Egyptian conquest, and British administrators were later keen to discourage it both on political grounds (as a check to potential nationalism) and because the promotion of Christianity and the English language would offer a route into a higher civilization. The south was thus largely excluded from the growing commercial and cultural networks and accompanying embryonic stratification. Other remoter areas were more connected, but still on the periphery: Darfur in the far west had been reconquered only in 1916 and remained somewhat isolated with attachment to Islam stronger than Arab identity, especially among the Fur themselves; while in the east the Red Sea hills were Islamized, but local Beja cultures remained strong.

In some respects Sudan was a typical imperial state. It was ethnically heterogeneous, it had a range of economic activity from export-oriented agriculture to largely self-subsistent communities, and it contained core areas linked to the international economy with fuller services of all kinds, and remote rural areas with far less impact of 'modernity'. But in important ways it was also atypical. It was physically vast (the largest country in Africa) and embraced extreme heterogeneity that ranged from the traditionally Arab and Muslim identities to be found in the north to the emerging African and Christian identities in the south. The policies of the imperial state had contributed directly to the politicization of religious identities (including rival Muslim sects) at the national level. And Sudan was the subject of an international dispute which impinged directly on the country's evolving indigenous politics.

Sudan's internal complexity was to be reflected in the rise of nationalism after the Second World War. Nationalism had its roots in a variety of themes. There were those who saw the Mahdist revolt as a precursor of nationalism; others were influenced, as so often in Africa, by Western education; while Egyptian nationalism after the First World War and Arab nationalism also had an impact. Nineteen-twenty-four was a year of disturbances that have been termed a revolt, and certainly shook the British rulers to the core, whereas, in spite of their countermeasures, the late 1930s saw the formation of the Graduates' Congress to give expression to the views of the intelligentsia. But when the Congress tried to negotiate with the government in 1942 it was rebuffed. Nationalists instead allied with the major Muslim sects, the Mahdists and the Khatmiyya, to produce two competing political parties, the Umma Party and the National Union Party (NUP). The Umma Party came to demonstrate its strength by outmanoeuvring the government and winning support through sectarian affiliation of tribal chiefs in the rural areas, and pressing for constitutional development. The latter included the decision to incorporate the south fully into Sudan as a unitary state, associated with the Juba Conference of 1947. But lacking the social, religious, cultural, linguistic and economic ties that had been growing for centuries in the north, the south remained largely peripheral to the political development taking place in the rest of the country. Meanwhile the 'unionists', the forerunners of the NUP, allied with Egypt (hence their sobriquet) to exploit the rivalry between the co-domini, including the boycotting of the British-backed constitutional development.

Thus the complexity of Sudan's domestic politics was magnified by its international context. Decolonization was always a coin that had two sides: not just African nationalism, but the domestic and international politics of the imperial powers. And in Sudan's case this was made more acute because of the involvement of two powers, Britain and Egypt, the nominal co-domini which were, in practice, ever keener rivals. The rivalry deepened after the Second World War as Egypt sought both fuller independence than that granted in 1922, which included the winning back of what it regarded as its former territory of Sudan. Unsuccessful negotiations between the two countries in 1946–47 and 1950–51 were backed by Egypt's forging of the alliance with the 'unionists', leaving the British to fall back on the historically anti-Egyptian Mahdists.

Deadlock had been caused for several years by Egypt's claim to sovereignty over Sudan, but the situation changed with the seizure of power in Egypt by the Free Officers led by Nasser in July 1952. By dropping the claim to Sudan, Egypt was able to win over all the Sudanese parties in 1953, even the small, weak Southern Party. Rapid steps were made towards full self-government and self-determination, which, to Egypt's disappointment, was on the basis of complete independence rather than unity with Sudan's mighty, radical northern neighbour.

In part, Sudan's decolonizing experience paralleled those elsewhere in Anglophone Africa. A fairly small group of mainly Western-educated men was able to mount a political challenge to the relatively light and thinly stretched imperial government, which was itself weakened by its liberal attitudes and the uncertain backing from the metropolis. Yet Sudan's particular character made it more complex than most. The largely Muslim and Arab-identifying north was politically dominant over a south which, though less homogenous and largely 'ethnically' structured, was evolving a small political elite, whose self-perception was increasingly 'African' and Christian, very much in contradistinction to the emergent political establishment in the north. But regionalism, often reflecting the imbalances of centre-periphery relations, is not in itself unusual in Africa. What was more unusual was the deep division within that nationalist establishment, especially since party rivalry centred on a long history of suspicion and ambition between the major sects, personified by the genuine antipathy of Sayed Ali el-Mirghani and Sayed Abd el-Rahman el-Mahdi. It ensured that party rivalry reflected deep social divisions as well. Simultaneously, Sudan was practised in the implications of international rivalries in ways that few other African states were, including a major regional power, Egypt. Independence at the beginning of 1956 finally ousted Sudan's British rulers, but it did little else to clarify the complexity and division of both Sudan's domestic politics and its international context.

Somalia

The drawing of the map of Africa had left the Somalis divided into five different territories: in the north Somalis comprised a major part of French Somaliland; next to it lay British Somaliland; the largest Somali inhabited area was ruled by Italy; in the extreme south Somalis lived in Kenya; and they also ranged into Ethiopia in the west. While Somalis shared a common culture and religion, at the heart of their social organization was a pastoral way of life. The harsh, arid environment gave rise to the evolution of this pastoral, migratory existence, involving camels, cattle, goats and sheep. Only in the south is there sufficient water for settled agriculture on a substantial scale, mainly in the area between the Jubba and Shabeelle rivers, though there is some in the north-west as well. For the pastoralists the colonially drawn borders would be an impediment, where they could not be treated simply as an irrelevance. The major migratory routes for many of the Somali clans are across those borders, particularly in the rainy season north–south and east–west into the Haud pastures of the interior which, under the imperial division, became Ethiopia.

The Somalis, like many people in Africa, have an identity myth that gives a common origin in the form of Samaale. But while of one nation, the Somalis also comprise a number of clans and numerous sub-clans. Among the pastoralists are four major clan-families – the Darod, the Hawiye, the Isaaq and the Dir – while in the agricultural south there are the Digil and the Rahanwayn. In addition to the major clan-families, there are numerous descendent clans and sub-clans, creating complex relationships which are:

> both centripetal, at once drawing the Somalis into a powerful social fabric of kinship affinity and cultural solidarity while setting them against one another in a complicated range of antagonistic clan interests. A person, for example, gives political allegiance to his/her immediate family, then to his immediate lineage, then to the clan of his lineage, then to a clan-family that embraces several clans, including his own, and ultimately to the nation that itself consists of a confederacy of clan-families. Each level of segmentation defines a person's rights and obligations as well as his/her standing in relation to others. The segmentary law dictates, for example, that two lineages that are genealogically equidistant from a common ancestor should stand in an adversarial relationship to each other but should be drawn together as allies against the members of a third lineage whose genealogical lines fall outside of the common ancestor.[1]

As a result of this, 'pastoral clan organization is an unstable, fragile system, characterized at all levels by shifting allegiances. Power and politics are exercized through temporary coalitions and ephemeral alliances of lineages'.[2]

While this organization may appear as a recipe for structured anarchy, there is also a form of institutionalism provided by *heer*, a form of social contract which is made between families and clan. Deriving from a mixture of Islamic law and local, traditional common law, *heer* is established through *ad hoc* assemblies (*shirs*) in which men deliberate on current problems. Although overwhelmingly male, *shirs* are also very open and egalitarian, leading to the comment that, 'all men are councillors, and all men politicians'.[3] This egalitarianism is accompanied by strong attachment to democracy and individualism. Although there may be individual leaders – wealthy men, sultans chosen by *shirs* or religious figures – they have not constituted longstanding offices: 'this lack of stable and formally defined political offices thus seems consistent with the extreme fluidity of political groupings'.[4]

While the Somalis were an overwhelmingly pastoral people, the coast was also dotted with ancient ports. Zayla', near modern-day Djibouti, and Berbera lay in the north; in the south were Mogadishu, Merka and Baraawe. Trade with the interior passed through Somali ports, especially from medieval Ethiopia via Zayla', and cultural contact with the outside world was maintained through these urban societies. The major influence absorbed from the outside world was that of Islam. The Somalis became a thoroughly Islamic people, especially from the thirteenth century. It was, of course, Islam adapted socially to the harsh environment, and was not to develop the extensive and powerful *turuq*, like the Khatmiyya and others that characterized northern Sudan.

The Somalis found themselves not only parcelled out among the various imperial powers, but affected differently by their policies. The harshest experiences in the early years were at the hands of the Ethiopians in the Ogaden. The herds in the Ogaden were an attractive target and raids were violent and ruthless. In comparison, the European colonialists were largely confined to the coastal areas initially, leaving the herders of the interior relatively untroubled by the new arrivals. It was thus the Ethiopians rather than the Europeans who appear to have been the first target of Somali resistance. The central figure of the resistance, Sayed Mohamed Abdille Hasan (known to the British as 'the mad mullah'), was himself of the Ogaden and began his resistance against the Ethiopians before later engaging the British and the Italians. An Islamic scholar of considerable charisma, he personified ethnic and national as well as religious resistance. He was inspired by the example of Ahmed el-Mahdi in Sudan, and the guerrilla tactics used by el-Mahdi's lieutenant, Osman Digna, in the east of that country. Abdille Hasan led over two decades of resistance in the north, and his threat was never fully extinguished until his death in 1920, whereas his vision of the unity of the Somali people became a great symbol of later Somali nationalism, indicating the capacity of Somalis to cooperate against the foreign invaders.

When resistance had finally been crushed, it was clear that the division of the Somalis among different imperial rulers meant different policies in the first half of the twentieth century. France was concerned mainly to develop Djibouti as a strategic and trading centre, soon abandoning any ambitions for her territory's small and unproductive hinterland. The port of Djibouti was established, and a railroad constructed from it which by 1917 had reached Addis Ababa, becoming the main link between the Ethiopian capital and the outside world.

Though having a larger territory, the British showed less inclination even to try to undertake development, largely putting the territory on to a 'care and maintenance basis' (as with southern Sudan). The secure holding of the territory facing the strategic port of Aden was seen as sufficient, and there was little attempt at military development of the main port of Berbera. At the same time, the provision of Aden with meat seemed the limit of British commercial aims, and thus the north experienced little in the way of social or economic development. Italy, however, was more ambitious, since Somalia was one of its few colonies and thus aspirations of colonial grandeur, as well as settlement of surplus population from the home country, were pursued there. The more fertile areas of the south were seen as suitable for settlement and commerce, and the coming of fascism in the 1920s gave an additional boost to these activities. The physical and social infrastructure was developed, including wells for the pastoralists, roads to encourage trade, as well as schools and clinics. During the period of the Italian occupation of Ethiopia from 1935 to 1941 there was common administration and some integration of Somalis on either side of the border. In the Ogaden the Ethiopians initially did little more than pursue their occasional quests for cattle. By the 1930s they had a more regular presence, but it was still primarily coercive and fell well short of being a recognizable colonial administration attempting constructive engagement with the indigenous Somalis.

Throughout, the Somali territories remained unusual in Africa in that the majority of the population continued to live as pastoralists: but that did not mean that they were unaffected by the colonial presence and divisions which resulted. There were times all through the colonial period when the various powers endeavoured to make a reality of the boundaries that they had imposed on the region and check the ancient patterns of migration, thus fragmenting clan relationships. The Mareehan clan was effectively riven as a result of the division of their traditional lands between Italian Somalia, the Northern Frontier District (NFD) of British-ruled Kenya, and Ethiopia's control of the Ogaden. Grazing lands and wells between which migration had taken place for centuries, were now separated by borders across which past free flow was by no means guaranteed in colonial circumstances. In the Ogaden there was access to both water and grazing, but trade through the port of Berbera was obstructed.

Ironically, the Italian invasion of Ethiopia in 1935 was to lead to a few years in which there was greater experience of unity among the Somalis, as almost all were under Italian rule. The Ogaden was unified with Italian Somaliland and there were moves towards administrative and economic integration. Then, at the outset of the Second World

War, Italy acquired the Somali territories of its British and French enemies. But soon Britain's pincer attack on the Italians from Kenya and Sudan led to Italy's defeat and expulsion from the Horn.

Britain's replacement of Italy following its victory led the new Labour government to propose the continued unification of the Somalis as part of the post-war settlement, but the proposal was stillborn: the Four Power Commission responsible for dealing with the former Italian colonies, comprising the USSR, USA and France as well as Britain, rejected the proposal. There were fears that Britain was trying to take advantage of the situation to expand its empire, especially when, on ousting the Italians, Britain had secured from Ethiopia temporary administrative responsibility for the Ogaden, only handing back the last of the reserved areas in 1954. The USA in particular, backed Ethiopia's claim to the Ogaden region and thus the old colonial boundaries were reasserted, while the administration of the Somalis was divided once more following the brief experience of common Italian rule. The *status quo ante* was further restored when Italy was allowed back into its old territory in the south in 1950, now as the administering power for the United Nations Trust Territory, for a ten-year period to lead to eventual independence. And in this period, as in the earlier one, the Italians were more active in development than Britain in the north or Ethiopia to the east.

These post-Second World War manoeuvres over the heads of the Somalis were to be one ingredient fuelling the growing Somali national movement. Other factors were more conventional African experiences, including the growth of a small Western-educated elite with perceptions of the changing international order, while the history of early Somali resistance was personified in Sayed Mohamed Abdille Hasan's vision and resistance to imperialism. The Somali Youth League (SYL), begun in 1943, was to be the dominant nationalist party in the years after the Second World War. However, it was not the only party, and the potential for fragmentation based largely around clans was observable from the outset. Party politics were encouraged in the Italian-administered region by the recognition that independence was definitely coming, as laid down by the UN. Throughout the 1950s it was clear in local and general elections that there were other, mainly clan, bases for parties apart from the SYL, though the latter remained dominant. In British Somaliland overt politics were repressed, though there was an officially unacknowledged presence, including the SYL, and then in 1959, perceiving the anomaly of the south, a general election was held.

Britain's belated acceptance of the need to keep in step with the UN Trust Territory to the south (and part of the post-Suez acceleration of British decolonization) was further seen in its decision

that Somaliland would become independent at virtually the same time
as the Italians were leaving, and that the two territories would then be
able to form one united country of Somalia. It was a hurried move for
which little planning had been undertaken, which meant that part of
the legacy of the new state was a very rushed unification. But at the
same time it was to be a unification of only two of the areas occupied
by Somalis. Approximately one-third of Somalis remained outside the
borders of the new state, mostly in Ethiopia, but some in Kenya and
what was still the French colony in the north-west. Thus the new
Somalia, though apparently a state unique in Africa in the cultural
homogeneity of its population, was from the outset confronted by
testing internal political questions, especially the joining of the less
developed north with the south, as well as the issue of Somali unity
which was now, thanks to the Somali's earlier colonial division, partly
an external issue.

Ethiopia

The late nineteenth century had been a time of rapid territorial expansion for Ethiopia. Under Menelik, in particular, it had expanded
its land by conquest, taking in much to the south and east, including
roughly a quarter of the Somali population, as well as incorporating
the whole of the highland plateau (except for a small area in Eritrea in
the north). This forcible expansion has been likened to the processes
of imperialism more generally. Ethiopia was shifting its character from
that of an African nation-state more in the direction of a multi-ethnic
empire, and consciously rivalling the European incursion in so doing.
And, as with imperialism elsewhere, the assessment of that process has
included both themes of exploitation and assimilation. In terms of
exploitation emphasis is put on the favoured positions in the new
lands of the empire. Menelik's favoured ex-soldiers received lands,
governorships and other forms of enhancement, and had sweeping
powers over their local subjects. Indeed, for what have been called 'the
predatory tendencies of the ruling class' the new territories even
became a source of expanded slavery, 'a hunting ground for humans as
well as animals'.[5] But there were also processes of assimilation for the
new local rulers of the freshly conquered territories who were not just
Shoan Amharas from the region around the new capital of Addis
Ababa, but included Oromo, Walamo and other leading figures who
had become allies of the empire in its southern and eastern expansion.
Assimilation, however, must not be exaggerated. Many small farmers
and peasants continued to be Muslims, or clung to traditional beliefs
and practices, and felt themselves ruled by alien intruders, who were

most generally referred to as 'Amhara', whatever their ethnic background. For their part, many of the intruders assumed an overall
superiority which has been likened to a belief in their 'manifest destiny'
to rule the peripheral areas of the country.

At the centre of the empire there was also political change. From
1855 there had been no established imperial dynasty and there was
rivalry for the title of ruler of the expanded empire. Yohannes IV had
come from Tigre and Menelik was from Shoa. Menelik's declining
years from 1908 until his death in 1913 were accompanied by portents
of a troubled succession, and even speculation that the empire might
disintegrate. In the confusion a group of noblemen were able to plot
a coup which in 1916 brought Menelik's daughter, Zawditu, to the
crown. One of their number, Ras Tafari, was pushed to the fore in the
expectation that he would be able to be manipulated as regent. However, Tafari established himself as the real power behind the throne,
and as Zawditu's heir on her death in 1930, he was proclaimed as
Emperor Haile Selassie I.

In addition to expanding the empire, Menelik and later Tafari were
keen to create a more modern state. The new capital of Addis Ababa
was one indication of this, and it was followed by the railway from
Djibouti and postal and currency arrangements. A small number of
students were sent abroad for education, and later, in 1930, a ministry
for education was established. A few hospitals were also started. Politically, a bi-cameral parliament was established. However, the senators
were appointed by the emperor and the deputies were nominated by
local lords, whereas the whole parliament was in any case only advisory
and of limited significance. The economic underpinning of the
modernization programme was based on the expansion of coffee
production, especially in the south and east, the export tax on which
was central to the state's financial structure. The impact of coffee
production on the empire's peasants was limited, though officially there
was a significant change throughout the country with the abolition of
slavery in response to Western pressures.

Menelik and Tafari were responsive to outside influences, but they
were also resistant; the means to maintain the African empire's unique
independence in the continent was to play off one power against
another, especially those holding adjacent territories. Menelik had appeared close to France, but following the Anglo-French confrontation
at Fashoda, he and his successor played off both those countries and
the Italians, as well as welcoming legations from other powers to the
capital. But this balance was to be destroyed by the rejuvenation of
Italy's imperial ambitions under Benito Mussolini. Mussolini had
sought for aggrandizement in Libya as well as Ethiopia long before a

pretext for invasion arrived in 1935 over a minor border incident. In a cruel campaign, in which Ethiopia was backed only by weak and ineffectual League of Nations measures, the Italians eventually conquered in 1936, driving Haile Selassie into exile in Britain.

The Italian occupation was tough and uncompromising, but not without positive effects both intended and unintended. The most obvious deliberate policy that made a long-term impact was the improvement in infrastructure, especially roads. In their determination to link their Eritrean colony to the newly conquered territory, major investment was put into roads straddling such obstacles as the towering Simean mountains and the plunging Blue Nile gorge. But from Italy's viewpoint it was all to little effect, for when the Second World War came it was unable to resist the British pincer movement which by 1941 had driven it out of all its East African territories. The attack included a significant role for the Ethiopian 'patriots' who gave an early indication of indigenous capacities for guerrilla warfare in the modern age.

It was in the wake of the war that the unintended consequences of the invasion were to emerge. Ineffective though the international community had been in 1936, there was considerable sympathy for Haile Selassie, which helped ensure that rather than foreign rule, probably by Britain, on behalf of the soon-to-be-created United Nations, the emperor would be restored to his throne. From Britain's standpoint Haile Selassie appeared to be potentially an effective ruler once more, and one who would feel indebted to his country's liberator. However, the emperor himself appeared to be something of a changed man. Though it was Britain that restored him to power, he showed after the war that he recalled the failings of the European powers in 1936, and he sought to diversify in his foreign policy. In particular, in the postwar years he was to forge a relationship with the USA, the acceptable superpower to him, at a time when the British empire was clearly waning and the USA was emerging as a major actor, especially in the Middle East and to a lesser extent in Africa. (In addition, Britain might have a different agenda since it had considered attaching the Eritrean lowlands to Sudan, as well as unifying the Somalis.) There was a special attraction for the USA, since it wanted a communications centre as part of its worldwide network, and built a base called Kagnew outside Asmara in Eritrea. But while the USA became Ethiopia's major patron, Haile Selassie sought to diversify contact internationally and also used Ethiopia's independence as the basis for playing host to the newly formed Organization of African Unity, founded by Africa's numerous emerging independent states in 1963, which established its headquarters in Addis Ababa.

A further change was the centralization of the running of the Ethiopian state, a process made easier by the improved communications to which the Italians had contributed. The emperor's court became ever more the seat of all effective power, as the authority of local rulers was undermined by the centralization of decision-making. Court life itself was Byzantine, with Haile Selassie at the centre of the web, shuffling officials and ministers and promoting and demoting at will, and showing considerable skill in handling rival personalities and factions. Although the deputies in parliament were elected from 1957, they were not permitted to form political parties through which to broaden their bases of support, nor did their institution have significant powers. This was reflected in the lack of popular participation. The 'patriots' wartime resistance to the Italians did enhance nationalistic sentiment, a feeling much promoted by the emperor subsequently, but beyond a general nationalism and patriotism there was little, if any, political participation encouraged by the system. As a result, though individuals might be assimilated, there were few links between particular communities and social groups and the state.

The most vivid example of centralization and eventual alienation was to be seen in Eritrea. The historic links between Eritrea and the Ethiopian state were open to interpretation and argument, but the experiences of the colonial era were clearly significantly different. As an Italian colony Eritrea experienced more social and economic development than Ethiopia, while under the British administration on behalf of the UN after the war a more liberal political climate evolved, including a parliament with significant powers – a marked contrast with the Ethiopia of Haile Selassie. The post-war political freedom served to encourage party competition that reflected Eritrea's heterogeneous society – Christians and Muslims, highlanders and lowlanders as well as ethnic and economic differences – and this mosaic made it easier for Haile Selassie to manoeuvre towards his goal of incorporation: a goal that the USA, with its eyes on a base in Eritrea, was happy to accommodate. The Eritrean parliament was encouraged in various ways to vote for federation and with the agreement of the United Nations this was achieved in 1952, with no requirement for wider consultation with the people of Eritrea such as a referendum. What few Eritreans realized was that within a decade the centralizing trend in Ethiopia would be extended to Eritrea and by the early 1960s federation had been replaced by incorporation.

Political control was matched by economic and social caution. There were areas of 'modernization' – the American-assisted national airline became as notable as the Italian-built roads – but there was no rush for economic growth. In the countryside, coffee remained the major export crop and the general conditions of agriculture remained tied to 'archaic tenure systems in the northern highlands and generally exploitative ones elsewhere'.[6] Industrialization was very limited and what there was of it tended to shift the centre of activity from Eritrea, notably its capital at Asmara, to the surrounds of Addis Ababa. It was also notable that a number of the larger enterprises were owned by Haile Selassie, his family and favoured courtiers. But for many of the fast-rising population living conditions were becoming increasingly harsh. The limited agricultural reforms in particular brought 'greater land alienation, concentration and commercialization of agriculture', and with this the growing impoverishment of many peasants.[7] This was underlined by the severity of the famine in the north in the early 1970s that immediately preceded, and contributed to, the emperor's overthrow in 1974.

Opposition to the emperor was not comparable with the nationalist movement of Sudan or Somalia. Clearly, Ethiopia was not decolonizing and therefore requiring mass popular mobilization for however brief a period: instead the emperor sought to project himself internationally as the personification of independent Africa, as indicated by his ready acceptance of the chairmanship of the Organization of African Unity (OAU) when that body was established in 1963 with its permanent headquarters in Addis Ababa. Yet there were centres of opposition, in particular to the continuing imperial form of government in an international context in which there were pressures for democratic and radical reforms. It had not been possible to isolate Ethiopia from these influences entirely, and the attempts at repression only encouraged further questioning. Western education, in order to provide a necessary cadre of modernizing technocrats, led to a student body that voiced growing criticism of the established order. At the same time the armed forces were also undergoing change, and as early as 1960 there was an abortive coup attempt based in the Imperial Bodyguard and which appeared, initially, to implicate the Crown Prince.

In the countryside, too, there was growing unrest. Peasant rebellions had punctuated Ethiopian history but their regularity and scale was increasing. In the 1940s, immediately after the restoration of Haile Selassie, revolt broke out in Tigre in the north. The next major revolt was to be in Bale in the south-east in the 1960s and at the end of the decade there was another in Gojjam, a central area of the country. These were only the most major revolts, and though repressed, they indicated the growing pressures on the peasantry from both agricultural development and the exactions of the state. An even more dramatic revolt in the long term also began in Eritrea in the 1960s.

In addition to a general sentiment for political change, there were more specific areas for criticism. The apparent indifference of the government to the famine in the north in the early 1970s was seen as a national disgrace and there was awareness too of the growing revolt in Eritrea, to which the government appeared unable to respond effectively either militarily or politically. Feelings towards the Eritrean movement were mixed but the inadequacy of the government's response was plain. It appeared to be all of a part with an ageing emperor who could no longer rule as effectively as he had in the past, but who had not constructed a form of government which could respond to the growing criticism.

Yet when the revolution began in 1974, it was not so much a national movement as an urban development reflecting the unrest among minority groups. It began as a mutiny in an outlying army unit and escalated into growing demands for reform from an apparently spontaneous movement in the armed forces. From rather shadowy origins a committee emerged known as the Derg, comprising representatives of different units from all ranks, some of whom were elected but by no means all. Outside the army the Derg found allies among the industrial workers, who were seeking to flex their muscles in what had been an authoritarian regime hitherto. The students also joined in: they too had been repressed, while some had been abroad and absorbed the Marxist-influenced student radicalism of the era, which had included the Paris revolt of 1968. The demands and moves of the Derg, backed by its new-found allies, rapidly outmanoeuvred the old emperor. Eventually, in September 1974, Haile Selassie was deposed and he was murdered in detention in the following year. His downfall marked an early step in the Ethiopian revolution but not the end of the road.

Conclusion

The European imperial system that had drawn the boundaries of the Horn and influenced internal political developments had collapsed with the independence of Sudan in 1956 and Somalia in 1960. And one of the major legacies lay in the newly independent states' frontiers themselves, in their potential impact for the intensification of relations between the states of the region, especially between Somalia and Ethiopia. At the same time there were important internal implications with relatively isolated regions within the individual states being rapidly brought together in new relationships: the colonially separated Eritrea's incorporation into Ethiopia; the isolated south's hurried inclusion in a unitary Sudan; and the joining of the former British and Italian Somalilands.

More broadly, in the post-Second World War period it was the decline of Britain as the major imperial power in north-east and East Africa that allowed a major change in the international politics of the Horn. (The UN's role was only a part of a transitional process towards independence from European rule.) Just as the Horn's strategically significant position on the sea route to the east and on the periphery of the Middle East had drawn European intervention in the region, so the same factors encouraged others to step into the international vacuum being created by imperial decline. The most obvious initial influence was that of the USA, through its contribution to Britain's decline in Egypt and Sudan, and more importantly through its growing involvement in Ethiopia. But the USA was to be challenged by the USSR, first in the Middle East and later, in their more radical phases, in all three major states in the Horn. With the superpowers playing out their rivalry on this Middle Eastern periphery, it was unsurprising that a variety of Middle East countries joined in as well. Egypt had been involved in the process of Sudan's independence and was to maintain the interest in the region from which the Nile waters flowed. Israel, as well as the USA, cultivated relations with Ethiopia, long perceived as an historic bastion against Islam and by implication Arabism; while radical Arab states such as Iraq, Syria and later Libya, supported Eritreans in their challenge to imperial incorporation.

European imperialism played a part, but only a part, in the shaping of politics within the Horn. Reasons of history and international politics ensured the deepening of the central involvement of Muslim sects in national politics in northern Sudan, an involvement that began long before the emergence of political parties. In Muslim Somalia, however, there were no comparable sects, and instead clan and sub-clan units remained the most characteristic structure for the emergence of political activity at the state as well as the local level. Yet the international divisions of the Somali peoples also involved divisions of those basic units ensuring that the structure of Somali politics would impinge on the post-colonial state's borders. In contrast to the largely localized political life of the pastoral Somalis, the traditions of state-building in Ethiopia had combined internal imperialism with enhanced centralization. This latter development had been aided by the West in the form of support to successive emperors (including the reinstatement of Haile Selassie), as well as acceptance of Ethiopia's case for expanded borders, including Eritrea and the Somalis of the Ogaden.

Those same indigenous and external experiences served to encourage reactions even within the imperial context. The manifestations were largely regional – the complaints of the southern Sudanese before independence and the revolt of the Eritreans in the 1960s – but other factors were involved as well, including not only social and cultural differences but also perceived socio-economic discrimination. Economic development of northern Sudan under British rule had not only led to neglect of the south, but a perception that ever since the slavery of the nineteenth century it had been partially at the expense of the southerners who were reduced to being huers of wood and drawers of water. At the same time Britain had neglected British Somaliland, while Italy had encouraged Italian Somaliland's economic development, albeit still modest in extent. Italy had also presided over economic expansion in Eritrea (mainly in the period prior to 1935 and the invasion of Ethiopia) that had been shifted to an emphasis on central Ethiopia after the federation of 1952. Regionalism, shaped by the era of imperialism, was to become not only a factor in the domestic politics of all three states, but eventually a major challenge to the whole state system of the Horn.

The mounting of a successful challenge to the structures of imperialism, whether external or internal, was to lead to a new political age in all three states and, in turn, to a challenge to the survival of all three as extant at the end of the age of imperialism. But the end of the age of imperialism was not the end of the era of external involvement in the Horn. The balance between external and internal was to alter; but just as imperialism had influenced rather than wholly transformed indigenous societies, so after independence those societies would remain influenced from without, though driven more directly by internal dynamics.

Sudan

The nationalists in power, 1956–69

Sudan's heterogeneity and political complexity, both externally with the struggles of the co-domini, Britain and Egypt, and internally with the rival sectarian-based parties and the isolation of the south, was contained rather than resolved with the coming of independence. On the face of it the choice of independence put an end to the question of union with Egypt, but it did not solve the question of the political relations between the two states, or completely end Egypt's penetration of Sudanese domestic politics, whereas the constitutional settlement only threw a simple and hurriedly constructed superstructure over the domestic political scene. Constitutional development had taken second, if not third, place behind the manoeuvres of the competing sectarian-based parties that had emerged after the Second World War, and their involvement in the rivalry between Britain and Egypt. Indeed, the unitary Westminster-style constitution adopted was described as an interim arrangement pending the introduction of a permanent constitution, but the political impasses resulting from the transitional constitution prevented that from occurring.

A Westminster-style constitution with its first-past-the-post electoral system and its winner-take-all outcome, is defended as producing firm government, yet in Sudan's context it delivered the opposite. The balance of two substantial parties with bases in the religious, economic and ethnic structure of much of the northern Sudan resulted in successive divided governments, based around unstable coalitions. The necessity for such coalitions not only strained relations between the two major parties, the Umma Party and the National Unionist Party (NUP), but also contributed to factionalism within them. The use of patronage to manipulate smaller, weaker, mainly regional parties, into government, or sometimes out of it, with promises of a better future deal added to the strain.

The pre-independence election of 1954 had the most decisive outcome of all Sudan's elections. It allowed the NUP leader Ismail el-

Azhari to form an NUP government, though intra-party factionalism
in the confusion of the independence choice resulted in a brief defeat
for him in November 1955 and then forced him into a coalition government in February 1956 with the Umma and the small Southern Party.
However, Azhari's Khatmiyya rivals in the NUP had created a separate
party, the People's Democratic Party (PDP), and in July 1956 it
combined with the Umma to oust Azhari and replace him with a new
coalition under Abdullah Khalil. The scheduled elections of 1958
produced no clear majority (like the later elections of 1965, 1968 and
1986) and the outgoing coalition was returned to power. But its internal
cohesion became ever more strained over issues of personalities and
relations with Egypt; it was this Umma–PDP division which resulted
in prime minister Abdullah Khalil inviting the army to intervene,
supposedly to calm the situation, in November 1958.

After the collapse of the military regime in October 1964, it appeared
briefly that Sudan might move towards significant political and
constitutional changes guided by the more secular intelligentsia and
influenced by a variety of radical themes including Marxism, Ba'athism
and Arab nationalism. But it was not to last, since the old parties soon
reasserted themselves, using their networks of support in the rural
areas to regain their parliamentary dominance at the elections of 1965.
The NUP and Umma Party were joined in a coalition government by
two regional parties, the Southern Front and the Beja Congress, under
the leadership of Mohamed Ahmed Mahjoub. (The Southern Front
represented southern leaders inside Sudan largely concerned with the
civil war in the south, while the Beja Congress was one of a number
of regional and ethnic groupings in northern Sudan which had emerged
on the political scene following the overthrow of the military regime.)
But the factionalism that had split the NUP in the 1950s now emerged
once more as a young Western-educated Mahdist, Sadiq el-Mahdi
(grandson of Sayed Abd el-Rahman), challenged the old guard, now
led by his uncle the Imam el-Hadi el-Mahdi. As a result, it was the
Umma Party's turn to split and in July 1966 a new government was
formed. Sadiq el-Mahdi became prime minister, with his wing of the
Umma Party supported by the NUP, Sudan African National Union
(SANU – another southern party) and the Nuba Congress (another
regional party from the Nuba mountains of southern Kordofan).
However, the following year the NUP cynically switched its support to
el-Hadi el-Mahdi's wing of the Umma Party and produced a new
government with the Southern Front, led once more by Mohamed
Ahmed Mahjoub. The 1968 elections saw the reunification of the NUP
with the PDP, now called the Democratic Unionist Party (DUP) and
the pre-election coalition was returned once more.

The failure of the parliamentary system to produce stable government after independence contributed to the growing alienation of the
south and the drift into sustained guerrilla war from 1963; parliament's
return in 1966 proved incapable of resolving the conflict. The lack of
effective development policies also led to growing criticism. Politicians
were widely perceived as simply seeking personal, factional and party
advantage; and by 1969 there was a growing sense of political dead-
end which led to rumours of new military intervention even before
the coup led by Ga'afar el-Nimeiri on 21 May.

The period of military rule from 1958 to 1964 had not itself sought
to re-shape politics radically, which was hardly surprising remembering
that a bewildered prime minister (himself once Sudan's senior soldier)
had invited the then senior officers to assume control. The conservatism implied in that move was underlined by the recognition of the
regime first by Abd el-Rahman el-Mahdi, the patron of the Umma
Party, and later by Ali el-Mirghani, the head of the Khatmiyya sect
around which the PDP was based. Moreover, the army itself was a
fairly stable institution. It was older than most armies in Africa having
been created as a separate Sudan Defence Force following the 1924
revolt, after which the Egyptian army had been expelled from Sudan
as potentially disloyal to the country's British rulers. There were some
challenges from within the army during General Abboud's presidency,
but none serious enough to pose a major threat to the conservative
leaders. There was an attempt to create a new political structure
through a system of Province Councils as a path to regionally rooted
'guided democracy' but the new institutions were still very young when
Abboud's regime fell in 1964.

The downfall was due to a combination of factors. Though there
had been some initial achievements, including revision in Sudan's
favour of the Nile Waters agreement of 1929 (which Egypt conceded
to gain approval for the Aswan dam and its flooding of part of Sudanese Nubia), the regime appeared to be running out of drive or ideas
for development. Meanwhile, the ousted politicians began to reassert
themselves. Northern Sudan at least had a culture of political tolerance
and of resistance to repression, and though detained for a while, the
former politicians later became protest figures calling for the army to
withdraw. But the old politicians were being out-organized by more
radical elements, such as the well-led Sudan Communist Party which
was preparing the ground, partly through the trade unions, for the
mass protests and strikes that eventually forced the soldiers out in the
'October Revolution' of 1964. In addition to the growing protests in
the north, there was an awareness that far from crushing the nascent
guerrilla movement in the south, the effects of repression and attempts

to enforce Islamization and Arabization were largely counterproductive.

While the north was largely preoccupied with the difficulties of evolving a stable government, the south was developing its longstanding suspicion over its place in the newly independent state into growing alienation and resistance. The southern politicians' relationships with their northern counterparts had always included a sense of historical marginalization and exploitation, socially and economically as well as politically, and this worsened after independence. The dominant northern parties, which had promised consideration of federalism in the permanent constitution and thereby acquired the agreement of southern politicians to independence, appeared to renege on it: indeed, they proved incapable of producing any new constitution let alone a federal one. Pressure from the south for proper consideration of a federal constitution was a factor encouraging Abdullah Khalil to hand over to the army in 1958, thereby hoping to shore up the emerging northern establishment in the face of southern and other regional demands. In addition to rejecting serious constitutional consideration, it was becoming clear that the most that was on offer was a few crumbs from the table of the northern parties and military rulers. The pre-independence arrangements had already ensured that the administration of the south was largely 'recolonized' by northern officials, and little more headway was made by southern politicians, enough of whom northern politicians could buy off with minor jobs, if not outright bribes, to prevent concerted revolt.

Nationally, the military intervention of 1958 ousted northern and southern politicians alike, though the resentments caused thereby were soon to grow. In addition, the military regime's heavy-handed attempts to impose measures of Arabization and Islamization in the south caused more resentment within the region. From 1960 a small number of politicians and southern officials began to slip across the border into Uganda (still under British rule until 1964) and the Congo (Zaire), where in 1962 they founded the Sudan African Closed District National Union (SACDNU) simplified a year later to Sudan African National Union (SANU). Meanwhile, within Sudan small groups of educated southerners in Khartoum and other cities and towns came together to form what became in time a rival organization, the Southern Front. It reflected what was to prove a longstanding problem in southern politics, the lack of a solid regional organization and voice. The southerners were divided along regional and ethnic lines; their lack of resources made organization difficult and left them vulnerable to the blandishments of northern parties seeking to divide and rule; they were strung out not only across the large area of the south itself, but from Khartoum to the Congo as well, while the depth of their links with the thinly spread heterogeneous people in the south itself was open to question.

The uncertain links between politicians and people in the south was reflected in the emergence of guerrilla groups known as Anya Nya in the early 1960s. The mutiny at Torit and elsewhere of the southern Equatorial Corps in 1955, ostensibly against being transferred to the north, has been seen as the start of the civil war; but though some soldiers escaped to the bush at that time, there was no sustained conflict until 1963. Indeed, it was less the escapees than those who were detained in 1955 and then released in 1961 who contributed to the formation of the guerrilla bands. Following their release, they were joined by a variety of discontented groups, including police, prison warders and others alienated by the heavy hand of the northern military regime in the south. By 1964, the region was fragmented and politically beyond the control of SANU or the Southern Front, while the Anya Nya groups were carrying the guerrilla war into all three provinces in the south. Their activities were influencing the atmosphere in the north as well, where the regime was unable to hide what was taking place several hundred miles away. Politicians of all generations and persuasions were utilizing the growing civil war to berate the military rulers and call for their downfall. It was a proposed debate on the south in the University of Khartoum, and the intervention of the security forces to stop it, causing the death of two students, that became the trigger for the uprising of 1964 which overthrew Abboud's regime.

With the downfall of the military there was new consideration of the south. Amidst considerable international attention, a Round Table Conference was convened in Khartoum in March 1965. But preparations had been limited and it turned out to be a disaster with all sides voicing different views. The conference collapsed without agreement, though a subsequent committee established in the wreckage of the conference was to go on to do some work of long-term significance for the later negotiation of regional government. Instead of peace, it became clear that as the old parties reasserted themselves, the conflict in the south would worsen. Instead of learning from the experience of Abboud's regime, Prime Minister Mohamed Ahmed Mahjoub in particular felt that the collapse of the Round Table Conference gave him *carte blanche* to allow the army to seek to crush the Anya Nya. From 1965 repression intensified, beginning among the educated communities in southern cities, and predictably it led to an intensification of the conflict. Though still fragmented, the Anya Nya were assisted by the collapse of the Simba revolt in northern Congo in 1965 which brought an influx of arms into the region; and closer contacts also developed between the guerrillas and the politicians of the two main southern parties, SANU and Southern Front.

The civil war in the south enhanced the impression of the imperial legacy that Sudan was divided into north and south, each proceeding along its own path. Yet the war in the south was also a culmination of processes alienating peripheral communities from core in a state in which related processes were already under way elsewhere. Other regionally based movements calling for improvements in their areas emerged in the Nuba mountains and Darfur in the west, as well as among the Beja of the Red Sea hills in the east. None was very successful, but they indicated a growing perception of the need for regional assertion in the face of domination of the political system by the centre. Furthermore, the dominant northern interests (whether under parliamentary or military system) appeared concerned primarily with looking after their own. The emerging elite seemed centred on riverain families and communities, from Nubia in the north to Kosti and Sennar in the centre. Their links with other rural areas in the east and west were partly through the long history of commercial diaspora, which had carried small merchants to these remote areas in search of trade and fortune, while after independence a number of parliamentary seats in these areas were filled by politicians from the riverain areas, such as Umma Party seats in Darfur.

As well as the rivalry for political power, the parliamentary manoeuvring was also a rivalry for commercial opportunities. In a country where the 'modern' sector was dominated by the import–export trade, which was officially regulated by government (as it had been in imperial times), there was good reason to want to have a hand on power, especially ministries such as finance and commerce, though other posts gave leverage and opportunities for patronage as well. Personal, factional and party rivalry was thus concerned with rewards that extended beyond the narrowly political, into the economic and social spheres as well. In addition, factions and parties needed constituency backing in the parliamentary periods, and the military officers, too, needed a measure of support in society.

This was where the sectarian networks were so important for they offered the widest opportunities for backing and, at election times, for mobilization. While the core of their existence was religious, they had long been connected to a range of economic activities, directly as in the case of the Mahdists, or more indirectly, as with the Khatmiyya; and they had been related to political development for decades, especially but not exclusively the Khatmiyya and the Mahdists, whether as collaborators or protagonists. At local level, the linkage for parties was not only with sectarian representatives, but also with traders and ethnic communities' leaders. The latter had been enhanced by native administration, which had largely survived the attempt at more democratic local government hastily introduced by the British in the early 1950s. (The radical elements in the October Revolution had sought the dismantling of native administration as a vital element of 'liberating the masses' but had been out-manoeuvred by both the native administrators themselves and their allies in the major parties.)

The overall effect of this network of powerful linkages was, however, perceived increasingly as benefiting the centre at the expense of the periphery. Much of the (limited) economic growth took place at the centre in the so-called 'golden triangle' between the two Niles – Khartoum, Kosti and Sennar. Light industry was concentrated in Khartoum North; the Managil extension was added to the Gezira scheme; and the central institutions of government, as well as the military, grew rapidly in size mainly in and around the capital. (Abboud did try some redress through regionally based projects but they were insufficient and inefficient.) The role of southern politicians in the growth of civil war included not only a strong expression of political marginalization, but also criticism of northern riverain commercial domination within the south. Profits of northern traders were frequently reinvested in businesses of various kinds in the centre, while economic development within the region was neglected. The alienation of other regions may have been less – there were greater cultural ties with the centre – but the outburst of regionalism following the downfall of Abboud was an indication that comparable, if less extreme, sentiments were felt elsewhere as well.

Sudan's descent into civil war after independence was the most dramatic manifestation of the country's political weakness, but it was by no means the only one. The situation of the south was the extreme case of the overall political, social and economic distortions between centre and peripheral regions right across the country. Yet the centre of the political stage was hardly equipped to dominate, riven as it was by personal, factional and party rivalries, supported by sectarian division, which gave rise to unstable civilian government, and unacceptable military rule.

Nimeiri in power, 1969–85

The coup of 21 May 1969 that brought Ga'afar el-Nimeiri to power was, in part at least, an amalgam of radical themes that had been central to the success of the 1964 October Revolution, but then had succumbed to the revival of the old parties and the old parliamentary system. The Communist Party, in particular, laid claim to having organized the 'masses' in 1964, and other radical ideologies with considerable popular appeal in the Middle East at that time, such as Nasserism, pan-Arabism and Ba'athism, were also prominent. It was also claimed that young officers, including Nimeiri, had checked any thought by Abboud and his senior colleagues that the army might suppress the 'revolutionaries'. At one level an important issue of the new regime was the compatibility of the various ideological strands, and the policy directions that would flow from them. But ideology was also about organization, and here there were two major institutions, the Communist Party and the army. The recognition of the potential confrontation of the two had hitherto led the Communist leadership to be wary of a coup as the route to socialism, but circumstances had conspired to overcome this caution in 1969. Thus the relationship was uncertain as the post-coup situation unfolded. While it was clear that the Communist Party's Secretary General, Abd el-Khaliq Mahgoub, headed an able and experienced team, relations among the new military rulers of the Revolutionary Command Council (RCC) were less clear.

At first things went smoothly with a move to the left that included sweeping nationalization of businesses and banks, and the opening up of closer relations with the Soviet Union. In 1970, as if on cue, the more conservative wing of the Umma Party that was led by Imam el-Hadi el-Mahdi attempted an armed Mahdist uprising, but this was forcibly crushed. However, in the following year tensions rose once more. The Nasserists and Ba'athists expected the Communist Party to dissolve itself into a new regime-led single party or movement of what was dubbed the 'May Revolution'; but the majority of the communists followed Abd el-Khaliq Mahgoub in resisting this and sought to maintain its autonomy. A related, though slightly lesser issue, was the wish of Nimeiri and his henchmen to form a union with Egypt led by their idol, Nasser (still a very popular figure in Sudan), as well as with the other newly radicalized neighbour Libya, where Colonel Qaddafi had also seized power in 1969. Nasser's record with regard to communism in Egypt was anathema to the Communist Party in Sudan. The tensions between Nimeiri and the communists had been building up for months when, in July 1971, communists in the army, led by RCC member Hashim el-Atta, staged a coup of their own; but within days a counter-coup was organized which released Nimeiri, restoring him to power and opening the way for him to wreak a violent vengeance on his former allies.

Following these events, Nimeiri and those loyal to him were in something of a political vacuum, having forcibly put down challenges by the two most organized bodies of the right and left, the Mahdists and the communists. With the old system and the most organized radical ideology discarded (as well as the death of Nasser in 1970, weakening the proposed union), the new approach that emerged was the creation of a fresh structure of government with a more centrist ideological orientation encouraged by non-party elements of the intel- ligentsia who became spoken of as the 'technocrats'.

One of those 'technocrats', Abel Alier, the leading southern minister after the execution of the communist Joseph Garang for alleged involve- ment in the 1971 coup attempt, was a major link in the peace settlement with the Anya Nya at Addis Ababa in 1972. Negotiated settlements of ongoing civil wars in Africa have been very rare, and the Addis Ababa agreement was much heralded at the time, subsequently attracting considerable analysis. Its making was helped by the military balance of the time with neither side in a position to make a major breakthrough, but the vacuum in the north and the flexibility of the 'technocrats', together with a favourable international environment, all conspired to contribute to its success. At the core of the settlement was a con- stitutional move, the recognition for the first time of the Southern Region, and the granting to it of regional autonomy. The Addis Ababa agreement was thus both the cornerstone of the second phase of Nimeiri's period in power, and the apparent ending of a civil war that had continued for a decade and contributed to the downfall of successive regimes in the north. It was also the start of an endeavour to constitutionalize the Sudanese political system, which even in its previous liberal-democratic manifestation had operated only on interim constitutional arrangements.

The belief that parliaments had hitherto been weak (a kind of Sudanese equivalent of the old French Fourth Republic) led to the deliberate creation of a strong executive presidency, though it was hoped by the constitution's authors that this would be contained by both the People's Assembly and the new single mass movement, the Sudan Socialist Union (SSU). More local accountability was to be ensured by a radical new local government system designed to replace native administration which had survived the attack on it at the time of the 'October Revolution' of 1964.

None of these products of the 'technocrats' was to work out as their creators hoped. The SSU, the intended cement for the building blocks of the new system, was to find that, bereft of influences of the left, and hostile to the old parties of more conservative hue, it was distinctly lacking in ideological inspiration. Instead, it fell back on the slogans of the 'May Revolution'. Moreover, organizationally, the mass mobilization was often less than apparent at the grass roots, or if present was seen as an agency for opportunists: one of its founders was later to call it 'a party of patronage run by cheer leaders'.[1] Aside from the activities of local SSU personnel, the new local government was often more noticeable, especially since its several tiers required a much larger number of officials, effectively making local administration more bureaucratic. (The distinction between SSU and local government activities was in any case not always clear at the local level.) Often the swollen local officialdom brought a heavy hand eased only by corruption, which became ever more open at all levels. Nor did the new local government structure obliterate the influence of the former native administrators, for often local leaders adjusted in order to maintain a more subtle influence where power had had to be formally surrendered.

But shortcomings in the single party and local administration were of less overall concern than the belief that Sudan had at last achieved peace, which for many observers, especially those outside Sudan, remained the touchstone of Nimeiri's success. Yet within the south itself there were problems in achieving stable rule. Politically, it was attractive to have a democratic legislature, and southerners took delight in contrasting the political freedom the region enjoyed with the continuing repression of the old parties in the north. But the Regional Assembly also became the seat of bitter and confused rivalries in which personal and factional attacks were marked. Amidst the blur of political manoeuvre one rough line of identity was between those who had been 'insiders' in the earlier civil war, and those who went 'outside'; with reference being made respectively to the old labels of Southern Front and SANU. Another rough division was between different parts of the south. Many Equatorians grew increasingly critical of what they saw as the ascendancy of the Dinka from Bahr el-Ghazal and Upper Nile under the leadership of High Executive Council (HEC) president, Abel Alier. Old divisions, together with new ethnic accusations, were thus arising to produce a fractious and potentially exploitable political scene.

Emerging charges of exploitation were to point to Khartoum in particular. It was said that the relationship between the two presidents, Nimeiri and Abel Alier (later to become a national vice-president as well as regional president), was used to bolster the latter within the south. Having been a central figure in the Addis Ababa agreement, Alier was declared the choice of the SSU for the regional presidency even before he could be challenged by two leading 'outsiders', Joseph Oduho and Ezboni Mondiri, in 1973. Such involvement was tolerated as long as Nimeiri remained a uniquely popular northerner in the south, enjoying a reputation as the region's saviour from the civil war, but his lustre was to fade. His involvement in southern affairs continued and, as these grew more confused, bitter hostility towards

Nimeiri himself increased. In 1978, as the 'outsiders' and Equatorian ethnic strands came together to build support for ex-Anya Nya leader Joseph Lagu's challenge for the regional presidency, Nimeiri persuaded Alier to stand aside at the elections rather than face defeat. But Lagu, though also patronized by Nimeiri, proved a far more mercurial and unpredictable character than the quieter, more detached Alier. Nimeiri's intervention became more overt as he intervened time and again. In 1980 he replaced Lagu with Alier once more, but events had swung too far away from the latter, and in 1981 Alier was replaced by General Rassas, a supporter of Lagu. In 1982 elections were held and another Lagu ally, Joseph Tombura, came to power. But by that stage uncertainty was rife, and a year later Nimeiri again intervened to announce the re-division of the south into three regions: Equatoria, Upper Nile, and Bahr el-Ghazal. For many in the south, the Addis Ababa agreement was dead and the reasons included not just Nimeiri's political interference, but his determination to exploit the south's emerging economic resources, oil and water.

Nimeiri's manoeuvrings in the south were typical of his political development in the north as well. The executive presidency had become the catalyst for his emergence as one of Africa's most notable 'personal rulers', a genre of political leadership (in his case allegedly Machiavellian style) that became a major feature of the continent in the 1970s and 1980s.[2] His survival of the armed challenges to him in 1970 and 1971 had set him on the path to executive presidency, and further major challenges in 1975 (from within the army) and 1976 (from the Mahdists again) served to sharpen the personal, manipulative character of his rule. Nimeiri, who combined being a forceful and even bullying leader with a measure of innate political cunning and instinct for survival, had become a master of manoeuvre in the several worlds that comprised Sudanese politics, both inside and outside the country. It was not only southern politicians, northern 'technocrats' and military rivals he was out-manoeuvring, but in the wake of his break with the Communist Party and the Soviet Union after 1971, he was learning to be an adept client of the Western powers and their emerging regional partner, Egypt, as well.

As well as seeking to escape from the post-imperial political structure, Nimeiri's 'May Revolution' perceived itself as seeking to break out of its economic system which was of a less than dynamic, if not stagnant, character. His ambition seemed timely with the oil price rises after the 1973 Middle East war creating ready capital, while the oil producers themselves sought new reliable food sources in the Arab world. The possibility that Sudan's vast savannah areas could become the 'bread basket' for the Middle East was too good to miss, and by the mid-1970s schemes of all kinds were being proposed, and some started. The most successful, in terms of eventual output, was the giant irrigated sugar scheme at Kenana on the White Nile, but it cost far more than originally estimated and by the time it came on stream world market prices of sugar had dropped, so that its operation required an effective subsidy from the Sudan government. With encouragement from the World Bank and the Mechanized Agriculture Corporation there was vast extension of rain-watered *dura* (sorghum) production, often by Sudanese trader-farmers with little concern for environmental damage caused by their ill-thought methods (a kind of mechanized shifting agriculture was widely practised, leaving infertile eroded tracts of land in its wake). Grandiose ranching schemes to expand the existing export of livestock and meat were planned, though in practice their scale was limited. There were also attempts at industrialization, with products such as cement and textiles expanded, but efficiency levels proved very low. A building boom also took place with new hotels for the swarming businessmen; and construction was expanded as many thousands of Sudanese found work in the Arab Gulf and remitted savings that contributed much to the mushrooming of luxurious houses and apartment blocks in new suburbs around the capital.

But Sudan's boom was a false boom, for the returns on new schemes failed to match the investment; the old schemes, notably the Gezira, were showing their age and in need of costly renovation, while the traffic-choked urban streets indicated the Sudanese adoption of expanded consumption patterns. By 1978 Sudan was increasingly in debt and had had to turn to the International Monetary Fund (IMF) and the World Bank. There was one last hope when in the same year it was announced that oil had been discovered and that there were significant reserves near Bentiu in Upper Nile in the south. But far from proving an economic asset, it soon became a political issue that contributed to the political squabbling and then renewed conflict in the region in the 1980s.

Meanwhile the political and economic changes were affecting the state as well. After independence the state had grown in scale, not least to fulfil the 'development' expectations of the era, but was noted in practice for having an over-sized, under-trained staff, leading to bureaucratic inefficiency and petty corruption. In the 1970s this grew in scale. The nationalization of 1969–71 in particular expanded the size and scope of the state; while Nimeiri's personal dominance, coupled with the capital inflow of the boom years, which was theoretically 'regulated' by various arms of the state, led to enhanced corruption. It was financed by printing money and thus contributed to inflation, which took off in Sudan for the first time in the 1970s.

The political and economic changes of the 1970s were having an impact on society. The relegation (though far from elimination) of businessmen clustered around the old parties made room for new-comers, sometimes from modest backgrounds, to prosper in the boom years, leading to later references to the emergence of a 'new class'. The expansion of mechanized agriculture led to rural upheavals in affected areas, including substantial migration from neglected areas to new growth points such as the mechanized farming around Gedaref in the east. There was also a drift to the towns: Khartoum was full of southerners attracted by the building boom in particular, with the Nuer prominent in this new 'trickle down' society.

Sudan's long decline in the 1980s was in many ways the outcome of the 1970s, and particularly the fragility of the search for a new political and economic order following the perceived failures of the post-imperial settlement. The continuing political challenges, especially those of 1975 and 1976 showed how fragile the new institutional edifice was, as well as creating the scene for the further development of the manipulative president. But few expected the degree of flexibility Nimeiri showed in 1977, when, after secret negotiations, he unveiled a new policy of national reconciliation, based on agreement with Sadiq el-Mahdi, the man whose supporters had violently attacked the regime in the previous year. Nimeiri had been cultivating minor Muslim leaders for some time in an endeavour to build his popularity in the north, but in reconciliation with el-Mahdi, as well as the Muslim Brotherhood, led by his brother-in-law, Hasan el-Turabi, Nimeiri was looking to the big battalions for support. To add to that impression, the old Unionists, with their Khatmiyya backing, were largely brought on board as well, though one faction, led by Sherif el-Hindi, chose to remain in exile. The price of reconciliation for Nimeiri was some promise of institutional reform, especially of the SSU, while the old politicians were being offered some pickings, though how much was not clear. It was also an important step in the alienation of southern politicians who had become more prominent in national politics follow-ing the Addis Ababa agreement.

It was the limited involvement in practice that was to frustrate el-Mahdi and led to his early effective departure, apparently recognizing that he had been out-manoeuvred by Nimeiri. But Turabi stayed inside and used the opportunity to develop the position of the Muslim Brotherhood both within and outside state institutions. The issue of constitutional reform in the direction of an Islamic state, which had been raised in 1968 but buried by the Permanent Constitution of 1973, was exhumed once more, while special encouragement was given to the establishment of Islamic banks, with Gulf Arab capital, in which the Muslim Brotherhood was prominent. Though there was apprehension at these developments, there was still an element of surprise when in 1983 Nimeiri suddenly pronounced the introduction of *sharia* law, and then went on an orgy of much trumpeted *huddud* punishments with the populous encouraged to attend public executions and amputations, all in a general atmosphere of enhanced repression.

Nimeiri's other innovations lay in the introduction of regionalism in northern Sudan. As an institutional innovation it resembled Abboud's provincial policy of the 1960s, and for comparable decentralizing administrative and political reasons. In reality, regional government for the five regions of the north was largely illusory. Financial dependence was still overwhelmingly on the centre, while even though governors were nominated from their regions, they were selected by Nimeiri in Khartoum.

In many ways the impact of the regionalization of the northern Sudan was greatest in the south, where there had been one regional government since the Addis Ababa agreement and with significantly greater powers than were now being accorded to its counterparts in the north. The issue became a dimension of southern politics, with Equatorians in particular, led by Joseph Lagu, campaigning for redivision of the south. But it was not the only issue. The growing Islamism in the north from national reconciliation in 1977 was also causing concern among southern politicians, while there was growing mistrust of Nimeiri, the former hero, for his interference in political development in the south, as well as his apparent plans to appropriate the newly emerging economic resources of the region. In 1983 the Addis Ababa agreement, which had been the product of delicate and difficult negotiation, was finally swept aside for redivision of the south into three regions by presidential decree.

By 1983 it was not just the political situation that had become one of growing turmoil in the south. Economically, the decline of Sudan's economy and the rise of inflation were having an impact that was compounded by the political storms surrounding the south's economic resources. The discovery of oil turned from dream to nightmare as politicians north and south wrangled over Chevron's discovery of the field near Bentiu. Southern hopes were for a refinery close to the field, but then it was announced that for 'technical' reasons it would be at Kosti in the north. Later still, policy changed once more and a pipeline was to be built to the Red Sea for the direct export of crude to provide urgently needed foreign exchange. Meanwhile plans were also developing for the building of a long-discussed canal, the Jonglei Canal, to take some of the waters of the White Nile around the vast swamps of the Sudd and thus reduce loss by evaporation. This would enable a

greater volume of water to be shared down river in the more arid
northern Sudan, and in Egypt. To sugar the pill there were promises
of local environmental and development measures, though there was
justifiable cynicism about these. Nimeiri's driving through what were
seen as essentially northern plans for both oil and water became a
source of growing resentment, including feelings that the squabbling
senior southern politicians were allowing themselves to be both
manipulated and out-manoeuvred in the process, thus contributing to
declining confidence in them.

There were also social tensions. Students in the south were
becoming restless over both their own position and the broader policy
issues, and in 1982 demonstrated against Nimeiri when he visited the
oldest southern secondary school at Rumbek. Among the less-educated
economic migrants to the north there was also discontent. The economic downturn was followed by arbitrary round-ups of southerners
and westerners in the capital and their forcible deportation, a crude
policy known as *kasha* which was widely seen as racist discrimination
against southerners in particular. Both students and returning labourers
were to be among those deciding to follow the 1960s example of
turning to guerrilla opposition.

Security problems were slowly but steadily worsening. There was
always an element that had rejected the Addis Ababa agreement, and
with the establishment of a revolutionary regime in Ethiopia increasingly linked to the Soviet Union, there was a potential new source of
support for dissident southerners. In addition to the new regime's
character, Ethiopia saw Sudan as a helper of Eritreans and other
guerrilla movements in northern Ethiopia, as well as a Western ally in
the region. Small groups of armed men, known generally as Anya Nya
II, were beginning to operate in Upper Nile in particular, and some of
them also crossed the border into Ethiopia where there were some
ethnic links. These groups in the bush and in Ethiopia were joined in
1983 by a larger body of soldiers following a series of incidents and
mutinies culminating in an attack by army units on the garrisons at
Bor and Pibor in May 1983. As a result of these attacks the two
garrisons, mostly consisting of supposedly assimilated former Anya
Nya units of the first war, decided to cross the border into Ethiopia.
One of the leaders, John Garang de Mabior, was an officer who had
gone to Bor shortly before the attack, apparently to mediate, but who
now threw in his lot with the mutineers.

A new force led by John Garang was swiftly created. He combined
ideological and military leadership in a way unprecedented in Sudanese
politics since Ahmed el-Mahdi in the nineteenth century. This new
force called itself the Sudan People's Liberation Army with a civilian

wing the Sudan People's Liberation Movement (SPLA/SPLM). Ideologically, the most notable feature of the movement was its aim not of secession for the south, but for a radical 'New Sudan'. Garang had a PhD in development economics and appreciated ideas of underdevelopment, from which it was a short step to associating the south with other deprived and exploited peripheral areas of Sudan: all should unite to challenge the minority, elitist, Muslim-Arab hegemony at the core of the country, that had dominated Sudan under successive regimes since independence. Other factors also encouraged an anti-secession stand: opponents of Nimeiri in the north and outside Sudan could be involved in the attack on his weakening position, while the SPLA's Ethiopian hosts would hardly be favourable to secession in view of the wars in Eritrea and Tigre.

Militarily, Garang and the SPLA had first to establish ascendancy over the southern groups, and there was a nasty little struggle with the group known as Anya Nya II. Numbers were increasing as the cycle of conflict and recruitment, so typical of such civil wars, developed. People would join the new 'liberators' or be ravaged and flee from the fighting, many to the outskirts of northern towns as well as into camps in neighbouring states (in this case initially Ethiopia), where the young men in particular would be natural recruits for the guerrillas and thus contribute to the intensification of the conflict. In terms of composition there was some denigration of the SPLA as a 'Dinka' army, with allegations of hostility first from the Nuer, often identified with Anya Nya II, and then later, as the war moved south, from Equatoria. While such characterization undoubtedly oversimplifies, there had long been an element of ethnic and 'provincial' identification within the south, as well as a 'southern' identity in national politics. It would have been surprising if such tensions and accusations had not arisen with regard to the SPLA, especially since the Dinka are the largest of the peoples of the south, and John Garang himself was a Bor Dinka.

The actual conflict began in eastern Upper Nile with the application of textbook guerrilla tactics by the SPLA, to which the relatively static and inefficient Sudan army was unable to respond, especially in the rainy season. Slowly the SPLA dominated the rural areas of Upper Nile, and spread its power into Bahr el-Ghazal to the west; but by 1985 it had suffered a rebuff in Equatoria where 'ethnic resistance' appeared stronger, partly encouraged by the government. As well as finding the going harder militarily, it was often observed that the SPLM wing of the movement failed to develop very significantly, and that in the 'liberated' areas the SPLA showed little of the concern for civilians displayed by guerrillas in northern Ethiopia. Indeed, neither of the major armies in the south showed much concern and appeared generally to behave with ill-discipline, brutality and exploitation.

Nimeiri's decline in the 1980s was a slow but palpable process. The economic downturn was leading to outbursts of urban unrest which showed the strain. After putting down one such outburst in 1982, the then first vice-president, Abd el-Majid Khalil, led a deputation of senior military officers to Nimeiri calling for reform, only to find themselves swiftly dismissed. Meanwhile, the rural areas of both east and west were hit by drought in the early 1980s and by 1984 large numbers of suffering small farmers were seeking help, many by heading to the towns and towards the Nile for relief. The regime was reluctant to recognize the problem, but a combination of growing awareness in Sudan and in the international community made it unavoidable. Politically, Nimeiri was deserted by all but the Muslim Brotherhood, and he broke with them as well early in 1985. Internationally, his major backers, the USA and Egypt, were appalled at the character of his introduction of *sharia* in 1983 and at his handling of the growing crisis in the south. It was notable that Nimeiri was in the USA when the intelligentsia began the *intifada* (uprising) in April 1985, which was soon joined by large numbers from urban and rural areas, and after a few tense hours it was clear that, as in 1964, the security forces were not going to turn their guns on the people.

The army's decision to side with the *intifada* was somewhat similar to its reaction in 1964, and showed similar ambiguities. Though having been expanded to some 70,000 and re-armed and trained by the USA, there were still deep uncertainties about the army's loyalties. Its decision was naturally presented as reflecting a clearly expressed national will, and as one of Africa's older armies (created in the 1920s after the 1924 revolt), it claimed a 'national' role. Indeed, it had shown past critical responsiveness to policy, as when a group of senior officers unsuccessfully expressed doubts to Nimeiri in 1982. Yet it was also an army which reflected the divisions in society and was thus capable of calculated political factionalism, hence the frequency of attempted coups. In the north the army's response to the *intifada* of 1985 was seen at the time primarily as a 'national' action, but the possibility remained that there was at least an element of personal, if not factional, calculation on the part of senior officers.

Return to civilian rule

While the *intifada* of 1985 seemed like a repeat of 1964, important differences were to emerge in its aftermath. Instead of a full-scale military retreat, the army's commander, Siwar el-Dhabab, intervened to announce the formation of a Transitional Military Council (TMC) to serve for one year to lead the country, together with a civilian cabinet. In the protracted negotiations it soon became clear that the TMC saw itself as more than a figurehead and that while it would negotiate with the National Alliance for National Salvation, which had led the *intifada*, it was also talking to the old parties. The upshot was continued uncertainty about where power really lay in the capital and a consequent inability to move forward determinedly on any particular front, as well as a realization that the time period for the transition was running out. That uncertainty was reflected in relations with the SPLA, for the latter was highly suspicious of the turn of events, especially since the TMC represented the army against which it was still fighting in the south. There were constant contacts through the Alliance, which led to a major declaration in March 1986 at a meeting of the Alliance and the SPLA at Koka dam in Ethiopia. But by then events had moved on and the indecisive transitional period had given way to a return to the old provisional constitution that had preceded Nimeiri's coup in 1969: back to the future.

Elections were held in 1986 (though not in many seats in the south) and parliamentary politics once more became much as they had been in the two earlier periods, save that the National Islamic Front (NIF – the party of the Muslim Brotherhood) now became a substantial third force with 51 seats, behind the Umma Party with 100 and the Democratic Unionist Party's 63. Sadiq el-Mahdi became prime minister and embarked on a series of unstable coalition governments which involved protracted negotiating, primarily with the DUP and NIF. At first there was an Umma-DUP coalition, and then in 1988 the NIF came in as well. The central concern was a share of power, and the central issue that of the *sharia* as Sadiq equivocated and vacillated as the mood and the moment took him.

Meanwhile, in the most crucial area, the civil war, the fighting intensified. Perhaps doubting the army's loyalty (though it now had Libyan and later other Arab backing), Sadiq encouraged the arming of Arab militias, known as *murahaliin*, in southern Darfur and southern Kordofan, and they raided south at will. Drawn from the Baqqara cattle-owning peoples on the Sahel frontier of the 'Arab' world, such as the Missiriya, Ta'aisha and Rizeigat, they had been associated historically with the Umma Party which Sadiq led. In addition, drought and environmental decay, affecting their traditional grazing lands, also encouraged their rapacious southward incursions, prompted, too, by the knowledge that there was a northern market for their seizures. In Equatoria, too, tribal militias were established, while in Upper Nile a pro-government Anya Nya II militia emerged once more. The SPLA hit back hard, but at the same time tried to have a more measured policy towards civilians. Coupled with its improving military performance, the SPLA was proving the most successful force overall in an increasingly fragmented, localized and destructive conflict that was reaching into all corners of the south, and even saw the SPLA briefly take the 'northern' towns of Kurmuk and Qessan on the Ethiopian border in 1987.

Southern war and northern politics were to become more deeply intertwined at the end of 1988 when the DUP partner in the then coalition announced that it had reached agreement with the SPLA; and early in the following year the army effectively backed the SPLA–DUP initiative. The NIF, horrified at the impending retreat of an Islamic state, left the coalition, but Sadiq and the Umma Party seemed impelled towards agreement. Tension was rising, with much speculation ranging from the best peace prospect since the outbreak of the second war, to the danger of another coup from one of several possible factions within the army. On 30 June 1989 the coup took place that was to mark the beginning of a new phase in Sudanese politics.

Islamic militarism, 1989–94

It was an indicator of the political expectations of Sudan that initial reactions to the 30 June coup consisted mainly of asking whose coup it was? Astute observers recognized the links of the new band of middle-rank officers fronted by Brigadier Omer el-Beshir with the National Islamic Front from the start; others were a little slower, since officially all parties were banned, and the Front's leader, Turabi, was briefly imprisoned (apparently in order to mislead deliberately and give the appearance that *all* political parties really had been banned).

But though the connections soon became clear to all, the military and security aspects of the new regime were still vital, and were ruthlessly tackled. Though there were challenges from within the army in the years that followed, they were vigorously suppressed and the officer corps was extensively and repeatedly purged. Estimates put the number of officers dismissed at between 600 and 2,000 out of an initial 5,000.

To augment, or potentially to counter, the regular forces, a new People's Defence Force (PDF) was created. Up to 150,000 people were enrolled, many as a requirement for later studies or public employment, and they were briefly trained, indoctrinated and armed. Elements of the PDF have been used against civilian demonstrators in northern towns as well as in the civil war in the south, with the latter portrayed as a *jihad* in which PDF units have taken heavy casualties.

Another growth has been the emergence of powerful security networks, apparently four or five in all. These have been far more intimidatory than even in the later years of Nimeiri and appear to have been primarily responsible for the well-documented expansion of human rights abuses of all kinds. Particularly notorious has been the establishment of 'ghost houses' where uncharged detainees have experienced maltreatment and torture of all kinds and where deaths have occurred. Other human rights abuses have focused on displaced people, many from the south, as well as on women in the streets and at work (often in the name of Islam), and the numerous vagrant children.

Regime security was understandably paramount, and central to other parts of what appeared ever more obviously to be an NIF-led 'revolution'. Indeed, one of its members had written before the coup that the NIF was out, 'To make a bid to control the state and impose their norms on society and hope to succeed where their opponents have failed by defining a new Sudanese community based on Islam'.[3] However, the ideology of the 'revolution' was less defined in past writings than in the organizational strength and stealthy infiltration in all areas of the state and the commercial world prior to seizing power. Clearly, Turabi, a British- and French-trained lawyer, was its ideological mentor. He had been influenced by figures such as Hassan el-Banna and Abu el-Ala el-Maududi, but he had offered fragments of his own interpretation of the Koran on many issues, rather than a major treatise. (He had also appeared somewhat liberal on a number of issues, including multi-party democracy.) In reality, it was arguable how extensive his influence was to be on the everyday workings of government after 1989, but he was certainly the senior promoter of the regime, not least in his extensive foreign travels.

The central theme in regard to the political system was the implementation of *sharia*. It had never been officially revoked since its introduction by Nimeiri in 1983, but it was formally reformulated and relaunched in 1992. *Sharia*, or for the south the lack of it, was also central to another constitutional development, federalism. The formal establishment of a federal system was heralded as providing the predominantly non-Muslim south with the opportunity to adopt other legal codes if its federal states so chose (though after Nimeiri's re-division there was no such entity as the Southern Region). Following its introduction, there was further division of the states, to the point where they more closely resembled earlier districts than the old regions. As well as federalism, a 'non-party' parliamentary system was established, based on a pyramid of 'congresses' supposedly transmitting upwards the wishes of the people in geographical constituencies and functional groupings (and loosely modelled on Libya).

In the absence of a competitive party system, the allegation was frequently made that the institutional panoply established was little more than a front for NIF control. While some state governors and members of the national assembly appeared to reflect backgrounds other than that of the NIF, all were regarded as acceptable to it, if not actually its appointees, and its power was thought always to hover in the background. This was accentuated by the changes made in the civil service. The inherited services were undoubtedly overmanned and corrupt, and sweeping changes in personnel were made. However, the criterion for promotion appeared to be attitude to, if not membership of, the NIF rather than efficiency or incorruptability. The upshot was a proliferation of keen youngish ideologues in many areas of government service – not just in central government, but ranging from the foreign service on the one hand to the numerous new states on the other. It brought new enthusiasm, of a kind, but no greater expertise, and no lessening of charges of corruption.

Taking over the state was only one part of the agenda. Equally important was the dismantling of 'civil society', that network of associations which in the Sudan had already been identified by the NIF as secularist in character, as well as leftist in inclination. Often referred to as the 'modern forces', the numerous, and hitherto relatively free, professional associations of all kinds were seen by the NIF as very much its true rivals – a rivalry which in many cases went back to shared student days. Many of the associations were repressed, with their leaders targeted for imprisonment and torture, while many more were among the thousands of Western-educated Sudanese to leave the country for voluntary exile, sometimes to re-establish their organizations abroad. In their place a number of front replacements were established. All were acceptable to the regime if not actively encouraged by it, and therefore scarcely constituted an autonomous 'civil society'.

The 'imposition of their norms on society' also led to inroads into the education system. Arabization was extended in higher education, while Islamization took place throughout. The involvement of many students in military training also provided further opportunities for indoctrination. Its results were hard to assess, but there is a possibility that after several years in power there may be something to show for the kind of psychological transformation for which the regime had been aiming. Beyond education, the control of the media also sought to promote Islamization, as did policies towards women in areas such as employment, dress and freedom of movement.

More difficult with regard to reshaping society was the policy towards the established Islamic sects, the largest of which were the Khatmiyya and the Mahdiyya, followed by the Hindiyya in the Gezira,

Tijaniyyah in the west, and the Qadiriyyah. Here there was a good deal of ambivalence, for while the ambition remained to define 'a new Sudanese community based on Islam', there had to be a degree of caution in the handling of the leading figures of the existing identities – no less than the 'holy families' of Sudan.[4] Thus former prime minister Sadiq el-Mahdi was imprisoned, then put under house arrest, but he remained a thorn in the side, still able to defy the regime and attract large numbers when he preached at the major festivals. In response, the regime sought to identify itself (rather than the Umma Party) with the Mahdist period of the late nineteenth century, claiming that it, too, had been a Sudanese Islamic state. Meanwhile, ironically, there was also the growth in popularity of the Ansar Sunna movement, an ultra-fundamentalist group critical of the corruption of government. Great was the public horror when in 1994 some twenty-six of its members were openly gunned down after prayers, allegedly by people connected to one of the security groups.

While the gaining of control of the state and attempts to re-shape society were clear, in two major areas, the economy and the south, there has been less change, only a worsening of the inheritance of the coup of 1989. In economic policy, the regime's oft repeated slogan for autarchy, 'We eat what we grow: we wear what we make', was belied by the extent of continuity. The NIF had already quite deliberately achieved substantial inroads into the commercial sector from the late 1970s through the rise of Islamic banking, with substantial funding from Gulf Arabs and Sudanese exiles. After 1989 that control was extended to force out many of the businessmen associated with the old parties. In their place came not only established NIF businessmen, but the new small entrepreneurs targeted by the banks. However, the long decline in Sudan's economy continued, while both economic weakness and political isolation made it ever harder to acquire credit internationally. The result was repeated shortages of many basics, most notably fuel, and spiralling inflation, lowering living standards sharply for most. These were accompanied by perceptions of widespread profiteering and continuing capital export by the dominant NIF businessmen. The resulting intermittent eruptions on the streets of northern towns and cities were scarcely surprising, though with vigilant security and repressed leadership from 'civil society' popular discontent found it difficult to produce the catalyst for change achieved in 1964 or 1985.

Like the economy, the war in the south went from bad to worse. There were attempts at negotiation, and there were some in the NIF who questioned the retention of the mainly non-Muslim south, but, like other new regimes before it, the eventual decision was to continue the war. Some thought from the outset that the south offered an opportunity for Islamic proselytism that could also be spread elsewhere into the Horn and East Africa. In addition, three developments were to occur which enhanced the military option.

First, the fall of Mengistu in Ethiopia in 1991 forced the rapid retreat of the SPLA, as well as the sending of hundreds of thousands of southern Sudanese from camps in western Ethiopia back into Sudan, whence they had fled. The extent of the significance of Ethiopia for the SPLA has yet to be assessed in detail, but the experience of the SPLA following its expulsion suggests that the military, political and strategic benefits gained were greater than those afforded by any other neighbouring country, as will be discussed in Chapter 6. The SPLA was thus made more reliant on Kenya and Uganda, in particular, for supply routes and contact with the outside world. But the East Africans, while broadly sympathetic to the southern cause, were not to be conduits for support on the scale that Ethiopia had been. And the important propaganda weapon of radio SPLA was also silenced in the process.

Secondly, the SPLA split soon after the expulsion from Ethiopia, when a faction under Riak Machar and Lam Akol based at Nasir in Upper Nile broke away. It called itself SPLA United (later Southern Sudan Independence Army), with Garang's faction becoming known as SPLA Mainstream. SPLA United described Garang as autocratic and they urged the need for new policies, calling now for secession rather than the over-ambitious 'New Sudan'. In late 1991 there was bitter fighting between the two factions, that appeared to have ethnic overtones, with United seen largely as Nuer while the Mainstream was predominantly Dinka. Later, other splits occurred so that by 1995 there were a number of increasingly localized conflicts within the south, as well as between the SPLA factions and the government.

The third advantage was the military assistance offered by Iran as Sudan's international isolation grew. Radical elements in Iran sympathized with their fellow political Islamists, and as well as weapons from Iran, more were bought from China with Iranian financial assistance. A number of towns were recaptured from the SPLA Mainstream but the government was far from achieving an overall victory. (There appeared to be some collusion between the government and SPLA United, with the former clearly benefiting from the divisions within the SPLA, though in 1995 the government captured its headquarters at Nasir in Upper Nile.)

With its ability to fight enhanced, there were always doubts about the seriousness of the regime's stance in the successive rounds of talks intended to try to bring peace. By 1994 it appeared that the most

successful outcome of such efforts was to bring the two wings of the
SPLA closer together. The central theme was self-determination, which
emanated from the United faction, apparently after the international
recognition of Eritrea's referendum and full independence. It did lead
to greater agreement but the factions were still far from at one, while
other breakaway groups had also proliferated.

The conflict on the ground, meanwhile, was devastating. Few in the
region were not affected to some degree: millions were forced to flee
to safer areas in Sudan or abroad, and there were repeated reports of
the growth of slavery reminiscent of the region's experiences in the
nineteenth century. The destruction of the means of subsistence for
the remainder was widespread, and relief efforts were hard-stretched.
The infrastructure built up after the peace settlement of 1972 was
largely destroyed.

The regime in Khartoum may have projected the war as a *jihad* but
the effects of it were felt by most Sudanese directly or indirectly. It
may have been an opportunity to make money for some, and become
a way of life for others, and in this may have lain a part of its
continuation: but only the callous would deny the need to end it.

The war in the south may have been the most dramatic manifestation of conflict, but it was not the only one. In the western regions of
Darfur and the Nuba mountains there was also substantial violence. In
Darfur it was related to the intervention of the SPLA into the region
in 1991, but was also associated with conflict between the Fur peoples
and Arab tribes, as well as cross-border themes which ran into Chad.
Government forces, with the help of local *murahaliin*, were successful
militarily and gained a degree of armed control of the region. A similar
cocktail worked to the detriment of the Nuba peoples in the Nuba
mountains of southern Kordofan, leading to charges of genocide. (In
the latter case in particular there were also indications of northern
businessmen seeking to acquire both land and labour for mechanized
agriculture.)

The regime that came to power in 1989 inherited a decaying state
and declining economy. In purging and dominating the state, its
capacity for political as opposed to coercive control declined as time
passed. There was awareness of this within the regime, which was
itself far from monolithic. Some prominent figures put out feelers
towards leaders of the old parties, but either they (the NIF figures)
were disowned by colleagues or they were received as a sinking ship to
which no helping hand was proferred. Without support the regime
could not retreat, not least because with its record and vested interests
it would not be let off as lightly as preceding military regimes. But
with economic deterioration and war continuing, it had no basis for

wider popularity in the country at large. It had thus manoeuvred itself into a cul-de-sac in which the end was hard to see, but from which there appeared no way out.

Conclusion

As a decaying or collapsing state, Sudan's case is by no means total, but there has been much breakdown. The sovereignty of the state has been challenged most directly by the civil wars in the south. What began at independence with calls for federation of the south turned into secessionism in the first civil war in the 1960s. It was ended by the negotiation of regional government for the south in 1972, but ten years later reverted to civil war in which the central issue for the SPLA was a radically reconstructed 'New Sudan' rather than secession. However, by the 1990s the now factionally divided SPLA had turned towards self-determination with the implication of possible secession. Thus the question of one Sudan or two is on the political agenda. The case for it rests on the manifest suffering of the south for much of its coerced incorporation into successive state structures since the middle of the nineteenth century, and in the feeling that since the referendum in Eritrea in 1993, in particular, there is now greater opportunity for the assertion of a right of self-determination. The sentiment in the south is understandable, for the exploitation and suffering has become increasingly apparent: yet the expected outcome of self-determination leading to a separate state is no easy option. There would be problems of agreeing the border and, if the regime in power in the north was hostile that would be no easy negotiation. The political and administrative creation of a new state would also pose problems. Political relations among southerners would need to improve substantially on those displayed in the years of regional government, while much of the (always weak) administration has been destroyed. Destroyed as well has been much of the economic infrastructure, such as roads and bridges, and though economic resources undoubtedly exist, exploiting them in such difficult conditions (and possibly with an unsympathetic northern neighbour) would be a most challenging task. Indeed, as a landlocked state, relations with several neighbours would have a special significance.

However, it still remains a real possibility that the south will not end up as an independent state. Military power may continue to give the government in Khartoum the capacity to control areas of the south and impose some form of administration on it, even though guerrilla fighters may maintain their opposition. Another possibility would be for some kind of confederal relationship between north and south, rather than the attempted resurrection of the now discredited regional self-government. However, such a prospect would probably necessitate a change of regime in the north to bring it about.

While there is no other comparable challenge likely to Sudan's sovereignty, the state's grip on other outlying regions, such as Darfur, has never been strong. One reason is another aspect of state weakness, namely the permeability of borders. For years Darfur's relations with Chad and Libya in particular have been a significant dimension of its regional politics, although with the emergence of independent Eritrea in the east, there are signs of possible parallel permeability there. It is conceivable that Sudan could tighten control of its borders somewhat, but given the limitations on its capacity and the length of its frontiers it is unlikely ever to be completely successful. As will be seen in Part Two, the most crucial political aspect of permeability comes down to relations with neighbours.

A second factor challenging the state's grip on outlying areas, and at the same time the survival of regimes in the historic riverain heart-land of state formation in Sudan, lies in the problem of legitimate government. It is of course fashionable in the 1990s to assert that liberal democracy is the currency of legitimacy globally, but in Sudan's case at least liberal democracy is no straightforward path to legitimacy and stability of government. Sudan has had three periods of liberal democracy based on a first-past-the-post electoral system in a unitary state, and the political system that re-surfaced each time was a repeat of its predecessor with no sign of any prospect of reforming its clear shortcomings. Major parties (Umma and Unionist) have not been national parties, while large minorities, most obviously in the south, have experienced political alienation. Military rule has survived for longer, but has also lacked broad legitimacy and stability; and civil war has three times intensified under military regimes. Even the separation of the south would not guarantee the better working of the old liberal-democratic system, especially its acceptabilty in other outlying areas. Legitimate government, whether of one Sudan or two, would involve something of a return to the constitutional drawing-board.

One major issue would be that of *sharia*. The inability of successive military and civilian governments to arrive at a clear and unambiguous position with regard to *sharia* is an enormous obstacle to constitutional progress. Yet without facing up to the issue, there cannot be unity and peace, and the spiral of conflict and decay that affects the vast majority of the country to some degree will continue. It is an issue that will require more concerted, imaginative and committed effort to resolve: without that effort it may be the rock on which a united Sudan founders. And even if the south were separated, the experience in the

1990s of an Islamic state imposed under a military regime may have altered attitudes to the character of Islamic precepts in relation to government.

There would be other issues too. There is real room for a debate on federalism, or some more effective form of regionalism than Sudan has experienced hitherto: the countries sheer size is a factor that calls out for some form of decentralization. Yet agreement on decentralization will be complicated by the probable requirement for special financial arrangements. It is likely that a degree of redistribution of resources would be sought, especially in view of the degree of devastation experienced in much of the war-torn areas. Even decentralization might not involve sufficient devolution in such a vast country, and an entrenched, rather than simply devolved, tier of local government might be required as well. That, in turn, could re-open old debates on native administration, and with it the underlying issue of the relationship of the state to local social structures.

In all probability it will be only when some decentralized arrangements have been established that the chances of effective policy-making and implementation will be put into practice. Since independence policy-making appeared all too often to be little more than the rapaciousness of political power-holders and their associates in the commercial and business world. Since 1989 that has been modified by the takeover of an ideologically driven regime pursuing its Islamic agenda; yet the tradition of the exploitation of state power for the benefit of the dominant party's activists continued and became even more intense, not least because for the first time Sudan has experienced genuine single-party rule. The concentration of so much political and economic power in the hands of so few, and the blatancy with which it was exploited, exceeded all that had gone before.

At the same time, any pretence at policy implementation has been the responsibility of an inefficient and corrupt state. There has been a sharp change in personnel since 1989, but political correctness rather than administrative expertise appears to have been the main criterion in the shake-up. In reality, services for most people have become scarcer and more expensive, and much economic and social life has ground towards a halt. Effective administrative decentralization would have to accompany whatever form of political decentralization is established.

A more stable state in Sudan would also require an economic dimension. The symbiotic relationship has to be developed between the state's ability to extract necessary resources from society while also playing a necessary role in promoting an environment of economic growth. Sudan experienced only a short burst of 'socialism', from 1969 to 1971, but it had inherited the imperial tradition of state overlordship of major aspects of the 'modern' economy, including basic infrastructure and the main export-earning Gezira scheme. Following the coup of 1989, there was some privatization, but it did more for regime supporters, who benefited from cheap sales, than it did to dynamize the economy, much of which continued to run down. The intensification of past trends maintained the patterns of domestic exploitation, including on the periphery, profiting from the growing war economy, as well as exporting much of such capital as has been accumulated. Sudan's exploitative political economy, both nationally and internationally, could well undermine any intentions with regard to effective political and administrative decentralization. A degree of economic management will be required to reverse that trend, as well as the provision of infrastructure for which the state alone has the capacity to take responsibility.

Clearly, both Sudan's limited capacity to intervene constructively in the economy, and the undesirability of doing so in the eyes of potential international donors and agencies, whose involvement is required for recovery, means that in economic as well as political spheres there will be a wish to see the resurgence of civil society. Sudan has traditionally had a more developed civil society than other states of the Horn, and as seen, it has come under attack from successive military regimes, most particularly that since 1989. The 'modern forces', as they are known in Sudan, have often been identified as leading institutions of civil society, especially the professional associations and trade unions, and in the early 1990s stood condemned as 'secularists' and 'leftists'. Their traditions and organizations in exile could probably be revived, but they have always tended to be urban if not elitist in character. Building a stronger civil society in rural areas is more problematic. The strains and changes for many in rural areas, especially in the south and central areas of the country, would require the total reversal of so much that has been experienced, including the widespread growth of violence. Civil war has extended well beyond armies, and even tribal militias, to conditions in parts closer to banditry; and in the areas affected few could remain wholly unarmed. Wholesale disarmament is probably unrealistic, but the addressing of the conditions that have contributed to violence is necessary. Only in that context is there likely to be a re-building of rural civil society. Nevertheless, there are traditions of local self-help groups and indigenous NGOs in Sudan, and in circumstances in which there was both governmental and international support it is possible to imagine them growing in significance. Support from both has, though, been put in question since 1989 (as will be seen more fully in Chapter 9). In brief, government suspicions with regard to civil society have been extended to NGOs, preferring those Islamic groups which the government itself encourages (sometimes known as GONGOs – government-organized non-governmental organizations). Western development aid of all kinds has been sharply reduced, largely on the grounds of the government's human rights record. What has been left (apart from GONGOs) is humanitarian assistance, which itself has led to continuing problems between international agencies on the one hand, and government and SPLA factions on the other.

Sudan is a semi-collapsed state. Its historic riverain core remains (though under regimes of declining legitimacy); elsewhere its presence lessens, especially in the arid areas of east and west, while in the south the majority of years since independence have been ones of warfare. Since neither state nor regime has collapsed entirely, it calls for reform as much as reconstruction, but in circumstances in which the regime in power from 1989 intensified rather than ameliorated the underlying problems, thus suggesting that significant change appears unlikely while it remains. Other states in the Horn may have experienced greater collapse, but they may also have reached a point from which reconstruction is possible.

3

Somalia

Parliamentary government, 1960–69

Somalia, like Ethiopia, was trying at independence to put together two territories that had been juridically distinct (southern Sudan had been only administratively distinct) but without apparently a problem of national identity, since all were Somalis. Indeed, the issue seemed initially to be that the Somalis were insufficiently united, since three territories regarded by the new Somali government as mainly Somali-inhabited, and therefore rightly parts of Somalia, lay outside its post-colonial boundaries. For a period at least it was to serve as a source of agreement between those Somalis who did find themselves in the newly independent state, and led to the pursuit of the struggle for the incorporation of the Somali-inhabited territories of neighbours. Sometimes the pursuit of Somali irredentism, symbolized in the five stars on the flag of the newly independent state, seemed to be the obsessive culmination of Somali nationalism.

Domestically, a major pre-occupation was to be that of establishing and maintaining a 'modern' stable government. The concern for 'modernity', as opposed to traditional ways and leaders, was another pre-occupation from the outset, with the major nationalist party having deliberately written 'Youth' into its title to symbolize its turning against the past. Also new was the country's liberal democratic constitution, established in 1961. There was a unicameral National Assembly elected by proportional representation on a list system. The Assembly elected the president for a six-year term, and he in turn had significant powers, including appointing and dismissing the prime minister, as well as dissolving the Assembly. There was some resentment over the constitution in the north since it was felt to reflect Italian-influenced southern thinking due to the greater advances made there before Britain's belated decision to withdraw from the north. As a result, there was a widescale boycott of the referendum on the constitution to demonstrate the strength of feeling, with the outcome that on the voting figures it was not in fact ratified in the north. The intention in adopting proportional representation was that it would promote a greater balance between regions and clans than the British first-past-the-post system (which Sudan used three times). Yet whatever the constitution, the underlying problem 'was how a vibrant democracy placed within an anarchic society could address itself in a sustained way to a broad agenda of problems'.[1]

The Somali Youth League (SYL) won an overwheming victory at independence in 1960, when the assemblies of north and south met jointly prior to the adoption of the united independence constitution of 1961. The leadership went to President Adnaan Abdullah Osman, who appointed Abdirashid Ali Shermarke as prime minister. Osman was from the Hawiye sub-clan in the south whereas Shermarke was from the Majerteen; a carefully balanced cabinet was also constructed. While the SYL was also the largest party in the 1964 elections, winning 63 of the 123 seats, it now had rival parties, especially in the north. In an endeavour to strengthen his own position, President Osman replaced Shermarke as prime minister with Abdirizaq Hussein, but this was to backfire on Osman after the 1967 elections. Shermarke succeeded in defeating Osman for the presidency, and then brought in a northerner, Mohamed Egal, as prime minister. The new ticket appeared once more to balance north and south, but there were policy differences between Shermarke, who was keen to pursue the irridentist claims, and Egal who preferred to downplay that issue in return for a substantial US aid package. Lack of clear political leadership and consequent policy drift contributed to the eruption of clan-based candidates (over 1,000) and parties (63) in the elections of 1969, pointing to the high potential for fragmentation in Somali domestic politics as individuals, sub-clans and clans competed for what were increasingly perceived as the per-quisites of power. This was apparently almost as swiftly reversed in the outcome, for when the Shermarke–Egal pairing was returned to power once more, the proliferation of parties imploded as members of parliament sought rewards from the ruling SYL. But the potential of 'ex-clan' (as they were known) rivalries was also seen in the murder in 1969 of Shermarke when on factional business. In particular, the utility of 'clan' as a unit had been demonstrated in national politics; for hitherto, the traditional clan family had been too large and unwieldy for the essentially parochial local politics in which sub-clans and *diya*-paying groups (groups of families among whom established compensa-tion systems existed, generally the most stable social units in the country) had been more significant. The intense rivalry from clan downwards, as demonstrated in the 1969 elections in which all the parties were clan-based, was destroying the hopes for democracy of the early 1960s and, ominously, replacing it with 'commercialized anarchy'.[2]

While the politicians competed, policy moved forward scarcely at all. The effort to promote the unification of all Somalis was popular but made little progress, while domestic issues went largely unresolved. One important question was that of a national written language: Somali was spoken, but public affairs were recorded in Arabic, English and Italian, and political advantage was inevitably discerned in any endeavour to promote a solution. Economically, a considerable amount of aid was received mainly from Western donors. It did contribute to improvements in the infrastructure, but few of the more grandiose schemes for development made progress, while the competition for those resources that were now attainable proved fuel for the intensification of political rivalries and intrigue.

Siad Barre, 1969–91

The confusion into which the parliamentary system was plunged following the assassination of Shermarke led to considerable relief and even hope when the army's senior officer, Mohamed Siad Barre, staged a bloodless coup on 21 October 1969. Siad was from the Mareehan clan and his mother was an Ogadeeni. He had joined the police in the former Italian territory, and this had later become part of the basis for the formation of a national army. The new military rulers quickly established a Supreme Revolutionary Council (SRC) which drew on talented civilians to take the ministerial positions, and there was a popular response to the denunciation of the former rulers for their large-scale corruption.

Siad's rule soon revealed itself as one that appeared to herald a sharp and deliberate turn to the left. The USSR had had ties with the Somali military since shortly after independence, and its numerous advisers in the country may have encouraged Siad's coup. The Soviet provision of arms rose after the coup, and in addition East Germany assisted in the creation of extensive intelligence networks that used informers to extend their tentacles well into clan structures. In addition, there was much ideological outpouring in the name of scientific socialism, and all secondary school graduates were inducted into the Victory Pioneers to ensure the enthusiastic dissemination of the new vision for society. By 1976 progress was thought to have been sufficient to found the Somali Revolutionary Socialist Party (SRSP). If parliamentarianism had threatened a descent into clan-based anarchy, Siad's answer appeared to at least threaten dictatorial 'totalitarianism'.

On the policy front Siad showed tendencies rather than a 'scientific' approach. He acted firmly to settle the language question on the side of a Latin script for the Somali language. This allowed for greater cohesion within the civil service, and a mass literacy campaign, reaching out into the rural areas, had some success, although there was criticism from Islamic leaders at the potential decline in the significance of Arabic script. Various steps were also taken to try to contain the expansion of a detatched, educated and salaried elite, including the encouragement of mass participation in programmes such as tree planting for environmental protection.

Economically, Siad nationalized the major economic institutions, while leaving small private businesses untouched, and had some initial success in starting new state-run enterprises. In the rural areas there were attempts to encourage co-operatives among pastoralists, but they met with little success. Indeed, the elements – in the form of a four-year drought from 1974 – worked against rural development, requiring instead large-scale relief to assist the impoverished pastoralists. It was tackled by relatively efficient distribution of food aid, mainly from the West; by a resettlement scheme towards the more fertile south; and by the encouragement of sea fishing. Furthermore, steps were taken to enhance the status of women in Somali society. (In this, as well as the language issue, Siad was criticized by leading Islamic scholars and caused deep shock and a longer undercurrent of resistance by publicly executing ten of them in 1975.) More dynamic efforts had been made than in the 1960s, but they had been partly offset by the drought, and Somalia remained a poor, predominantly rural country exporting livestock from the north to Arabia, and bananas to Europe, while being more closely linked to the USSR.

Yet Siad was not content with scientific socialism and at various times detained a number of leading leftist ideologues, perhaps fearing possible rival power centres emerging. Meanwhile, his efforts to contain clan rivalries were only partially successful. One method was to outlaw references to clan allegiance, but this was only to push the whole reference to such identity underground. Another was to try to isolate the more powerful clans that had dominated the preceding liberal-democratic era – the Majerteen, Hawiye and Isaaq – which led in time to the relative over-representation of Siad's own Mareehan clan. He also came to rely heavily on the Ogaden and Dulbahante clans, creating an alliance referred to generally as the MOD, all three being part of the Darod clan-family.

The tensions became greater following the revolution in Ethiopia which began in 1974. Ethiopia appeared to be in national turmoil which presented opportunities for discontented regions that might even lead to the country's fragmentation. With clans with a presence in the

Ogaden involved in Somalia's Supreme Revolutionary Council, the pressure on Siad to risk war built up to the attack of 1977. Not that the eventual decision was in any way divisive, for the attack could be seen as fundamentally nationalistic in character and as such a source of unity for all Somalis which overcame the rumbling clan issues, at least for as long as the war was being waged successfully.

The public emergence of the hitherto subterranean clan rivalries came with the heavy defeat in the 1977–78 war. The importance of that defeat cannot be overestimated, for it was a defeat for a long-standing ambition which lay at the heart of Somalia's self identity. Instead of achieving the addition of a third (and large) star for the Somali national flag, the dream had been crushed: instead of successful expansion, Somalia began in the wake of its failure on the path to an implosion of clan rivalry as earlier frictions and tensions multiplied. The response to defeat came quickly in the form of an attempted coup, mainly by Majerteen officers, which was swiftly crushed. Those who escaped established the Somali Salvation Democratic Front (SSDF) in Ethiopia and endeavoured to wage guerrilla warfare, but found the Majerteen within Somalia subject to vigorous repression and their campaign met with little success.

The next to take up arms against the regime was the Somali National Movement (SNM) of the north. Founded in London in 1981, the SNM had an Isaaq core, but also a territorial heritage in the old British Somaliland which linked it to other smaller clans, thus somewhat diluting its exclusive clan identity. The SNM sought refuge and assistance from the old enemy, Ethiopia, as well as receiving arms from South Yemen (PDRY), both of which were hostile to the now Western-backed regime of Siad Barre. It was more successful in its guerrilla activities than the SSDF, and the reaction of government across the north was fierce. An experienced visitor in 1985 commented that the north 'began to look and feel like a colony under a foreign military tyranny'.[3]

It was not only the security situation in the north that indicated the growing problems of the post-war situation. The economic position was worsening. Trade restrictions on livestock by Saudi Arabia from 1983–85, as well as renewed drought, were weakening the pastoralists in the north in particular, and some northern traders were funding the SNM. Financially, the war had pushed up Somalia's debt, and with insufficient exports the country was forced to turn repeatedly to the International Monetary Fund, where it met with an increasingly reluctant response due both to its own profligacy and to international recognition of growing political instability and a worsening human rights record. Rivalry for government posts and contracts was increasing, with clan favouritism ever more observably the basis of appointments and awards. Once in positions of authority, corruption was the norm with kickbacks of 40 per cent commonly demanded. Financial irresponsibility and the printing of paper money led to rampant inflation, with the real living standards of many employees falling, together with those of most of the population at large.

The government tried to utilize the refugee problem to excuse much of the dislocation and to enhance economic aid. Not that the problem was illusory, for after the war of 1977–78 many fled from eastern Ethiopia to Somalia, fearing reprisals for involvement in the upsurge of violence that preceded the Somali army's invasion. Even allowing for the discrepancy between the government's own figure of 2 million and the UNHCR's estimate of 650,000, it was the greatest proportion of refugees to indigenous population in the world and beyond the capacity of Somalia to harbour without substantial aid, let alone absorb. It required a major international effort, and with it came attempts by various parasitic elements in and around the regime to profit from the relief (as will be seen in Chapter 9).

Siad's response to the mounting difficulties was increasingly auto-cratic and repressive, which in turn led only to rising opposition. Writing in 1985, Laitin and Said Samatar were already warning of a climate of 'interclan animosity, political alienation, and personal cynicism' which they predicted would lead to growing violence (a situation made worse by uncertainty when Siad was seriously injured in a crash in 1986).[4] However, even they did not foresee how far Siad Barre was to go in 1988: in an effort to control the situation Siad was even prepared to surrender Somali pride and sign an accord with Ethiopia's President Mengistu. The two would cease supporting each other's opponents so that Siad could tackle the SNM in particular, while Mengistu could move more troops to his hard-pressed northern fronts in Eritrea and Tigre. The growing Somali opposition likened the accord to the Hitler–Stalin pact of 1940.

The result was a rapid upsurge of fighting in the north. Sensing what was to come, the SNM staged large-scale assaults that brought them close to capturing the major inland towns of Hargeisa and Burao; but the attacks were met by a fiercesome response from the government forces, particularly the massive bombing of the towns. Thousands were killed, and an estimated 400,000 fled to Ethiopia. As well as en-couraging the military, Siad armed others of the Darod clan-family and encouraged them to turn on the Isaaq. Yet the Darod clan-family, especially the three parts of it in the MOD (the Mareehan, Ogaden and Dulbahante clans) was itself under growing pressure, largely because the accord with Ethiopia had, in effect, meant the abandonment of the Ogadenis to the advantage of the anti-Siad Ogaden National Liberation Front (ONLF). (The ONLF itself stood for a multi-ethnic Ogaden state as opposed to rule by either Somalia or Ethiopia.)

Neither the accord with Ethiopia, nor the repression in the north halted the conflict. Instead, it continued on both sides. Villages were attacked and burned and their people killed or forced to flee to the refuge of Ethiopia and Djibouti, while Isaaqs in the armed forces were detained in numbers to prevent them joining the SNM. But such measures were inadequate to contain the situation; indeed, they were often counterproductive as the conflict raged across the north.

Conflict also spread elsewhere in the country in 1989 as groups and clans turned against Siad, often using weapons with which his regime had provided them. In the far south, in Kismayu, Ogadeni soldiers deserted. Ogadeni troops had been widely used in the repression in the north, but disaffection had grown following the perceived betrayal by Siad of Ogadenis in particular through his accord with Ethiopia. Among the Ogadenis of the region the Somali Patriotic Movement (SPM) was formed, and with it came the reprisals from troops still loyal to Siad. Many Ogadenis fled into Kenya seeking refuge, though on occasions the fighting spilled over the border as well.

In the centre of the country, too, violence was growing. Among the Hawiye long-running tensions were giving rise to widespread conflict. Disputes between local sub-clans of the Hawiye and Mareehan had been worsening, and the army increasingly showed the government's tendency to discriminate in its involvement in favour of the latter. Opposition among the Hawiye generally grew rapidly, leading to the formation of the United Somali Congress (USC). Mogadishu itself was in traditional Hawiye territory, and from the summer of 1989 conflict grew in and around the capital.

Siad's response was to step up the use of force, particularly against civilians. Yet the army itself was disintegrating. Though expanded to over 60,000 men after the war with Ethiopia, it had manifest weaknesses. At the top it was increasingly clannist in promoting senior officers, mainly Dulbahante, Mareehan and Ogaden in that order, to the alienation of other clans. At the bottom, the introduction of unpopular conscription in 1984 was leading to increasing desertion, while, in spite of earlier US help with 'defensive' re-armament, the army was running out of resources by the late 1980s. Heavy armaments were running down, and since the army was mostly unpaid, it survived and even sought to accumulate by looting, thus contributing to the growing atmosphere of unconstrained violence and banditry. Furthermore, the core of the regime became ever more a family affair with a growing number of the senior positions being taken by close relatives of Siad. Small wonder that his occasional attempts to present a reformist front were met by cursory dismissal from his mounting enemies. The naming of an Isaaq as prime minister had been suggested as early as November 1988, but to no response; so there could have been little surprise that the appointment of an Isaaq to that post in January 1991, as rebels closed in around Mogadishu, had no effect.

Militarily, the conflicts involved not a single campaign, but increasingly fragmented acts of violence of all kinds. Defections from the army, often on clan lines, have already been seen. And while the various opposition movements had impressively nationalistic titles, these, in reality, cloaked clan-based identities, and within them actual militias on the ground that often centred on sub-clans. This fragmentation of armed groups spilled over from violence ostensibly for political ends – most immediately the downfall of Siad and his henchmen – into armed banditry where the months and years of conflict had made violent extraction from any available source a way of life for a significant minority. Siad fled south from Mogadishu in a tank on 26 January 1991, minutes before the USC finally captured the presidential palace, but the situation he left was closer to anarchy than liberation.

The downfall of Siad was not brought about by the arrival of a united force already encompassing a degree of ethnic incorporation and seeking to take over the state, as was the case in Ethiopia at almost the same time. Rather, the forces of the USC that approached Mogadishu, though predominantly of the Hawiye clan, were loosely coordinated militias centring on sub-clans and even sub-groups thereof; and their target was a battered city in which the last remnants of the Somali state were fast collapsing. Their main leader was an experienced soldier and former Siad prisoner, Mohamed Farah Aideed, by reputation a somewhat autocratic and uncompromising figure from the Saab sub-group of the Habre Gidiir sub-clan of the Hawiye. More political leadership came from Ali Mahdi Mohammed, of the Abgal sub-clan of the Hawiye, who had closer links with the old political and merchant communities of the capital. The two men were apparently the main candidates for the political leadership of Somalia, at least as far as that was represented by the growing rivalry for the capital. At the same time, in the city army units were bombarding enemy-controlled areas and indulging in a rampage of looting, inciting an upsurge of popular violence that produced widespread destruction.

Siad Barre had presided over a major attempt to strengthen the Somali state, and build a state-led economy. But from the climax of nationalist aspiration in the attack on Ethiopia in 1977, there was a long record of state decay. Government became ever more personal, narrowing at first on favoured clans (MOD) and finally on Siad's family, to the growing alienation of the majority, who in turn identified increasingly in clan terms in national political issues. Coercion had increasingly become the means of seeking to cling to power, encouraging opposition to reply in kind to a degree that finally brought down the remnants of the state with Siad's departure. The formal economy, increasingly reliant on foreign aid, was largely used for the enrichment of the remaining state incumbents, while the informal economy grew in significance. It was the bleakest inheritance left by any of the three major dictators in the Horn; Siad Barre, Ga'afar Nimeiri and Mengistu Haile Mariam.

After Siad Barre

Though Siad had departed, the attempt of Ali Mahdi to form a new government remained checked by his rivalry with Aideed in particular, but this was only the tip of the iceberg. The Minority Rights Group identified no less than eight main militias in April 1991, and it was far from clear that these were fully inclusive. While mainly having various forms of clan identity, they did not represent clan 'control'. In particular, young men were being drawn into militias without any sense of the traditions of the leadership of the elders in the management of the clan and sub-clan militias. A report from the time stated that in Siad's downfall:

> Almost everyone got hold of guns. ... Armouries are empty. Police have no weapons. There is no army as such. The elders of the clans do not seem to be able to control many of their armed youth, and there are conflicting inter-clan interests which prevent their elders from acting jointly to improve security.[5]

Almost the only sign of overcoming such fragmentation lay in the emergence of military alliances, particularly of Darod clan-family militias against the Hawiye, but it proved the loosest of relationships in the multi-faceted violence that waxed and waned. And even within groups cohesion was limited, with some of the so-called warlords by no means in full control of their armed young followers, for whom guns from a variety of sources across the ravaged Horn, and outside, were easily available. (The coincidental downfall of Mengistu unleashed many more weapons – even tanks were for sale!) 'Warlords', always a pejorative term, were a product of the emerging interstices of localized and perhaps limited 'traditional' authority on the one hand, and the collapsing state on the other. There was a pressure for clan and sub-

clan formations to assert themselves in the scenario of the state itself
retreating into Barre's clan-based coercion, as well as the presence of
men of ambition, local 'warlords', to lead such emerging forces. However, these were not just against the state, but potentially against each
other as well since the clan mobilization of both Siad's regime and his
numerous opponents ran counter to the emergence of a national
opposition. It was not that the forces were large – clan militias were
only up to 2–3,000 in number – but that there were so many groups
and factions deploying weapons, and with so little apparent structure
of control. (It was the looting of these groups among the cultivators
of the south, rather than simply drought, that contributed to famine
in the early 1990s, a situation that was worsened by the depravities of
the remnants of Siad's troops as they first retreated and then tried to
counter-attack against Mogadishu.)

While violence continued, efforts at political reconciliation proved
predictably difficult. The government of Djibouti managed to convene
a conference of six groups in July 1991, but it proved incapable of
achieving any clear agreement. Instead of a political solution, the
continuing violence was promoting economic distortions that fuelled
the conflicts further. From Siad's downfall looting had become an
increasingly important form of survival, and this included the agricultural areas in the south as well as the towns and cities. In addition,
the trade in the narcotic *qat* grew rapidly. Business interests connected
to Kenya regularly flew in loads using small planes, while the situation
in Ethiopia released trade from there from the constraints of the former
marketing board. Thus, for some, there was a new rapacious and
destructive economy to be joined, and in the absence of a state (and
without even the pretence of government as some of Ali Mahdi's
'ministers' fled) it centred around the armed groups and factions, to
the growing suffering of the majority of the civilian population.
Indeed, the numbers of refugees continued to grow with estimates of
up to 300,000 in Kenya, as well as 500,000 in Ethiopia and more in
Djibouti and Yemen, and with some even reaching Italy.

The situation was thus not just one of collapse, but a new destructive dynamic, whose political, social and economic focal point rested
on the gun and the armed trucks known locally as 'technicals'. It was
in this context that humanitarian organizations began to come to
prominence, trying to counter a man-made 'famine' and recognizing
that 'aid' was not enough. Early in 1992 James Jonah of the UN
visited Somalia, and even suggested a UN force to divide the warring
factions. This fell on deaf ears, though instead he appeared to make
some progress towards a cease-fire between Ali Mahdi and Aideed, but
it was a stand-off rather than a solution and thus fragile and short-

lived. While it lasted, relief aid moved more freely, under the umbrella of the United Nations Operation in Somalia (UNOSOM); but it, in turn, became subject to the emerging economy of banditry, and the small band of 500 UN troops was confined to Mogadishu airport and unable to protect supplies adequately. The major relief supplies came by sea, and as they were unloaded in Mogadishu port and trucked to the city and inland they became subject to protection rackets, demanding both a part of the load for the gunmen, and payment to 'guard' the delivery of the remainder. On occasions it proved impossible even to off-load and deliver as racketeers proliferated around the port and routes. (According to Drysdale, the term 'technicals' arose as the NGOs entered these armed guards in their accounts as 'technical assistance'.[6])

The approach of the senior UN official appointed to Somalia in April 1992, Mohamed Sahnoun, an Algerian diplomat, was to try to work through the existing political and traditional leaders to restore some degree of order and facilitate relief. He also proposed dividing the delivery of relief into five regions to reduce the significance of Mogadishu, and thereby the importance of the rivalry for control of the city. However, he rapidly became frustrated with the UN institutions of which he was publicly critical; and when he in turn was criticized in public by the Secretary General, Boutros Boutros-Ghali, Sahnoun resigned. The two men also differed over policy, for while Sahnoun had opposed the deployment of a UN force, at least until it had the agreement of Somali leaders, Boutros-Ghali was becoming an increasingly open advocate of armed UN intervention, a step that would stiffen the UN globally as well as bring accelerated relief to Somalia. He replaced Sahnoun with one of his allies, an Iraqi diplomat, Ahmed Kittani, a man of less conciliatory approach than his predecessor. It was an open sign of the policy differences developing within the UN bureaucracy itself. Boutros-Ghali's views coincided with the loss by George Bush of the American presidential election and his wish to go out with a final flourish. After consultation with his opponent Bill Clinton he announced on 24 November 1992 that US forces would be deployed on behalf of the UN in Mogadishu. With this action relief had finally become not peripheral but central to the politics of one country in the Horn, and a new chapter in the relationship between domestic violence and international force was about to be opened.

Yet while international intervention was about to occur in the capital, elsewhere in the country the situation was more stable. In the far south it was an uneasy peace as the USC fought off a final attack from forces loyal to Siad in April 1992 (though it still left one of his sons-in-law, Mohamed Siad Hershi Morgan, in the field, together with the Somali Patriotic Movement under Omer Jess). In the north-east the situation was better still with the Somali Salvation Democratic Front (SSDF), a Darod-based force, in control and, more importantly, traditional leaders such as the elders beginning to restore some of the mechanisms of dispute settlement. Most notable of all was in the north-west where the SNM had really opened the conflict in 1988. Here, a new independent state of Somaliland was proclaimed as will be seen shortly, but without receiving international recognition.

Meanwhile, in the area of the south around Mogadishu and down to Kismayo there was such apparent anarchy and suffering that the UN was about to embark on military intervention in what was still legally a sovereign state. The absence of any government or quasi-governmental structure was to make it the first time a UN operation had been mounted without the consent of the belligerents involved in a conflict.

Yet even as the US-led UN operation prepared for action there were those, including some in government circles in member states of the Security Council (including the USA itself), who queried the whole operation. But in spite of the voices of caution, intervention won the day. Boutros-Ghali was keen for action to demonstrate a new capacity of the UN for peace enforcement, rather than simply peace-keeping as hitherto. To him it was to be a new era for the UN and one for which he had been eager for some time. For President Bush it was an opportunity to go out in a blaze of glory of the kind he had enjoyed in the Gulf, demonstrating one last time his capacity for decisive leadership in international affairs, and the US dominance in the New World Order of which he spoke so bravely. His successor, President Clinton, was less sure, but found it difficult not to concede the humanitarian character of Operation Restore Hope, especially when he had been critical of the morality of Bush's foreign policy. There was too the US media which was projecting images of Somalis as the victims of famine, denied relief by the warlords: a simplified picture that cried out for intervention. The Europeans may have failed to act with sufficient decisiveness in Bosnia; but the USA would show how it could be done with a swift large-scale intervention in Somalia. The Pentagon gave assurances that it would be 'do-able' and would not involve significant loss of US troops. On 3 December 1992 UN Resolution 794 was passed calling for the establishment of a safe environment for humanitarian aid in Somalia. Above all, it was to be a Chapter VII operation which meant that for the first time a UN force under the overall direction of the Secretary-General would be deployed for peace-making, rather than simply in a peace-keeping role, since it was the violence, partly directed to the exploitation of the aid itself, that was ongoing when the force was committed.

Thus on 9 December the first of 30,000 US troops, the major part of a Unified Task Force (UNITAF), landed at Mogadishu in an operation carefully timed for live prime-time television in the USA. The aim was to take control of the ports of Mogadishu and Kismayu, to ensure the passage of relief supplies to the food distribution centres, and then to prepare to handover to UNOSOM II. On the question of disarming the gunmen, there appeared to be uncertainty: Boutros-Ghali for the UN seemed to think that this was implicit in securing 'a secure environment for humanitarian relief operations', but this view was not to be shared by President Bush or the US commander on the ground who regarded the delivery of relief supplies as possible without such dangerous and possibly widescale operations being necessary. Bush had assured the American public that the operation would be complete by 20 January, but it was clear from the outset that such a timetable was optimistic (indeed, it was revised to 120 days), and that in reality intervention was more open-ended, particularly since the political objectives were unclear in a country that had no government and very limited prospects of establishing one in the foreseeable future.

Initially, there was comparative success as far as the delivery of relief was concerned, but predictably the political problems soon surfaced. While the USA's special envoy, Robert Oakley, was keen to promote agreement between Somali leaders, and Ethiopia and the UN convened conferences of faction leaders in Addis Ababa in January and March, Aideed in particular was concerned to defend his own position in south Mogadishu. At first, both he and Ali Mahdi had welcomed the UNITAF intervention – they had little option – but thoughts of disarming them brought manoeuvres to avoid any such action. However, by February Aideed perceived that the UN's action in the port of Kismayu showed clear favouritism towards one of his rivals, Hirsi Morgan (related to Siad Barre), and against Aideed's ally, Omer Jess. He was also concerned that Ali Mahdi was stealing a march on him and that there was a danger of Ali Mahdi's claim to head an interim government being recognized. Heavy, if brief, fighting broke out in the capital.

Though the position remained tense, the withdrawal of the majority of US troops did take place by 1 May, when, as planned, a new UN force took over. UNOSOM II under Security Council Resolution 814 went into Somalia on 1 May and comprised forces from a number of different countries. (The international composition of the force was itself to prove a problem in terms of overall coordination; there were also accusations of different national agendas, directed particularly against Italy, and also against the USA which provided a separate Rapid Reaction Force under US command which was the force largely used in the conflict with Aideed.) The clashes with Aideed in particular soon developed, especially in June. There was a feeling that UNITAF had done insufficient to pursue disarmament generally, and that faction promises to this end were not to be relied upon. For his part, Aideed appeared to feel that it was time to test the strength of the disparate new UNOSOM II force to see if it would be as feeble as the first UNOSOM force had been in 1992. Though still few in numbers, his faction showed skill in organization and propaganda. He was able to deploy in such a way as to use civilians as cover for anti-UNOSOM operations, and when the latter responded with increasing violence, he used his radio to expound his message of resistance. Within weeks UNOSOM forces were scarcely able to venture out of their quarters even in vehicles; and in unsuccessful attempts to capture Aideed, US helicopter gunships and heavy weapons were deployed. With forty-seven UN forces and an estimated 300 Somalis killed, it was soon being suggested that the UN was becoming the biggest warlord of all and the greatest threat to the people of Mogadishu, and that the UN favoured Ali Mahdi against Aideed, with potential consequences for the followers and clansmen of both. Moreover, throughout its activities the UN was accused of displaying manifest bureaucratic inefficiency in spite of moves to restructure its operations. By early September doubts were being expressed both internationally and in the US Congress about the objectives, and in particular the attempt to criminalize Aideed and concentrate on his capture to the apparent exclusion of almost all else. Not only had there been discussion of his trial, but a price of $25,000 had been offered for his capture. In contrast, the UN appeared to have little concern about broader disarmament in Somalia: it did not appear to put much energy into pursuing the clan reconciliation attempted earlier in the year, and was spending far more on military operations than humanitarian relief.

The picture of political uncertainty was exacerbated as more Americans and Somalis were killed in October 1993. Pressure in the USA was understandably raised, but the response was potentially contradictory. President Clinton ruled that US forces would be strengthened, but he also put a time limit of 31 March 1994. The impression was of reinforcing to facilitate withdrawal rather than sustained long-term commitment to an operation in which it had been the USA that was at the centre of the UN action. However, the political legacy being sought for Somalia was less rather than more clear. Instead of pursuing Aideed as hitherto, it appeared now that he was once more to be rehabilitated through talks, as had been sought initially when the US forces first arrived. Once more it appeared that political vacillation prevailed, in the midst of preparing for an early exit of American troops. Militarily, future policy remained uncertain, while politically it appeared that the UN and neighbouring states would once more be handed the initiative of trying to patch together some kind of national agreement from those who had emerged as leaders from the wreckage of Somalia, irrespective of the blood attaching to them. (In preparation for such a role, Aideed even produced his personal credo on the future marriage of local Somali democracy – 'the most democratic people in world' – with national non-clan-based parties within a system of proportional representation to ensure stable coalition governments.)

In the end time ran out for the UN before the 'warlords' and in March 1995 UN troops were finally withdrawn. There was no immediate explosion of violence, but nor was there a legacy of conciliation and peace. Instead, the major factions continued to manoeuvre with respect to one another, including intermittent skirmishes. That situation in turn threatened UN efforts at the local level. While in Somalia the UN had contributed to the reviving of local and district councils in the south, but its departure, and the continued existence of the rival armed factions, put the future of such local institutions in doubt, especially when the UN had been strongly criticized for 'politicizing' the councils and trying to use them to sideline Aideed's supporters.

Meanwhile, in the north-west the new self-proclaimed state of Somaliland had emerged from the struggles of the Somali National Movement. Founded in London in 1981, the SNM had an Isaaq core but also a territorial heritage in the old British Somaliland, which linked it to other smaller clans, thus somewhat diluting its distinctive clan identity. The SNM had been a relatively egalitarian and democratic organization, eschewing radical ideologies not least because it had been opposing in Siad Barre a former scientific socialist. The Siad–Mengistu accord of 1988 was the catalyst for the explosion of conflict in the north, and by the time of Siad's downfall in 1991 the intense wave of violence had largely passed on, albeit leaving a ravaged and confused legacy.

The SNM was now the main power in the former British territory, However, after some discussion it became clear that it was not just about regional peace. In May 1991 it declared the independence of a new state, Somaliland, under President Abd el-Rahman Ahmed Ali 'Tour', the SNM leader. The claim, like Eritrea's, centred on the creation of a new state from two hitherto separate colonial territories in 1960. Somaliland claimed that in the light of events after 1960, in particular the increasing domination of government by the south and discrimination in its favour, Somaliland should have the right to secede. To this end it officially repealed the Act of Union of 1960. In any case there was now no government or even state in the south, whereas Somaliland claimed to be establishing both. Somaliland's claim, however, met with no recognition in the international community (including neighbours Djibouti and Ethiopia, which both hosted peace talks at which the SNM declined to be represented), and instead Somaliland was left to manage as best it could with only a trickle of aid to an area in which the conflict of 1988 had devastated the infrastructure. The UN, and in particular Boutros-Ghali, was felt to be strongly opposed to recognition: the SNM recalled that when, at the Egyptian foreign ministry, he had supported Siad's regime.

By the end of 1991 predictably reports were surfacing of clan and sub-clan rivalries and consequent instability within the newly created army and police, especially in the towns of Burao and Berber. The SNM government, its critics said, had not only failed to win international support, but it was so weak that it could not even pay for its own personnel, or deliver services. But instead of the feared descent into conditions such as those in the south, Somaliland became more settled, though not without some difficult moments. There was a significant outbreak of intra-Isaaq clan fighting in 1992 over control of the port of Berbera, and Tour's government lost the conflict, having to leave control in the hands of the Habr Awal sub-clan. After 1993, when Egal, of the Habr Awal, became president, Tour's Habr Yunis sub-clan was resentful and was involved in some subsequent clashes. However, any fears of vengeance by the Isaaq majority on other smaller clans proved misplaced; instead, they were given minor positions in government in Harage, while locally clan and sub-clan units were incorporated into local administration. Central to this has been the growing authority of a variety of 'traditional' leaders. 'Sultans' emerged as local political leaders, and lineage elders in the sub-clan groups. Traditionally, the clan leaders' title of sultan had been largely honorific, but with the growing significance of inter-clan politics, they gained a greater importance. Processes of mediation and the peaceful settlement of disputes and grievances were resuscitated. The clans and some sub-clans restored their own *guurti* (councils of elders) that could arbitrate between clans, especially in such important and sensitive matters as grazing rights. These bodies were backed by various other inputs, including those of holy men, popular oral poets, and women who have sometimes been in a position to utilize their marriage networks to reduce tensions. (This apparent building of working relations between local communities and Somaliland government also appears to owe something to the war fought by the SNM in which it had sought to work with the grain of local social structure, as in the creation of clan-based military units.)

The various steps to reduce clan conflict in Somaliland culminated in a national conference or *guurti* at Boroma from February to May 1993. A new outline was agreed for the maintenance of law and order, and in the course of the proceedings 97 of the 140 Central Committee voted to replace President Ali 'Tour'. The perceived failure of central government to develop effectively brought an assertion of power by local leaders; and they also backed a new leader, Mohamed Ibrahim Egal, who had been prime minister of Somalia from 1967–69. Somaliland thus established a loose political structure which its supporters said offered a form of synthesis of national government on the one hand and local leadership on the other, rather than the schizophrenic relations between 'modernity' and 'tradition' of the former parliamentary and socialist periods. A government executive in Hargeisa was maintained, and although its authority was relatively weak, it effectively shared power with *guurti* at 'national', clan, and in some cases sub-clan, level. These, in turn, were cross-cut by sultans, the influence of Muslim leaders (including growing fundamentalist groups), and other fragments of 'national' civil society, especially among the intelligentsia, all of whom appeared to gain in influence somewhat with the collapse of the old Somali state. The influence of these leaders was seen particularly in their often successful efforts to defuse the intra-clan rivalries mentioned above. The failure to achieve international recognition may even have helped the search for stability since its pursuit encouraged Somaliland identity, whereas disorder would have only damaged the case being presented to the world. Doubters, however, feared that the very looseness of the young state reduced its capacity to function in the face of obvious developmental needs, and there were fears for minorities and the place of women.

Conclusion

In terms of state collapse, Somalia appears to be the most complete experience in the Horn. The building of Somali socialism in the 1970s contributed much to making state and regime increasingly synonymous; the reverse of that coin was the long political narrowing of the regime after the 1977–78 war with Ethiopia, which finally brought the destruction of the state with the overthrow of the regime. The collapse of state sovereignty had another dimension as well, for from the ashes of the destruction of the north rose the new self-proclaimed, but internationally unrecognized (though increasingly accepted), state of Somaliland, which appeared determined not to be reunited with the south.

While the destruction of the Somali state as constituted from 1960

was primarily due to domestic factors, the issue of the permeability of
the state's borders was also relevant. Indeed, in Somalia's case the
relationship between borders and the survival of the state was particularly crucial. Somalia was one of the minority of states in the world
with irredentist claims. These were actively pursued by promoting
cross-border activity for part of the 1960s, and then most spectacularly
by the invasion of Ethiopia in 1977, as well as being continued at a
lower level thereafter. Yet border permeability was to work against
Somalia from 1978 as Ethiopia hosted Siad Barre's growing number of
opponents. The agreement between Siad and Mengistu in 1988 had
the sealing of the border from both sides as its main objective, but
instead precipitated the major conflagration in the north which contributed so much to the weakening of regime and state thereafter.

Perhaps because the state collapse in Somalia has been so complete,
much of the discussion of its causes and possible recovery has centred
around analysis of the legitimacy of the state in Somalia. This has
concerned not just the particular reasons for Somalia's collapse, but
also the conception of state–society relations in what was for so long
a stateless area, and where state-building was exclusively an alien
undertaking in origin (unlike the historical experience of at least parts
of Sudan and Ethiopia). This discussion has thrown up a number of
related themes, rather than a single consensus.

The complexities of Somali society, which were briefly alluded to
in Chapter 1, were an obvious starting point for the experts, and ones
which called for the insights of social anthropologists in particular,
notable among them being Ioan Lewis, who has been such a pioneer in
the field. Writing in 1989, Lewis emphasized that in spite of public
claims by successive post-independence governments to end clan
politics in national affairs, they were back more virulently than ever:

> In the present Somali vortex, then, clan and lineage ties are definitely
> born again. In fact of course they never died. ... Somali nationalism
> evidently retains its segmentary character and has *not* been transformed
> into a modern organic mode.[7]

However, Lewis was not suggesting that politics in Somalia were simply
'primordialism' writ large; rather, he was claiming that Somalia represented the 'perfect application of segmentary lineage principles at the
highest levels of segmentation', arguing that Siad had sought 'to exploit
to the full segmentary lineage rivalry'. In addition, there was, as Lewis
has argued, a newness to 'clan' as a unit. In 'traditional' politics clan
was too large a grouping for relevant political action since such action
was predominantly local and therefore small-scale at family and sub-
clan levels. However, in the context of the modern state it emerged as

a new force (though, as noted, often with sub-clan dimensions and even further divisions as well).

Few would argue with that, but Somali writers in particular have sought to bring out the changes wrought in the nature of 'clan' itself by the political and economic context. In an unpublished paper in 1990, Ahmed Samatar made the useful distinction between 'kinship' and 'clanism'. In brief, traditional production was for pastoral subsistence and the importance of kinship reflected the reciprocal relations of production. Colonialism had introduced commodity production for a people on the fringe of the international economy which brought major rewards only for the few, most notably the merchants and later state personnel, and contributed to the relative or absolute impoverishment of the many. Such has been Somalia's marginality in the international economy that a more 'modern' economic system could not 'take off', while its 'traditional' system has been undermined in various ways. As a result ruthless competition developed that turned regulated local kinship into a new unfettered national clan rivalry. In addition, Britain's relative neglect of economic development in the north gave the south a head start which was compounded by the favouring of southern-based interests and clans by post-independence governments.

Abdi Samatar contributes a similar line of analysis, arguing that 'traditional' society, based not just on clan but a 'complex of *Xeer* (*heer*), Islam and blood ties'[8] was broken down by the combined weight of peripheral commercialization and state-building. It amounted to a partial transformation of Somali society, but one which lacked the capacities to fulfil itself and instead imploded into the tragedy of recent years. Ominously, he concluded that 'In the absence of an organized indigenous agency which can establish peace ... the Somali people must rely on the international community to save them from the horrors and the savagery of petit-bourgeois fascism'.[9] (A cynic might remark that it was from the 'international community' of the past that Abdi Samatar's twin horsemen of the Apocalypse descended in the form of partial commercialization and the building of a coercive state capacity.)

There are political implications, as Abdi Samatar has argued. The colonial and post-colonial state was equally alien in its development. As well as being distorted towards the south in the independence period, it became itself the origin of a state-based class under first liberal-democratic and then military regimes. Rather than existing to provide services to society, the incumbents of the various arms of the state became instead ever more extractors and consumers themselves; and when the regime was increasingly challenged after the war with

Ethiopia, this state-based ruling class resorted to enhanced repression. However, instead of coherent opposition to the real nature of the crisis (that is, state-based class exploitation), clanism prevailed both in the defence of what became an ever more narrowly based regime, and in the manifestation of opposition giving rise to numerous clan-based fronts.

Related ideas are advanced by Said Samatar in terms of the alien post-colonial state, though his argument (like that of Lewis) is couched in more traditional terms. However, the level of violence reflects the existence of a state in the modern world: 'Somali state politics is nothing but traditional clan politics writ large, with the difference that the society is today armed with modern, mass-destructive weapons – with Stalin organs and assault rifles. Hence the massive level of the violence.'[10] The lack of legitimacy of not only the state itself, but the political process operated within it, has also been a major weakness. Parliamentary politics were remote and meaningless to most, while a military ruler (Siad Barre) rose only through membership of the colonial police – an alien institution.

The theme of alienation is also expressed by Hussein Adam, albeit in a more consciously cultural form. Somali society is about the expression and recognition of worth, including a degree of tension and rivalry in the maintenance of finely balanced systems of 'reciprocal recognition' at all levels.[11] For Somali society to survive within the context of a state requires the balancing of clans politically as competing socio-economic pyramids. The logic of this is towards political arrangements that are consociational in character, creating a balance of political forces in government. However, first a constitution that promoted a search for majority rule (which even though including proportional representation produced distortion towards the south) and then later military rule, destroyed any vestiges of balance, replacing it by an extreme clan rivalry (in which, as Said Samatar points out, Siad Barre, with his power and patronage, was a hero figure to his own Maraheen).

These lines of analysis bring out a number of strands with regard to political reconstruction. The significance of clan, sub-clan and even family units continues, though their character and relative significance have changed. The relevance of this lies in thinking of constitutional reconstruction in Somalia, in contrast to the earlier attempts to deny officially clan in national politics. The example of Somaliland, and even UN efforts to build local administration, provide an indication of what could be attempted in the south in the future, as indicated in Hussein Adam's suggestive comments. The importance of achieving an effective balance between society and the state is enhanced by the greater absence in Somalia than in Sudan of traditions of civil society as an intermediary layer of social organization of a national character. There may be possibilities for the development of indigenous NGOs, for instance among women, but these are likely to be of a very localized character and thus of limited significance in some form of wider reconstruction.

Meanwhile (as in Sudan), the issue of the compatibility of decentralized politics and economic development arises. The building of Somali socialism in the 1970s intensified the competition for state power as the access to financial and economic resources, and that is unlikely to be repeated. However, commercial activities, some of a parasitic character such as the supply of *qat*, took over as alternatives for political and armed rivalry and can be sustained even in the context of a collapsed state (in which trade can still be undertaken in, for instance, US dollars). There have been winners and losers in these ugly clashes, including dispossessions in the more fertile southerly regions, and addressing economic grievances may be a necessary aspect of political reconstruction.

The proliferation of weapons is a further significant theme. Arms have become associated not only with the pursuit of political power, but also with rivalry for control of economic resources. Total disarmament appears unlikely; indeed, for many, weapons appear a justifiable need in the Hobbesian world they inhabit. But any reconstruction will have to address the issue of heavier weapons which, by their existence, help to create a core around which the survival of competing military factions has been built. The state, then, may not be expected to have a monopoly of weapons of destruction, in the short to medium term at least, but it will need a preponderant force if it is to be reconstituted.

The aspect of collapse and reconstruction that attracted most attention on Somalia has been international involvement. The UN and US intervention in Somalia (which will also be discussed in later chapters) was the most dramatic intervention in the Horn. Though the final US forces departed in March 1994, and UNOSOM II a year later, the UN had contributed to a new form of international involvement that could not be abandoned without implications for Somalia, the region, and the international community.

The UN's role by 1994 had become, at one level, facilitator of agreement among those self same warlords who had previously been castigated and in Aideed's case even pursued. On the one hand this appeared to involve encouraging negotiation between the faction leaders, and on the other seeking to make them think flexibly about some appropiate form of constitution, possibly including federalism or confederalism that might have some appeal to Somaliland. Furthermore, the UN backed its position not with significant sticks, which had been so maladroitly and disastrously deployed in 1993, as through the carrot of recognizing that any new leader or leaders would require sufficient stability to allow the foreign aid to function that would be necessary for reconstruction. However, there was to be an element of idealism in this. Indeed, towards the end of 1994 there was a fear that instead of having contributed to the framing of a solution, the UN had become the target for armed groups in the south of the country. It seemed a re-run of the situation before the UN's intervention when the foreign intervention had become inadvertently a cause of, rather than a solution to, suffering. A role that had once fallen on the shoulders of aid agencies of engendering violent conflict for resources (a pattern that in turn went back to the later years of the Siad Barre regime), had now been taken over by the UN itself, especially as a result of its failure to achieve any effective disarmament of the rival factions. Small wonder that calls were heard for the UN to withdraw entirely and let Somalis come to terms in the absence of the resources for predatory banditry by 'warlords' and their followers.

At the local level the task is also difficult. As already mentioned, the UN did contribute to the establishment of local and district councils in the south, while the Somaliland experience is often raised as indicating the significance of 'elders' and other traditional leaders, (though the legitimacy of at least some 'elders' in the case of the south has been questioned, together with accusations of the appropriation of land by some such figures during the Siad Barre years). Optimists will no doubt hope that by constitutionally limiting the powers of a future central government, Somalia will not only strike a more workable relationship between 'clan and country', but also overcome the schizophrenia that it has appeared to exhibit under both parliamentary and military rule in the past.

The international community is also likely to be a dimension of future relations of Somaliland with the rest of the country. In Somaliland itself, the UN is seen as hostile to its independence, a position which is viewed critically in the light of the latter's acceptance of Eritrea, though there is growing informal recognition, especially by NGOs. Decisions of the international community regarding the recognition of Somaliland will remain a dimension of the reconstruction of Somalia as a whole, whether as one or two recognized states.

The UN, most actively encouraged by the USA, appeared to stumble into an involvement in Somalia from which it eventually had to retreat ignominiously. Its presence was requested by Ali Mahdi, but he was a self-appointed president, and certainly not the head of an effective government. The UN was stepping into a violent factional morass, without a clear party or parties with which to negotiate its purpose and eventual way out. It thus seemed singularly uncertain of its long-term intentions in a way that was to have serious consequences. It fell between two stools which were largely of its own making: Sahnoun had wanted a 'softly softly' approach while Boutros-Ghali had sought a tough intervention force under UN command and with disarmament as a high priority. Some even believed that nothing less than an effective UN trusteeship would suffice, however anachronistic that might sound in the 1990s. What in the end happened was an intervention in which the USA became the largest single voice and which sought, in effect, to drive a middle way between these one-time rival views in the UN. Perhaps the Boutros-Ghali approach was always impossible: to seek to disarm factions on their home ground was inevitably to confront Somalis in such numbers as to put the whole operation in doubt, and therefore jeopardy. In the event, it was the loss of UN (more particularly US) forces as much as the effective waging of war on at least some Somalis (with contrived and accidental civilian casualties) that brought the revulsion that forced Clinton, rather than the UN, to lead the retreat. Once it was accepted that there was no military way forward, the only route was backwards to the slow patient dealing with ambitious contenders, which was clearly not ideal with a number of incidents still arising, but was the only realistic option.

From the first UNOSOM intervention in 1992 to UNITAF at the end of the year the UN had also shown uncertainty of purpose. The contending approaches indicated above meant that the organization was drifting with regard to both the content of policy and resolution to carry it through. In addition, the experience in Somalia called into question the UN's organizational structure. It proved to be riven with problems in the smooth working of its supposed chain of command, with considerable internal frictions being shown publicly at various times. It also had problems over the means at its disposal, especially its reliance on member states to supply forces; and when they did contribute, there was often concern for their own national agenda and command structure rather than simple incorporation under the UN (for which this was so obviously a first). It was suggested that regional organizations and local forces should play a greater part in operations of this kind, but that raises the question not only of their willingness and capacity, but the extent to which they are perceived as partisan: some Somalis clearly perceived Boutros-Ghali as still at heart an Egyptian with past links with Siad Barre's regime. A further negative consequence of the UN operation was that it made any prospect of a similar peace-making operation in Sudan recede rapidly, though there the only thing on which the parties to the conflict were sufficiently sensitive to agree was the need to allow relief supplies through to areas most affected by the war (or perhaps it was the food for their forces that they sought).

4

Ethiopia

Revolutionary government

While not being colonized itself, the nineteenth-century scramble for Africa had given the opportunity for Ethiopia to become a form of indigenous imperial power in the Horn in its own right, as emphasized by the subsequent promotion of the idea of its long tradition as a multi-ethnic empire. But while claiming to be an old order, what had sprung from Menelik had been largely a new one, paralleling in its own way the European imperial acquisitions in Africa. Yet because it was an indigenous creation it stood apart from the later nationalist challenges to imperial rulers across the continent. Indeed, it was part of the success of Haile Selassie that having lived with, and been a part of, the era of imperialism, utilizing after his restoration the resources of the USA in particular, he then transformed himself and his country into a symbol of African freedom, crowned by his assumption of the leading role in the founding of the Organization of African Unity in 1963, with its headquarters in Addis Ababa.

But it was not to last, and forces for change were building up which the ageing emperor was unable to contain. Perhaps because it was held back for a time, when change did come it proved one of the most dramatic and revolutionary experiences on the African continent. In retrospect there had been a number of pressures which were at best contained, but rarely alleviated. Students, soldiers, workers and peasants at different times and in different regions had shown signs of unrest, and open revolt had been growing for years in Eritrea. Then, in 1973, came the news of widespread famine in Wollo and Tigre provinces that the government appeared to treat with a disregard that bordered on disdain. Furthermore, it took foreign media to expose it, thus further highlighting the shortcomings within Ethiopia itself. It proved the spark that ignited a revolution.

Yet the revolution took time to gather pace. At first Haile Selassie hoped that reform, in the shape of a new prime minister, Endalkatchew Makonnen, a courtier of predictably moderate views, might suffice;

but it was not to be. Within the armed forces in particular emerged a very unusual body, the Provisional Military Administrative Council (PMAC) better known as the Dergue (Committee). It was an unusual body in that coups are generally conducted by particular units or strata of the military, but the Dergue consisted of 108 men of various ranks and from different units. It was thus an unusually representative body, and in marked contrast with the unrepresentative nature of Ethiopia's previous rulers. The formation of such a body indicated just how out of touch they had become, even with the military. But though its composition was mixed, it did not behave like a representative forum with public information and support, but instead developed as a powerful and secretive group, even the membership of which was known only to a few. That secretive character (itself very reflective of Ethiopian political circles traditionally) was illustrated by the unfolding of events. Few knew quite what was going on in the Dergue as it moved in more violent directions first internally, and then with regard to the former rulers.

At first the Dergue appointed as head of state a popular and well-known figure of Eritrean family background, General Aman Andom, who had not been a member of the Dergue, but by the end of 1974 policy differences within the Dergue had led to his shooting together with two other colleagues. This was to be only the start of a violent path within the Dergue leading to the eventual emergence of a middle-rank officer, Major (later Lieutenant-Colonel) Mengistu Haile Mariam, as head of state and dominant figure of the regime. Mengistu was supported by the NCOs and junior officers in particular because he was more radical than senior figures and less tainted by proximity to the old imperial government. In the course of this process of radicalization the Dergue made inroads into the old aristocracy and courtiers, eventually leading to the detention and death of the emperor himself.

As often with soldiers, the Dergue had only the loosest of ideas about the direction it should take. But the existence of such a stratified and illiberal society as that which had existed under the emperor had been a factor in encouraging one of the most radical student bodies in Africa, and soon Marxist ideologues both at home and abroad were converging on the Dergue. They had lived through a period in which there had been a resurgence of revolutionary thinking: in the USA it had been encouraged by the Vietnam war, and in Europe by the Paris-led student upheavals of 1968. In Africa there was growing demand for more than nationalism as exemplified in the growing popularity of the ideas of Frantz Fanon. Marxism-Leninism seemed particularly appropriate to Ethiopia, despite its having one of the most backward economic systems in Africa. A comparable backwardness had not stopped Russia from becoming the home of Marxist-Leninist revolution in Europe, and there were obvious parallels with Ethiopia. Under the tsars, Russia had also had a ramshackle, hierarchical, imperial political system trying to contain a multi-ethnic population, and the communists appeared to have established powerful state control. This appealed to both the new rulers and revolutionary ideologues in Ethiopia. Marxism-Leninism, moreover, appeared to offer an economic development programme which, from the understanding of Soviet experience since 1917, was still perceived as offering substantial achievements in unpropitious circumstances. It also called for greater exercise of power by the new rulers rather than the dilution apparently offered by free-market capitalism, which at that time had few proponents in Africa. (The Ethiopian revolutionaries, however, did not confine their attentions to the USSR, but scanned the world considering other Marxist-Leninist experiences, including, ironically, that of neighbouring Somalia.) The determination to proceed by this route was also strengthened with the support given by the USSR from 1978.

The combination of intellectual revolutionaries endeavouring to lead such groups as urban workers, and the military leadership in the Dergue fell apart by 1977. Two of the main factions of the intellectuals, the Ethiopian People's Revolutionary Party (EPRP) and the All Ethiopia Socialist Movement (MEISON), had themselves emerged as bitter rivals. In part it was simply factional rivalry for power, though there were also policy differences. The EPRP was seen as more populist with sympathy for the Eritreans, whereas MEISON wanted the establishment of a hard-line communist party. MEISON encouraged the Dergue to smash the EPRP in the early phase of the Red Terror in 1977, but the Dergue followed this by crushing MEISON as well. As a result the Dergue had destroyed its revolutionary inspirers, killing thousands of idealistic young Ethiopians in the process, but it had largely inherited from them a Marxist-Leninist ideology which it had lacked when it launched the revolution three years earlier. The Dergue had taken sole charge of the revolution by 1977, and Mengistu had taken control of the Dergue. Yet while taking command, Mengistu had also absorbed: Marxism-Leninism was to be no mere window-dressing, but a way forward, to be annually rubber stamped by the 'elected' National Shengo – Ethiopia's equivalent of the Supreme Soviet.

Perhaps wary of the character of political participation of the populous, the increasingly autocratic Mengistu was slow to develop a revolutionary party, in spite of growing urging from the USSR. There had been an early start with the formation of the Provisional Office of

Mass Organization (POMOA) in 1976, but following the Red Terror it came under tighter military control and was replaced in 1979 by the Commission for Organizing the Party of the Working People of Ethiopia (COPWE). Senior COPWE officials, many drawn from the military, slowly established their presence across the country in such a way as to ensure the centrality of the organization in the administration. When the Workers' Party of Ethiopia (WPE) was finally constituted in 1984, it drew very directly on COPWE and became a major political force with power flowing down from its General Secretary, Mengistu, through generally loyal lieutenants to the countryside. Those local officials reflected not just a personal stake in the system but, initially at least, many seemed to have a real ideological commitment to their cause. And in addition to the WPE, there was also a range of complementary associations, for women, youth, etc. Mengistu behaved increasingly like the emperor (especially after a visit to North Korea), and he was also in the habit of invoking the example of Tewodros and his attempts to centralize power in the nineteenth century. There was also a quasi-religious element to the way that the Holy Trinity had been replaced by the new trinity of Marx, Engels and Lenin who were prominently depicted in the capital, dominating the square in which Mengistu presided over grand parades. As well as his trappings and symbols, Mengistu had established a more powerful political instrument in the WPE than his predecessor had commanded. In addition to revolutionary legitimacy he also claimed nationalist credentials, particularly during and after the war with Somalia in 1977–78.

Mengistu also headed a more powerful administrative structure. The imperial state had looked to the notables in the northern regions to head the local administration, and to its own officials or settlers in the south. The revolution removed these strata, with a weakening of the state that some of the revolutionary intellectuals hoped would be replaced by popular local movements. But hierarchically inclined soldiers were not likely to concur, and the defeat of the intellectuals' factions meant the re-assertion of the centre, largely by rejuvenating the administration through the promotion of younger cadres. There was thus a continuation of the administrative centralization of the state that was to grow with the new tasks being undertaken, particularly that of directing the economy.

As significant, and in the many troubled areas of the country more important for the reconstruction of the state, was the growth in the size of the military. Ethiopia had had one of the largest armies in Africa since the restoration of the emperor in the Second World War, much of its build-up having been assisted by the USA, but the combination of the Somali attack of 1977 and the spread of violence across swathes of the provinces led to a rapid multiplication of the size of the armed forces. The regular forces and the militia came to total some 300,000 men, many of whom were conscripts with varying degrees of reluctance to serve. (There was also a local People's Militia which may have reached some 150,000.) But willing or not, with the help of Soviet advisers and equipment from 1977 (obtained on relatively easy terms) and stiffened by the Cubans, the Ethiopian forces were able to pacify most of the countryside outside the north.

In addition to the administrative and coercive structures, the regime also embarked on new forms of control of both urban and rural areas. In the towns, local *kebelle*s (neighbourhood associations) were established with which the people were registered. These had a range of functions which included local policing, the allocation of housing (one per family, eliminating the private rented sector), distribution of rationed commodities, and aspects of social development. Inevitably, the actual performance varied from one *kebelle* to another but the growth of their overall importance was undoubted. Politically, there were links with COPWE/WPE but many *kebelle* leaders were not known party men, though *kebelle*s were expected to turn out for political parades when required, especially in the capital.

While the *kebelle*s extended urban control, they made less of a contribution to the urban economy which saw an overall decline in living standards. The revolution's inevitable Ten-Year Plan introduced in 1984, envisaged a growth in industrialization from the 11 per cent of GNP in 1974. However, rapid nationalization ensured the virtual cessation of what little Western private investment there had been, and reliance had therefore to be placed on Eastern Europe. This did result in some new industrial enterprises but at relatively high cost and low efficiency. The many small craftsmen and traders (petty trade was allowed to remain in private hands) were encouraged to form co-operatives, but with limited success. Above all, the urban economy remained short of foodstuffs, a major factor in the falling living standards. The combination of shortages and control in turn gave rise to a parallel economy with corruption and an active black market. With the towns reduced as magnets for migrants, and the rural population increasingly tied to the land, Ethiopia experienced less of the urban drift that characterized much of Africa in the 1970s and 1980s.

The vast majority of the population (nearly 90 per cent) lived in the rural areas, and the tying of peasants more tightly to the land was a major feature of the revolution. At the policy's heart lay a system of across the board land redistribution which replaced the varied forms of land tenure of the pre-revolutionary era. Peasants were to be allocated small plots of land in their home areas and from time to time plots were re-allocated, supposedly to promote fairness of opportunity. The central mechanism for the process was the establishment of the Peasant Associations (PAs), of which some 20,000 were eventually set up with an average size of 281 households. Initially, there was some enthusiasm. There were peasant grievances and exploitative situations, but now the peasants were empowered to address these issues themselves, and there was spontaneous support for PAs. In addition, students were sent down to the countryside to encourage the new local dynamism, as well as promoting literacy. However, from the late 1970s the PAs increasingly became arms of the state that imposed a growing burden on the peasants. Officials of the Agricultural Marketing Corporation allocated grain quotas for the PAs, which were expected to deliver the crops for low fixed prices. Unable to move as freely as hitherto, and with government quotas to fulfil, there was little incentive for peasants to expand production. Consequently, there was a drop in grain supplies to the towns, and this was exacerbated by the need to give priority to the burgeoning armed forces. (PAs were also forced to produce conscripts for the army; a very unpopular requirement that contributed to low morale in both villages and barracks.) Levels of control were steadily extended in a counterproductive attempt to alleviate the situation, and finally, in the mid-1980s, an ambitious villagization programme was launched. It brought some 12.2 million people into collective villages by 1988, but state-led villagization proved as unsuccessful in Ethiopia as elsewhere in the world, as well as being increasingly unpopular. The major area of investment in agriculture was in state farms. These partly comprised the nationalized estates (formerly in private hands), which had been expanding production before 1974, and also newly cleared lands, including those used for the re-location of some 600,000 peasants moved (many forcibly) from the north during the famines of the 1980s. State farms remained the backbone of the export sector, dominated, as before the revolution, by coffee, but their record of production was weak in spite of the investment; some of the new farms for the re-settled were particularly deplorable.

The famines themselves were the product of the conjunction of a number of factors. Historically, the less fertile north had been particularly prone to famine, one reason for which was drought. The rains had not in fact been noticeably sparse in the early 1980s, but there was a poor year in 1984. In addition, the longstanding relief for a rising population of southward drift had been curtailed by the reform that had locked the peasants more tightly to home areas. In Tigre in particular civil war also played a significant part, with accusations that the Ethiopian army had pursued a scorched earth policy against the growing guerrilla insurgency.

The return of famine was a considerable embarrassment, even for such an autocratic regime as Ethiopia's had by then become. It brought back memories of the 1970s and the part that famine had played in weakening the *ancien régime*; and it was an indictment of the achievements of the revolution. In fact the government's own Relief and Rehabilitation Commission (RRC) had raised the call of famine relief before the Western media picked up the story, demonstrating both the relative autonomy and effectiveness of that organization, as will be discussed in Chapter 9. In the short term, however, neither the famine of 1984–85 nor the less publicized one towards the end of the decade led to a political threat to the regime of the kind seen ten years earlier. The control at the centre, as well as over much of the central and southern regions of the country, was such that economic policy shortcomings did not in themselves constitute the source of a threat to the regime's survival. That threat was to come from conflict in the north which, as already seen, pre-dated the revolution by several years, though famine, and the government's part in it, did contribute to the growth of resistance.

Revolt

The revolution of 1974 appeared to hold great opportunities for the Eritrean movements. These might have included a serious dialogue, but the slaying of General Aman Andom early in the revolution effectively precluded that possibility. Instead, it was the new military opportunity of a power struggle within the Dergue, the ruling military council, that provided a fresh incentive to the Eritrean factions. In addition, the Somali invasion of 1977, sucking the bulk of the Ethiopian forces to the south-east, also provided a new opening. Strengthened by an influx of revolutionary youthful volunteers to their ranks, by the end of 1977 the Eritrean Liberation Front (ELP) and Eritrean People's Liberation Front (EPLF) between them had captured most of rural Eritrea and the smaller towns. But once having pushed back the Somalis, and aided now by Soviet supplies and advisers (though the Cuban troops who had been imported to fight the Somalis in 1977–78 refused to serve in the north out of sympathy for the Eritrean cause), the Ethiopian forces went on to the offensive. The ELF was particularly hard hit with splits, heavy losses and even defections to the EPLF, added to which there was internecine strife in 1980–81 between the Eritrean factions. The outcome of the dual conflict was the virtual elimination of the ELF, which thereafter was little more than a small guerrilla force in the west of Eritrea, whereas the EPLF was forced to retreat to the far north where it dug in at the town of

Nacfa and the war settled into a protracted period of trench warfare reminiscent of the First World War. To its leaders, Ramadan Mohamed Nur and Issayas Afewerki, who had been trained in China, it must have seemed like the EPLF's Long March, but it remained a disciplined and organized force. In addition to the core army in the trenches at Nacfa, there were also guerrilla groups which harassed the Ethiopians behind their lines.

The EPLF also sought to encourage other groups in Ethiopia, and another major area of revolt had already opened up in Tigre from 1975. Tigre was both part of the historic heartland of the Ethiopian state and also the poorest region. It had been marginalized by the southward movement of the state from the nineteenth century. In addition, the revolution, with its land policy, had put greater pressure on this area of rising population, coupled with agricultural degradation. Resistance came first from established local leaders responding to the new revolutionary upstarts in Addis Ababa, but this reactionary phase of the revolt soon passed. Instead, from 1977 a new radical movement developed, supported initially by the EPLF, which was keen to see a fresh uprising that would put a kind of buffer between Eritrea and the Ethiopian army. But though helped by the EPLF, the Tigrean People's Liberation Front (TPLF) had a core of radical Tigreans and other Tigrinya-speaking people. Some had been in the EPRP and had escaped the Red Terror in Addis Ababa, which encouraged the ideology of the TPLF. It too was broadly Marxist but, after some early dissension, wanted the revolution to bring about radical decentralization. The TPLF thus evolved not as a secessionist movement like the EPLF, but with the aim of achieving the eventual overthrow of the regime in Addis Ababa and installing its own version of revolution, which at various times appeared to be modelled on different Marxist-Leninist variants, including Albania.

In its operation it showed great skill and commitment to the mobilization of the peasantry. The weakening of 'traditional' local leaders was one factor helping the TPLF. Another was the revolution, for the control by the state of this rather distant region had been weakened, and when it did seek to re-assert itself it was through coercion which promoted alienation. (Northern Tigre had suffered particularly from being adjacent to the conflict in Eritrea.) There was thus something of a political vacuum into which the TPLF penetrated by successfully linking its own struggle with the peasants' accumulated grievances. The TPLF not only championed the peasants but also organized them. They encouraged elected people's assemblies known as *baytos* to run the villages and promoted the position of women and other hitherto oppressed groups. It was to prove an attractive form of organization for the peasants, and encouraged their own involvement as soldiers. TPLF forces grew to an estimated 20,000, together with some 40,000 armed militias. The TPLF was also fortunate that in its early years the government appeared preoccupied with the Somali and Eritrean challenges, and did not take sufficiently seriously the threat from an historically more core area. The TPLF's leadership was a tight secretive vanguard, and prone to occasional struggles, one of which brought the group around Meles Zenawi to power in 1985. It both resembled and owed something to the neighbouring EPLF. But relations were not always smooth, and the TPLF, though an ally, was also something more than simply an offshoot of its fellow revolutionary organization to the north.

Significant though the TPLF was, the core of the conflict in the north still lay in Eritrea, and in 1984 (after desultory but unproductive talks with the government for two years), the EPLF staged a major breakout from Nacfa and the war moved into a more mobile and fluid phase. Militarily, it was by no means clear which side seemed to be gaining the upper hand, at least until a major victory by the EPLF at Afabet in 1988. That proved a major blow to the Ethiopian army: its commander in Eritrea was executed by Mengistu, and the already shaky morale of the troops swiftly plummeted. In addition, particularly large quantities of arms were captured by the EPLF for Afabet had been a major army strong point. In the following year there was an attempted coup. Mengistu survived, but took harsh retribution, executing a number of senior officers and imprisoning others. The retreat of the Ethiopian forces proceeded apace. Meanwhile, the Soviet Union had been re-thinking its whole policy towards commitments in the Third World, and its support for continued conflict in Ethiopia waned rapidly. (The 13,000 regular Cuban forces, who as mentioned had not served in the north, had left Ethiopia in 1984 when the rest of the country had seemed under government control.)

The success of the EPLF in turn encouraged the TPLF and also a number of smaller movements. The TPLF had itself created the Ethiopian People's Democratic Movement (EPDM) in fresh revolts in Wollo and Gondar provinces; and in 1989 the two merged to form the Ethiopian People's Revolutionary Democratic Front (EPRDF) whose forces had pushed right up to the border of Shoa province and threatened the capital itself. The EPRDF also became an umbrella for other developing groups, of which the most notable was the Oromo Liberation Front (OLF). Though the most numerous ethnic group in Ethiopia, the Oromos were scattered and somewhat amorphous, with many having been absorbed historically into the state. But in the late 1980s the OLF became a more potent force, operating particularly in

Hararge province (bordering Somalia) and Welega (neighbouring Sudan).

The growing success of the EPRDF reflected both its own strength and the decline of the Ethiopian army. For its part, the EPRDF was being assisted by the EPLF, including even the OLF on the new fronts it was establishing. The EPRDF was also the unintended beneficiary of Mengistu's last-gasp attempt at economic liberalization, which included measures to promote freer agricultural activities, including decollectivization, and permitted peasants to pass on land to their descendants. Popular though these measures were, they served less to generate new support for the hard-pressed regime than to undermine the control of the WPE in the countryside, since everything the party had been pursuing now appeared to be hastily abandoned. It added insult to injury for the WPE officials when their party was also renamed the National Democratic Party, and with it the old Marxist-Leninist ideology was confined to the dustbin. To all intents and purposes it was a major retreat by the state, and the loss of authority in rural areas eased the rapid advances of the EPRDF.

The collapse of Africa's largest army in the face of determined but less numerous guerrillas was due also to its steady demoralization following the surprise attack and defeat at Afabet in 1988. With half its forces in Eritrea, it was the setbacks there that really weakened the Ethiopian military. After Afabet the EPLF was virtually unstoppable, and in the following year captured the main port of Massawa, in spite of the damage wreaked on it by the Ethiopian airforce. The heavy losses suffered by government forces in Eritrea led to executions and demotions within the officer corps, but instead of stiffening the military's resolve to fight, such actions contributed to the coup attempt of 1989. Though that attempt failed, more executions of many senior and respected officers served only to weaken the army further. The new, swiftly promoted officers, were no match for their enemies. In addition, the troops being pushed in to try to shore up the position were increasingly young, untrained conscripts with little if any stomach for the fight and were increasingly ready to surrender or turn and run when the conflict intensified. The EPLF was also attracting new support as its success grew. Many of the arms used by all the fronts were captured from the Ethiopian forces, but some useful additions were acquired elsewhere. The capture of Massawa was helped by five Kuwaiti-supplied patrol boats with Syrian-donated ammunition. Increasing help was also coming from Sudan, including transport to assist the EPRDF. Mengistu's belated embracing of reform was thus perceived as much as a response to the declining military situation as to a genuine conversion from his hitherto doctrinaire Marxism-

Leninism, and it did little to win fresh support either at home or abroad. There were hopes that it might appeal in the West, and that a formal reopening of relations with Israel in 1989 might bring military assistance to compensate for the withdrawal of Soviet support, as well as an influential new friend with the USA, but it was all too late, and instead Mengistu fled the country on 25 May 1991.

The collapse of Mengistu's regime was more than simply a change of rulers. It was the end of the most far-reaching Marxist-Leninist experiment in Africa that had gone further than other self-proclaimed Marxist regimes. This reflected not only the determination of Mengistu and his comrades to pursue their chosen ideological path, but the fact that Ethiopia was a more hierarchical and statist society than virtually all others in the continent and thus one relatively structured hierarchy had been replaced by another. But the character of that state was also now in question, since it was from Tigre in the north that an apparently decentralizing force had come that appeared to be challenging not only the character of the state but also its personnel, as power appeared to be passing back from the centre-south of the ancient country to the centre-north once more. The downfall also provided further evidence of the potential of revolt in African politics. Though the challenge in Eritrea was Africa's longest-running continuous war, few were confident that it would lead to the kind of military victory that eventually occurred. In the end it was not the first such movement to lead to the overthrow of an African regime – that accolade belonged to the National Resistance Army in Uganda in 1986 – but the EPLF and EPRDF were clearly the largest and most successful such movements and achieved their victories against the continent's largest army.

Given that it was such a large army, part of the explanation for the collapse of the regime has to lie with its failure to sustain the armed forces. Perhaps a question hangs over the military from the outset? Though successful against Somalia in its first major post-revolutionary challenge, it was only after major setbacks not only on that front but in the north as well. Much of this may be put down to revolutionary confusion, but if so it was a confusion that affected the armed forces themselves as well as the wider society. It took massive Soviet support and thousands of Cuban troops to push back the Somalis, and though Cuban participation in the reconquest of much of the territory lost in the north was withheld, the Soviet advisers and equipment played a role there too. The failure to stem the tide of revolt that swept down from the north from 1988 in particular was a military failure. It appears to have become an army increasingly in disarray and measures to stiffen it were inept. The coup attempt of 1989 indicated the division within it and the hasty executions thereafter were also a cause of shock, reflecting a degree of sympathy for the plotters and their cause. Morale plummeted thereafter, contributing to the feeble resistance. The hasty and often forcible conscription also threw into the fray ineffective forces whose poor performance itself contributed to the unexpectedly rapid military collapse. At the same time, it was already clear by 1988 that there would not again be large-scale external intervention to save the regime, even though outside parties were still generally favouring the retention of the unity of the Ethiopian state, albeit in some new and negotiated framework.

Of course, had the 'nationalities question' been solved politically, the issue of military survival might never have been put to the test; and there were attempts to broker negotiations at various times, as will be seen later. However, from a regime standpoint its view of the question had been essentially Stalinist and, in consequence, in the mid-1980s it had been willing to lay down terms itself for 'regionalized centralism' rather than embarking on a potentially more open-ended approach to negotiations. In these circumstances it had to ensure the effectiveness of its chosen alternative – coercion – and this it failed to sustain against more effective adversaries.

As well as failing militarily, it was also failing economically, and, as a result, in terms of social support. The decline in living standards was palpable, even in urban and rural areas not directly affected by war until very late in the conflicts. Food shortages were widespread and contributed to renewed famine at the end of the decade. The hardship was due not only to the failure of agricultural policies in particular, but also to the belated and hurried drafting of large numbers of boys and men to try to stop the advances of the fronts. It was also a product of the situation in which some 55–60 per cent of the budget was going into the failing armed forces.

Politically, the regime relied primarily on the state itself and particularly on the single party. Though it appeared to have a core of ideologically reliable cadres, there was little that they could do to maintain political support in the face of economic hardship and the exactions of the conflicts, and in the end they were to find themselves effectively discarded even by their own leaders as Mengistu hastily sought to rename as well as redefine the party, while abandoning the economic policies on which the whole enterprise had been centred.

After Mengistu

The seizure of power in 1991 by the EPRDF, led by Meles Zenawi of the TPLF, raised many questions about the future directions of Ethiopia. From its early days the TPLF looked as if it might become a replica of Mengistu's regime: Tigre style. Though having a regional core from the north, it was was not secessionist (historically, Tigre had been at the heart of Abyssinia), while its early predeliction for some of Marxism's hardest cases – most famously Albania – suggested little change from the record of political and economic centralism. But the TPLF had discarded its leftist apparel as easily as Mengistu had done, and then created an alliance of People's Democratic Organizations (PDOs) with essentially regional and ethnic bases.

Once in power it became clear that this was no mere tactical move for military victory, but rather the outlines of future policy as well, albeit under the guiding hand of the TPLF leadership as forged in the years of conflict. The core of the policy was to lie in ethnic federalism as a political and administrative structure, under the leadership of the EPRDF and the regional PDOs. A national conference in 1991 led by the EPRDF, but also involving numerous other groups, mostly hastily constituted, led to the establishment of the Transitional Government of Ethiopia (TGE) to operate for two and a half years. A seventeen-strong Council of Ministers began by including representatives of seven ethnic groups, though some became identified with growing opposition and withdrew, leaving Amharas and Oromos in particular poorly represented. In addition, there was a Council of Representatives, which was also dominated by the old EPRDF and its allies. Ethnic federalism was the basis for the redrawn map of the regions that appeared to reflect political strengths as much as administrative rationale (for example, Tigre now had a border with Sudan which had been such a significant opening in the war). Initially, fourteen regions were designated, though by 1995 this had been reduced to ten.

The next step was the holding of local and regional elections in June 1992, but this proved a more difficult experience. It appeared that political control was to be built by TGE encouragement for ethnically based parties in the regions, with which the former would maintain alliances. However, in an endeavour to ensure the victory of those allies over rival parties, international observers monitoring the elections recorded a series of abuses which led to the general refusal to judge them free and fair. (In the wave of democratization in Africa, Ethiopia stood out in regard to this criticism in spite of fairly relaxed standards being applied in some other countries.) In addition, the longstanding tension between the old EPRDF and the OLF, which did not necessarily represent all of the numerous but dispersed Oromo people, came to a head with the OLF's decision to withdraw from the elections, with many of its leaders retiring to the role of opposition in exile. Some Oromos had turned to guerrilla tactics as early as 1992, though with little activity or success. In spite of efforts to reconcile the TGE with opposition groups (including encouragement from the USA), when federal elections and regional assembly elections became due in 1995, the opposition boycotted once more, leaving the future of political relationships extremely uncertain, though the government appeared in the stronger position.

Conclusion

The issue of the survival of the sovereign states of the Horn was most dramatically resolved in Ethiopia with the emergence of Eritrea as a separate independent country, recognized by the rest of the international community. However, with the acceptance by the TGE in Ethiopia of Eritrea's independence there arose the question of whether a precedent had been set with regard to other areas of the country. The response of the TGE was to reject any such claims, and to embark instead on a policy of defining new regions and devolving major powers to them. The rationale for the TGE's actions was not hard to see. Ethiopia had had a century of increasingly intensified centralism that had given rise to marginalization, especially in the north, as the political and economic centre shifted southwards; and regionalism was a timely reversal of that process. At the same time, the Tigreans of the TPLF at the heart of the downfall of Mengistu were from what is now the northernmost province, and one which is comparatively small, numbering only some three million people. Yet there are dangers in the policy, most obviously the maintenance of central-regional relations, if the encouragement of regionalized ethnic politics is not to become a basis for strong centrifugal tendencies, a possibility that led some to question the readiness of the TGE to agree to the separation of Eritrea, as will be seen in Chapter 5. The avoidance of such an outcome will depend heavily on political management. In the past the military has had a central role in maintaining the state but, in the end, reliance on coercion failed; in any case, the army and police had dissolved with Mengistu's fall. Their replacements were drawn heavily from the ranks of the Tigreans in particular, but over-reliance on coercive forces from a single region carries dangerous risks. Clearly, skilful political management from the centre is required to avoid the potential for greater dissolution of the kind that occurred in the former Soviet Union. In endeavouring to pursue its chosen policy, it began to appear as if the EPRDF was balanced between two main opposition sentiments. The Oromo and Ogadeni (Somali) opposition in particular seemed to be on the centripetal wing, with concern not only for devolution but also for a real right of secession, while on the centrifugal side were more conservative elements, especially Amhara officials and intellectuals, who feared the dismemberment of the historic state, which they felt was presaged by the independence of Eritrea.

While the issue of the maintenance of the (reduced) sovereign state was being addressed through regionalism, Ethiopia had less to concern itself with in regard to the permeablity of borders than other states in the Horn. The former TPLF leadership was itself well aware of the potential danger, having exploited such opportunities itself in the past. In the event, its preoccupation with internal affairs, which themselves had few implications for neighbours, avoided any immediate significant threat from that quarter. Nevertheless, in agreeing to the independence of Eritrea, Ethiopia had made itself the largest landlocked state in the world, which might have implications for the future.

While regionalism might placate centripetal tendencies, the problem of the legitimacy of central government still continued. In modern state-building in Ethiopia legitimacy had centred first on the symbolism of the emperor and then on revolutionary ideology, but these were past, leaving only a residual attachment to Ethiopian statehood. As elsewhere in Africa, there were hopes that liberal democracy would emerge as a legitimate form of government, though unlike other states in the Horn, Ethiopia had no experience of such a system. In addition, there were questions about the EPRDF's approach to the issue. The encouragement of regional parties allied to the EPRDF was construed as checking rather than encouraging national opposition parties which could contribute to a competitive liberal democracy. And when a group of parties did seek a national conference of reconciliation, of the kind so fashionable in democratization in Africa in the 1990s, the EPRDF chose not to participate and, indeed, arrested several of those attending as they arrived in Addis Ababa. Opposition parties have also questioned the government's approach to the development of an autonomous civil society and human rights. Ethiopia has had little experience of civil society, though certain civilian groups played a part in the revolution; but there have been accusations of harassment of opposition elements by the TGE. Human rights is a theme to which the government is alert, especially through its policy of indicting those accused of horrendous human rights abuses during Mengistu's rule. However, the TGE in turn has been accused by the opposition and some international monitors of being somewhat cavalier in its own approach to critics, though nothing like its predecessor.

Policy-making and implementation in reconstruction has also produced problems. The one part of the Ethiopian state to survive Mengistu's downfall was the central civil service, but relations with the victorious EPRDF involved tensions on both sides. For the new government there was the question of confidence in officials who had

served the former regime. This led to accusations that it was secretive
and authoritarian in policy-making, while some officials looked with
askance on the new rulers, predominantly from remote Tigre. In
addition, the policy of regionalism was aimed at reversing the ac-
cumulation of power in Addis Ababa and devolving it to the regions.
These, however, were not the regions as formerly constituted, but
wholly new entities. The policy involved creating new administrative
structures, to which new powers were entrusted and for which finance
had to be arranged.

The issue of balancing the extraction of resources for government
with incentives to produce was particularly sensitive in Ethiopia, in
view of the experience of state-enforced disincentives under Mengistu.
There was a somewhat delayed beginning to economic liberalization,
and there was also the prospect of a peace dividend with the decades
of conflict apparently over, but these did not presage immediate
recovery. Ethiopia had always been poor and its experiences had
accentuated that condition. Peace and liberalization could hold out no
instant panacea, though understandably there were increased expectations. The policy set by the TGE, and supported by the World
Bank and the International Monetary Fund (IMF), was very similar to
that to which Mengistu had belatedly retreated; and it faced the same
problems. Agricultural production was low, and the population rising
fast (around 50 million with a 3 per cent birth rate). There would be
a need to absorb the demobilized armies, and security problems arose
in some parts of the south and south-east. The infrastructure was
poor and world coffee prices depressed. This daunting picture had to
be married with the devolved administrative and financial arrangements
already mentioned, a task requiring deft management at the centre
combined with skill in the handling of the much needed external
support. In a context in which economic marginalization had contributed to the development of conflict, it added up to a crucial factor
in the maintenance of a stable and united country.

In spite of the daunting prospects, Ethiopia was helped, as indicated
by a general sympathy in the West, led by the USA, the IMF and the
World Bank. When that is combined with its intention to avoid
antagonizing neighbours, Ethiopia, of the major countries of the Horn,
is now in the most favourable position internationally for state reconstruction.

Ethiopia was the only existing state in the Horn where actors central
to state collapse, notably insurrectionists in the north, were put in a
position to takeover and address the task of state reconstruction. It
had the advantage that the past rulers were effectively excluded, and
that a degree of control was fairly smoothly established in their place.

However, against those advantages had to be set the task of trying to reconstruct a state in the largest country in the Horn in population terms, and one in which the experiences of revolution had been felt in varying degrees, some very traumatic, all over the country. There might be few obvious obstacles from the past, but there was inevitably some fragility in any reconstruction process.

5

Eritrea and Djibouti

Eritrea

On attaining official independence in 1993, following a referendum on its future, Eritrea culminated over three decades of struggle which has already been reviewed in Chapter 4. Perhaps the clearest of the EPRDF's policies in Ethiopia had been to agree to the holding of an Eritrean referendum in the confident expectation that it would result in the independence of the former province. The EPLF had always made a referendum the centrepiece of its aims, because it was central to its case that the UN had denied it one in 1952, allowing federation to go through on the vote of an allegedly corrupt assembly. Thus Eritrea was not seceding, but exercising a right denied in the past when, as a separate former colony and then a UN Trust Territory, it had been attached to Ethiopia and then unilaterally incorporated.

That argument was backed by a powerful political one. It was the EPLF that had encouraged the formation of the Tigrean People's Liberation Front (TPLF), and for the most part the two had been mutually supportive in the military campaigns that had seen the defeat of the vast Ethiopian army and the downfall of Mengistu. In view of the fragility of the political situation that both *de facto* sets of rulers faced with his departure, the maximum political cooperation would be necessary, and potential independence for Eritrea promised rather than ended that. Furthermore, neither set of new rulers would regard Eritrea's achievement of independence as a precedent since it had a unique juridical case. (Even if the transitional government of Ethiopia had sought to contest the referendum for Eritrea, there was little it could have done since the EPLF army was probably the stronger of the two, and in any case the former was in no position to put it to the test. As it was, a friendly independent Eritrea seemed better for Ethiopia.)

The referendum in Eritrea did not take place immediately after Mengistu's downfall, but as planned after a two-year delay, during which time the territory had been completely self-governing and independent in all but name. This allowed for a period of consolidation before the referendum which was appreciated in Ethiopia as well as Eritrea. When the UN-sponsored referendum did finally take place in April 1993, it was approved overwhelmingly with an official 98.5 per cent turnout, of which 99.8 per cent voted for independence rather than remaining in Ethiopia. (The EPLF's former third choice – federation with Ethiopia – was no longer an option!) The plethora of international observers who attended that vote were far happier than they had been with the earlier elections in Ethiopia, and Eritrea was duly introduced to the international community of nation-states. It was the first time that a new African state had been recognized as formed from an existing independent state, a fact that reflected not just the achievement of Eritrea, but a new attitude internationally to the prospect of new states in the international community. It was an attitude that had been brought about in large part by the ending of the Cold War. Eritrea's new status also gave it greater access to international sources of aid which had been limited in the intervening two years.

The end of conflict in Eritrea had left a political legacy very different from that in Ethiopia. Instead of a coalition of forces led by one small remote region, Eritrea had a unified command which had asserted ever more control over the territory during the course of the war. At the centre of that achievement had been the army itself which had evolved from a guerrilla force into a highly organized regular army numbering some 100,000 by the end of the war. It had been an outstanding military achievement not only in African but also in international terms. As well as excelling as an army in the field, it had developed a high degree of self-sufficiency, especially in the repair of captured weaponry, and proved able at such disparate activities as road-building and medical services. In addition to being brave and skilled, EPLF cadres were committed and disciplined. Even after victory in 1991, the forces were required to remain intact and without pay until 1995. Although there were incidents resulting from this situation, most notably in 1993, they were defused without serious consequences. In the long term it is planned to reduce the army to 30,000, though this also raises the problem of demobilization and subsequent employment opportunities.

The EPLF had also had years to develop relations with the in-digenous communities. Though regarded as recruited predominantly from the Coptic, Tigrinya-speaking highlands of Eritrea, the years of organizing the transportation and distribution of food supplies from Port Sudan to the lowland peoples had helped develop support there, especially after the defeat by the EPLF of the ELF. In addition, while more highland territory was being 'liberated' in the 1980s, land reforms were also being implemented in consultation with the peasants that proved popular and contrasted with the autocratic agricultural policies of Mengistu. Indeed, instead of the EPLF remaining a force that had had to learn to survive among the peasants, it was in many ways the rural population of Eritrea that had come to need the EPLF.

The military strength of the EPLF had thus been used for political ends, but it was far from clear what kind of political development would follow the coming of peace. Decision-making was firmly in the hands of the Central Committee of the EPLF, now established in Asmara. EPLF departmental officials and Eritrean civil servants from the outgoing administration headed the new government's departments (Ethiopian officials having been expelled). Beyond the capital, Asmara, there was an attempt to fuse central and local control which extended the practice during the war of establishing (under EPLF guidance) a pyramid of elected councils. That practice has now been spread to the whole of the country, together with centrally appointed province governors. The aim is to encourage the maximum decentralization possible to the nine provinces (reduced to six in 1995). Also at a local level, the organizations established by the EPLF during the war, such as those for workers, peasants, women and youth, have been turned into indigenous NGOs, though still with a significant element of government control; some of these cooperate with their international counterparts that have arrived since 1991.

The first 'national' political objective was the referendum, but beyond that there were plans to wind down the EPLF and replace its control with multi-party politics. However, it was to be a multi-party system without permitting ethnic, religious or provincial identities to form the basis of mobilization and lead to what the country's new president, Issayas Afewerki, termed 'pseudo-multipartyism'.[1] The alternatives, where interest and ideological differences at the 'national' level were so constrained, were hard to foresee. For its part, the EPLF leadership, now reborn as the People's Front for Democracy and Justice (PFDJ), is likely to continue in one guise or another for some time to come. That was underlined by the decision that the transition period for the writing and presentation of the new constitution would be extended until 1996, with elections not expected before 1997.

For all the unity built up within the movement during the years of war, the potential lines of division within the boundaries of Eritrea are obvious, and have been seen to some degree. The possibility of religious differences being mobilized has been raised by the emergence in the west of the country of a shadowy Islamic Jihad movement. Small Islamic factions existed from the early 1980s, especially after the defeat of the ELF, and grew stronger towards the end of the decade. How far they represent indigenous dissent, and how far external influence, is open to argument, but there have certainly been a number of incidents. The other obvious dimension of possible divisive mobilization is ethnic, and on this front the most significant query initially was raised by the Afar of the east. Divided between Eritrea, Ethiopia and Djibouti, some Afar have called for self-determination, an appeal which falls on deaf ears in government circles in all three countries. Nevertheless, the potential for the expression of ethnic discontent is real, and the Eritrean answer of pyramidal incorporation of the new provinces will be a testing ground. Political tensions could also arise between the former EPLF fighters, who have dominated since the end of the conflict in 1991, and returning Eritreans, who may have the expertise and even economic resources and expect opportunities in the new Eritrea, though thus far their numbers have been comparatively small. There are also some so-called 'collaborators' with the former Ethiopian government, some of whom have had military training.

Economic policies centred upon the revival of agricultural output following the devastation of war and the ravages of drought. As in Ethiopia, decisions relating to land tenure were necessary and built on the previous work of the EPLF. Land ownership was retained in the name of the government, but peasants were allocated land, which could be inherited, on a lifetime's usufruct basis. By these means it is hoped to encourage investment. Agricultural output did rise, but Eritrea remained dependent on the importation of grain. The 1991–92 season saw widespread crop failure due to drought, though, while subsequent yields improved, 60 per cent of the population were still dependent on some form of food aid in 1994–95. The limited industrial plant that survived both removal to Ethiopia and war was capable of restoration where equipment and spares were available or could be bought. Vital, too, was the rehabilitation of the port at Massawa following the bombing by the Ethiopians. Given its limited natural resources, hopes for economic recovery have focused on the possibility of Eritrea becoming an important trading centre at the southern end of the Red Sea and with established overland connections to Ethiopia and Sudan. (To compensate Ethiopia for becoming landlocked once more, it was given preferential access to the port of Assab which had been developed following dislocation of the railway between Djibouti and Addis Ababa during the Ethiopia–Somalia war of 1977–78.) Few of the numerous Eritreans who left the country during the long war have returned – many having made themselves other lives overseas – but they do make significant remittances to their families. The refugees in neighbouring

Sudan have also been slow to return, a process made more difficult by strained relations between the two countries.

In leading the successful liberation of Eritrea, the EPLF seems, in retrospect at least, to provide a virtually classic textbook case. A cohesive leadership emerged, especially from the late 1970s; an effective force was developed that made the transition from guerrilla warfare to more orthodox combat, and did so, moreover, in the context of surviving being forced on to the defensive in the early 1980s; relations with the civilians were built upon to the advantage of both fighters and peasants; and external alliances were struck that ranged from relations with other governments, to encouragement for, and generally effective relations with, the neighbouring TPLF and later the EPRDF in Ethiopia. Much of this is to judge the outcome, for the EPLF remained generally secretive, revealing only what it wished the world to see, including conducted parties of journalists and academics, most of whom emerged to sing its praises. Clearly, there were setbacks and blemishes along the way, not only the retreat of the late 1970s into the far north but also the two periods of conflict with the ELF. Yet what emerges above all is the combination of determination and control on the part of the leadership in particular. In this circumstance it is hardly surprising that, as Afewerki's remark about avoiding 'pseudo-multipartyism' indicates, Eritrea is not about to embark simply on the sunny uplands of full-blown liberal democracy and economy. Rather, there will continue to be a significant degree of direction and control in political and economic life for some time to come. The newly named PFDJ may have abandoned its one-time penchant for Marxism-Leninism, but it clearly sees the significance of a reasonably strong and interventionist state – for instance, the Red Sea Trading Corporation, which was established originally to purchase equipment for the EPLF, became the biggest trading organization after the conflict ended, with preferential treatment from the government.

Economic liberalism will not be unrestrained with the continuing sentiment of egalitarianism in what is a poor but active country, a view which led to the rejection of a US aid package because it had too many economic policy strings attached. (It did, though, join the World Bank in 1994.) But if the pitfalls of Eritrea's social heterogeneity can be contained by the vision and organization of its political leadership, then its comparatively small population, and potentially economically exploitable location, could enable it to have a better future than some other states in the present structure of the Horn.

Djibouti

While Eritrea is the newest independent state in the Horn, and the product of years of instability and eventually the break-up of Ethiopia as it had existed for over a quarter of a century, the even smaller state of Djibouti was for long seen as a paradox of vulnerability and stability. As seen earlier, French Somaliland, as it was known for much of its history, was essentially a French foothold at the mouth of the Red Sea. With the early hopes that it might serve as a base from which to penetrate westwards into Africa frustrated, it then became the base from which the French navy could reach out into the Indian Ocean, and so it has remained ever since. Though called French Somaliland, in the years before independence the French were accused frequently of favouring the Afar community: in 1967, in a move to emphasize its even-handedness, the name was changed to that of the French territory of the Afars and Issas. Ten years later, in 1977, this tiny country of around half a million people finally became the independent state of Djibouti.

As Djibouti's former name indicates, there are two major ethnic groups. The largest are the Issas who comprise about 33 per cent of the population and live in the southern part of the country. The Afars account for a further 20 per cent of the population and live in the north; as mentioned earlier, they are linked to Afar communities in neighbouring Ethiopia and now Eritrea. Other significant elements of the population include two other Somali groups, the Gadaboursis and the Isaaqs; Arabs, mainly from Yemen and involved in trade; the French, especially the armed forces and their dependants; and there is also a floating population from the neighbouring countries, some of whom have arrived as refugees. With an arid hinterland and few natural resources Djibouti has had to rely on its port and railhead to Addis Ababa to try to become a significant regional trading centre as well as on the wealth generated by the presence of the French forces. Its attempt to create a free port since 1981 has been handicapped by its growing number of rivals in the vicinity, and there has been little development of industry, though there has been some success in the service sector, especially banking. Inland there is little more than impoverished pastoralism, though there have been attempts to tap underground water supplies for wells and even some irrigation.

Politically, Djibouti's independence in 1977 was not a time of change. The French had already bestowed their favours on Hassan Gouled Aptidon, an Issa who was loyal to the concept of Djibouti and had no ambition of participating in any Greater Somalia project. There was no significant nationalist challenge to France, but there were changing regional circumstances in the states around Djibouti which made it appropiate to put France's position into a new context. Thus a colonial system was replaced by what swiftly emerged as a presidential system under the leadership of Gouled. With no formal constitution until 1992, his powers appeared substantial, but for a long time they were exercised with caution. It became his practice to appoint successive Afars as prime minister and other government posts were likewise distributed proportionately, as was, in effect, the 65-member National Assembly. But for all this apparent balance, there was too a requirement for loyalty to the president personally, which was supported by the single-party system that operated under the Rassemblement Populaire pour le Progres (RPP).

The aim of Gouled's rule seemed to be simply to maintain stability and thereby hope to ensure the survival of the Horn's smallest state in the midst of the political turmoil that went on around Djibouti, hence the regular references to it as the 'eye of the hurricane'. Its two largest ethnic groups, the Issas and the Afars, appeared to indicate in themselves the dangers inherent in the situation, linked as they both appeared to be to larger and rival neighbouring powers. The war of 1977–78 between Somalia and Ethiopia was a particular strain in which tensions did arise and there were some violent clashes. Nevertheless, Djibouti's survival relatively unscathed, appeared to justify its system.

However, the end of the 1980s saw Djibouti entering a new era of uncertainty. The years of consolidation under President Gouled were being seen increasingly, by Afars in particular, as having entrenched the power of the Issas behind a façade of proportionality; and various other critical voices were also trying to surface in Djibouti's semi-restricted environment. The major expression of discontent emerged from an Afar group which formed the Front pour le Restauration de l'Unité et la Démocratie (FRUD) in 1991, and grew to a force of about 3,000. It was far larger and more threatening than the limited guerrilla movements that had surfaced in the past.

One factor in the emergence of the FRUD was the ending of the Cold War and the era of re-democratization in Africa which appeared to fit in well with demands that Djibouti become a multi-party system. This would give political space for the Afars with their growing sense of grievance. Another factor was the ready availability of arms, especially after the downfall of Mengistu in Ethiopia. The flow of arms across the border, and of some Afars as well, allowed President Gouled to blame the FRUD attacks on outside elements, but there appeared to be a significant element from Djibouti itself, inspired not only by the factors mentioned above, but also by the apparent example of what force could achieve in overthrowing established rulers in the region.

(There had been an Afar Liberation Front in Ethiopia but the FRUD
did not appear to share its objective of an autonomous homeland for
the Afars so much as proclaim their goal to be the reform of Djibouti.)

Under pressure from France, the government responded to the
political challenge from both the FRUD and the growing critical voices
among civilians by introducing a constitutional reform process in 1992.
The proposed new constitution called for a multi-party system with
up to four parties, though with a substantial registration fee. However,
it still maintained strong powers for the president at the expense of
the legislature and for this reason the referendum on the constitution
was boycotted by the opposition, though this did not prevent the
government announcing an overwhelming victory. That result was also
repeated in the elections at the end of 1992 when the ruling RPP won
all sixty-five seats in the National Assembly against the two other
parties that entered the lists. In 1993 presidential elections were held,
and in spite of earlier speculation that having served two terms Gouled
would stand down, he once more triumphed over four other candidates
and began his third term in office. Following his success with political
'reform', Gouled then turned to deal militarily with the FRUD which
had boycotted the elections and appeared capable of operating in many
of the rural areas as well as in its original northern bases. But the
FRUD was vulnerable against a strengthened army, now up to 15,000
men, and had little external support or space in which to fall back. In
consequence, a determined advance inflicted significant defeats and
the immediate outcome had been to repel the military as well as the
political threat. However, there were repeated allegations of abuses
against civilians and many sought refuge in Ethiopia and Eritrea, as
well as swelling the impoverished Afar quarters of Djibouti city, thus
suggesting a potential for resentment rather than reconciliation.

President Gouled is the longest survivor from among the 'personal
rulers' who beset the states of the Horn (Barre, Nimeiri and Mengistu).
Unlike them he has fought off the main military threat from the FRUD
with strong and decisive action. Like them he attempted reforms which
had the effect of consolidating his power. In this he has been assisted
by the international support that he has received both from the region,
where he has avoided provoking enmity towards his tiny state, and
from Djibouti's major backers, not only France but also the USA,
which welcomed the availability of Djibouti's position to the UN action
in the Gulf War. Perhaps the very smallness of Djibouti in both area
and population, which made it appear so vulnerable, has also contributed to its remaining so stable, for both control of the political
system and military action was swifter and easier than in the larger
neighbours. Nevertheless, the democratic reforms appear to have been

little more than the addition of a fig leaf of respectability, and the discontents, especially the ethnic resistance from the Afars, have been repressed rather than accommodated. For the present Djibouti may have survived its shaking, but the future of both president and system have become more uncertain in the last few years, and the experience of the Afars in particular may lead to a longer-term polarization of relations between the two major ethnic elements that could threaten the survival of the only state in the Horn whose boundaries have not been seriously challenged in the past three decades.

PART TWO

International Politics

6

Neighbours and Conflict

It has been a premise of this book that the concept of the Horn, as it has expanded in the past decades, has centred on the relations between Ethiopia and its two major neighbours: Sudan to the west, and Somalia to the east. While Part One reviewed the indigenous developments in all three countries, the position has now been reached when their relations with each other can be examined. However, the interaction of the three states is only one aspect, though possibly the most important in some cases and at some periods, of their foreign policies.

The foreign policies of individual African states, like all states, are partly a matter of international initiatives taken by them (for a variety of motives) and partly their responses to the activities of other states and international actors. The relative weakness of African states leads to their frequent depiction as being more in the reactive position than able to take positive leads. Nevertheless, African states can take initiatives that are of significance both with regard to neighbours, and perhaps at a wider regional and even, on occasions, global level.

A number of factors are involved. First is the linkage with Part One, for the structure and character of domestic politics have a direct impact on the foreign policies pursued. The degree of instability within a particular country may well be reflected in attempts to exploit external linkages for regime, if not state, survival; and when support is forthcoming, regimes may feel strengthened in their domestic policies. Secondly, and probably more frequently alluded to, are economic factors in policy-making. Economic development in Africa has often been viewed largely in terms of external trade, but instability and poverty may contribute to conditions such as famine and become a part of the equation for both African and non-African actors, with the latter, in particular, delivering aid packages which seek to enhance the position of the poor. A third factor, and one clearly vital to the Horn, is strategic significance. One has only to mention the discussion of the significance of the building of the Suez Canal for the scramble for Africa, to be reminded of the continuing importance of the Horn; an importance later re-emphasized as new Middle East priorities emerged, especially oil. Finally, ideology, broadly understood, may play its part, not least because ideologies of various kinds have been a significant aspect of international politics in the mid to latter part of the twentieth century. These include the emergence of nationalism that was central to the ending of imperialism and the independence of states in Africa and elsewhere.

While the above are the kind of broad factors that influence foreign policy, there is rarely a single foreign policy, but rather varying policies tailored towards particular countries. High on the list has to be neighbours, simply because of their immediate proximity. But another reason for one dimension of state collapse is the inability to control borders effectively. The immediate answer appears to be to build up a capacity to police frontiers, but the realities of large comparatively weak states in Africa means that policing cannot be relied upon. In consequence, an important aspect of control of frontiers lies in effective cooperation with neighbouring states. Some neighbours will be more important than others, but none can be entirely ignored. The very fact of sharing a border may be an issue in itself, and even if that is not the case in most of Africa, the virtual inevitability of cross-border transactions of all kinds makes some consideration necessary. Furthermore, while being independent states, there may have to be a sharing of resources. An obvious example is the flow of a river, with water a growing issue in the Middle East in particular. But shared resources may also be reflected in the cross-border movement of pastoralists, whose long-standing and vital migrations may have been subject to a colonially imposed formal division of territory; or in more recent times 'modern sector' economic migrants. The political instability of neighbouring states may well spill over borders, however much the neighbour has sought to remain above the fray. Overall, Africa has become the continent generating more refugees than any other in recent years, as will be considered in more detail later. Suffice to note here that refugees may have their own agendas with regard to their countries of origin and they may seek to pursue these from the relative safety of their sanctuaries. But it also has to be said that neighbours may be less than innocent with regard to instability. In spite of the strictures of the Organization of African Unity (OAU) to the contrary, there has been covert and, on occasion, overt interference in the affairs of neighbouring states for a variety of motives. Some of these motives involve the ambitions and activities of neighbouring states directly, and some the activities of influential third parties.

Ethiopia and Sudan

As areas of ancient state formation, Ethiopia and Sudan had experienced the interaction and clashes of neighbouring countries. One such conflict had led to the death of King Yohannes of Ethiopia in battle with the forces of the Mahdist state in 1889. But that had not been indicative of major ambitions held by either state towards the other; the general picture had rather been one of two core areas of state formation – Highland Ethiopia and riverain central Sudan – between which the normal atmosphere was one of live and let live. However, the imperial period had given a reminder both of the strategic significance of the area and the scale on which major powers could confront each other in the Horn. Mussolini's invasion of Ethiopia in 1935–36 had served as a reminder of the region's strategic significance, and British forces had ousted Italy's army by a pincer movement from Sudan and East Africa. With the coming of independence to Sudan in 1956 there was little sign that the underlying pattern of relations would change. Sudan's preoccupations in the advance to independence were entirely towards the north with Egypt, and her south-eastern neighbour was of little concern. Meanwhile, Ethiopia's strategic significance globally was acknowledged by the building of an American communications base near Asmara in Eritrea.

For both countries the subsequent evolution of their relationship was to centre around the continuation of the same factors of growing regional and superpower rivalries. That rivalry in turn led to important alliances propping up increasingly challenged regimes – with a major part of the challenges emanating from the respective peripheral areas within Ethiopia and Sudan. Those centre–periphery struggles have already been considered; what has to be illustrated now is the way in which they brought periods of rising tension between Ethiopia and Sudan.

It was Sudan that took the lead in what was to become a long and bloody game of tit-for-tat. Yet, as so often in Sudanese politics, it began less as a conscious policy option and rather as a build-up of various factors. In origin, the revolt in Eritrea was indigenous and the first arrivals of refugees in eastern Sudan were largely unnoticed. When they were acknowledged, it often seemed beyond the capacity of the lax, under-resourced and inefficient Sudanese security authorities to do much about preventing their arrival. Nor was there much attempt on the whole to restrict the refugees, either because the policy was poorly implemented, or because the government had other priorities. Two elements of Sudanese politics already discussed, religious sects and ethnicity, played their part. The Khatmiyya sect, usually influential

in politics whether in periods of liberal democracy backing the Unionist Party, or in an even more subterranean manner under the military
regimes of Abboud and Nimeiri, felt a sense of solidarity with fellow
tariqa members in the lowlands of Eritrea. The fact that the spiritual
centre of the *tariqa* was in Kassala, close to the border, emphasized
this link, and put a basic sympathy for some at least of the Eritreans
at the heart of the generally somewhat confused Sudanese policy-
making milieu. (Kassala was also the home of the ELF's Revolutionary
Command in the 1960s.) Ethnic links were, inevitably, of a more
parochial character, though not without effect. The Beni Amer, the
southern extension of the Beja peoples of the Red Sea Hills, straddled
the border and thus contributed to the sympathy and receptivity of
local communities in eastern Sudan, especially when numbers of
refugees were relatively low.

In addition to these structural influences evoking sympathy for the
Eritreans in Sudanese politics, other aspects of foreign policy were to
play a part, especially Sudan's nascent Arabism. The emergence of the
ELF coincided with, indeed was influenced by, the rise of pan-Arabism
under the charismatic leadership of Gamal Abdel Nasser; Radio Cairo
gave early encouragement and the Front de Libération National (FLN)
in Algeria provided an operating model. A number of Arab states
showed concern, Saudi Arabia and other Gulf states as well as Egypt,
but the major commitments as arms suppliers in the early years of the
ELF were provided by more distant states, Syria and Iraq – the two
Ba'athist states determined to demonstrate that they were more radical
than each other, as well as more active than the rest of the Arab world.
Thus weapons began to flow towards Eritrea, via the most obvious
route of Sudan. This placed successive regimes in Sudan in something
of a quandary. On the one hand they wanted to maintain their credentials with Arab states, especially in the growing confrontation with
Israel, which was also assisting Ethiopia (and both backed by the USA);
on the other hand there was a growing awareness that southern Sudan
was the Achilles heel which Ethiopia could exploit. These uncertainties
were reflected in Sudanese policy: Abboud was naturally somewhat
conservative and sought to play down pan-Arabism, while from the
Six Day War of 1967 Prime Minister Mohamed Ahmed Mahjoub
endeavoured to placate Ethiopia. In contrast, in the intervening period
from the October Revolution of 1964 Sudan identified more fully with
radical Arabism and was active in encouraging and assisting the
Eritreans. In any case, even when not being positively encouraging, the
situation in eastern Sudan, from Port Sudan southwards, was such
that in practice the Eritreans were able to operate across the border,
even when Khartoum's policy was one of obstruction.

As for Ethiopia, it mattered less what posture was being adopted by the regime of the moment in Sudan, than that a guerrilla war was being conducted against her in which both men and supplies were coming across the border from her western neighbour. Thus, while continuing diplomatic efforts to restrict activities, including an agreement to that end with Mohamed Ahmed Mahjoub in 1967, Ethiopia also countered by allowing the Anya Nya the use of its territory. Ethiopia was helped in this by Israel which from 1967 was supporting the Anya Nya with arms and training from both Ethiopia and Uganda. Meanwhile, on a broader African canvas, Emperor Haile Selassie was promoting the cause of the sanctity of Africa's state borders, especially in the Organization of African Unity (formed in 1963 and with its headquarters in Addis Ababa), of which he was first chairman. (This latter point was of course relevant with regard to the Somali as well as the Eritrean question.)

The logic of the situation was increasingly obvious to governments in both states, but it required a major political change in one or other, and it was Sudan (as usual) that proved the more unstable and thus provided the circumstances for an apparent breakthrough. Nimeiri's military coup of 1969 set in train the eventual process towards a peace agreement with the Anya Nya. But the fact that that agreement was signed in Addis Ababa in 1972 was not just a piece of good neighbourliness as far as Ethiopia was concerned. Haile Selassie was not himself a mediator, but his government did act as a facilitator for the peace talks (and behind the emperor were his Western friends, encouraging the peace process with hints of aid). The expectation was that in exchange for Ethiopia's help in the peace process, Sudan would then clamp down on the Eritreans with greater vigour than it had managed hitherto.

Nimeiri did endeavour to maintain the spirit of Sudan–Ethiopian relations embodied in the Addis Ababa agreement. He made efforts in the following years to mediate between the Eritreans and the emperor, with the example of the Ethiopian-assisted Southern Region in Sudan as evidence of what could be achieved. However, negotiated peacemaking was not what Haile Selassie had in mind when he looked for reciprocation, and Nimeiri's efforts were in vain. Later, during the revolution, he tried to save Haile Selassie's life, and after his death felt less obliged to even make a pretence of containing the Eritreans. (In addition, Sudan was increasingly borrowing from Arab states that were supporting the Eritreans.) In practice, Nimeiri did not have strong control over the Eritreans operating from Sudan, and in any case they were involved in their own internecine strife as the EPLF emerged to challenge the ELF in what became an intra-Eritrean civil war.

However, it was the direction of the revolution in Ethiopia that really strained relations anew, especially when the death of Aman Andom marked the Dergue's determination to fight rather than talk with the Eritreans. In its efforts to cut the Eritreans' lines with Sudan, the Dergue had, by 1976, committed a series of attacks, a number of which transgressed Sudan's borders. Also in 1976, the serious coup attempt mounted against Nimeiri by Sadiq el-Mahdi involved the infiltration into Khartoum, via Libya, of Mahdist followers who had previously been sheltered and trained in Ethiopia following the defeat of the previous attempted uprising by Imam el-Hadi el-Mahdi at Aba Island in the White Nile in 1971.

The Dergue's major offensive in the north in the late 1970s again saw Sudan offering to be involved in mediation, but once more with little success. The Dergue felt that it was strong enough to dictate terms, while Sudan (and her Arab allies) found that its influence was much weaker with the EPLF than with the ELF and the ELF–PLF (a short-lived faction from 1972 to 1975), and that it was the EPLF which was developing by far the most significant force in Eritrea.

Instead of mediation it was the renewed tension between the super-powers in the late 1970s, which became known as the second Cold War, that was really to show the importance of the two states for their respective guerrilla opponents. One important marker was the Aden Treaty of 1981 linking Libya, Ethiopia and South Yemen (all armed by the Soviet Union) into a pattern of superpower checkers on the board of north-east Africa, with the USA supporting Egypt, Sudan and Somalia. In the following years, Sudan was to become an ever more important base. The EPLF's use of the route from Port Sudan as well as the camps in eastern Sudan was not just known but well publicized, and, at the same time, there were a variety of rather shadowy activities, with Western as well as Middle Eastern backing in Eritrea and northern Ethiopia, the most spectacular of which was Operation Moses to extract the Falasha (the 'black Jews') in 1984. It was not until the downfall of Nimeiri in 1985 that something of these activities became clear and by that time a new impetus had been given to the fronts, especially the EPLF and the TPLF, that was never to be stopped.

As well as support for military activities there was also a developing cross-border traffic in aid. The Eritrean Relief Association (ERA) was established in 1975 to be followed in 1978 by the Relief Society of Tigre (REST), both of which operated from bases in Sudan. A group of Christian-based NGOs established an Emergency Relief Desk in Khartoum, through which supplies were funnelled to ERA and REST and into guerrilla-held territories. The famine of 1984–85 brought increased demands, and even the preference on the part of some of the needy, encouraged by REST, to trek long distances to Sudan rather than go to Ethiopian government-run relief stations with the risk of forcible resettlement. In 1985 USAID was finally convinced of the desirability of helping cross-border relief in the form of trucks, on the grounds that it would help to prevent mass movement to over-burdened camps in Sudan.

On the other side, meanwhile, Ethiopia had seized her opportunity with the emergence of the Sudan People's Liberation Army (SPLA) in 1983. Security had been worsening in southern Sudan for some time, and resentments with the north were growing. But it was Ethiopia that imposed unity on the groups in the south that were attracted to seek its shelter and support, and backed John Garang as the new leader. Apart from personal reasons, Ethiopia was quick to support Garang's view of a radically changed Sudan (the so-called 'New Sudan') rather than the old Anya Nya message of secession for the south, a position that had obvious parallels in Ethiopian eyes with its own enemies in Eritrea and Tigre. Having identified the SPLA's leader, assistance was then given with arms of Soviet origin, as well as with finance and logistics; some of the training was provided by Cuba, including flying SPLA soldiers to Cuba itself for courses. A radio station was supplied that became essential listening right across Sudan, while the Ethiopian army was closely involved in the bases in western Ethiopia from which the SPLA launched its successful campaign, spreading inexorably, if seasonally, across the south. For its part, the SPLA partially repaid the assistance from Ethiopia by assisting the government with security in the south-west, including acting against local units of the Oromo Liberation Front (OLF).

Sudan certainly made the most of depicting the SPLA as an Ethiopian-backed movement. Nimeiri tried to use the charge to win direct American and Egyptian support in the south, but to no avail for both blamed him for the turn of events in the region rather than seeing Ethiopia as the main culprit. When Sadiq el-Mahdi became prime minister in 1986 he showed the same attitude as Nimeiri, but sought a deal with Ethiopia by which both countries would abandon support for the other's rebels, though this strategy failed as well. The accusations against Ethiopia therefore continued, especially in 1987 when the SPLA's brief capture of the 'northern' border towns of Kurmuk and Geissan brought charges of active involvement by the Ethiopian army, as well as a partially successful call for Arab solidarity in the face of Soviet-backed Ethiopian attack.

In response, the Sudanese army increased its covert relationship with the EPLF and the eventual EPRDF. Trucks and supplies were provided, and when Mengistu finally fell in 1991 Sudanese forces were in evidence in Addis Ababa, apparently keen to capture the SPLA leaders in the capital. Though the latter were able to stage a fairly orderly withdrawal via Kenya into southern Sudan, the loss of its bases and support from Ethiopia, as well as the radio station, proved a serious blow to the SPLA, which soon split into its bitter faction-fighting. Meanwhile, tens of thousands from the SPLA-controlled refugee camps were forced to flee back into southern Sudan, contributing another chapter to the long story of 'disasters' in the region.

While neither Ethiopia nor Sudan can be said to have started the conflicts in the neighbouring country, their actions were significant in bringing about radical change in both countries. Sudan's political crisis deepened in the 1980s as it went from the personal rule of Nimeiri, through transitions, to liberal democracy (again) before the decade culminated in the seizure of power in 1989 by an organized ideological minority. The major single challenge in that protracted crisis was the reopening of civil war in the south, a development that Ethiopia deliberately and significantly sustained until 1991, as the SPLA's subsequent fragmentation and retreat demonstrated. In return, the EPLF in particular was far more independent than the SPLA, but nevertheless both it and the TPLF/EPRDF benefited from the attitude of successive regimes in Sudan which thus played at least an indirect part in Mengistu's downfall. And Sudan then sought to capitalize on its friendship with the EPRDF to isolate and pressurize the SPLA.

Relations between the two neighbours had not been consistently hostile. There had been times when 'deals' had been attempted, most notably at the time of the Addis Ababa agreement of 1972 between north and south in Sudan. But the fact that the conflicts were overwhelmingly domestic in origin and lasted for far longer than the years of peace meant that low-level animosity rather than positive cooperation characterized relations for most of the period from the outbreak of civil war in both states in the early 1960s to the downfall of Mengistu in 1991.

Thus 1991 appeared something of a victory for Sudan's rulers rather than their past rivals in Ethiopia. The new rulers in Asmara and Addis Ababa were aware that Sudan regarded them as somewhat in its debt, and that Sudan could, if it so wished, still pose a significant threat to their fragile new regimes, especially should it endeavour to play the potentially destabilizing Islamic card. They thus sought to maintain effective working relations with Khartoum in spite of their different ideological complexions. Eritrea in particular exchanged a string of official visitors in the run-up to the independence referendum, and Sudan cracked down on the Jihad Eritrea movement which had bases around Kassala in the east, sending its leaders to seek refuge in Saudi Arabia. Sudan was, however, in something of a quandary given the declared intention of Hassan el-Turabi, the regime's *eminence grise*, to promote a swathe of Islamism in north-east Africa. Support for both Jihad Eritrea and Oromiyya Islamiyya, an Islamist faction among the Oromo in Ethiopia, was also pledged by Turabi's Popular Islamic and Arabic Conference, which was established in Khartoum in 1991. In January 1994 Eritrea felt it necessary to issue Sudan with a public warning over increased Islamic activity in the new state, and at the end of 1994 broke diplomatic relations on the same issue. It had a ring of the past about it which begged the question of how much the political changes in the region had really altered relations fundamentally. The new government in Ethiopia, meanwhile, felt some concern lest Sudan offer any direct assistance to the disaffected Oromo, and it was certainly the case that Sudan carefully scrutinized the political advancement of the Muslim community in Ethiopia. Ethiopia also linked Sudan to the attempted assassination of President Mubarak in Addis Ababa in 1995.

It might of course be argued that at times Sudan and Ethiopia were acting not just as neighbours but as proxies for others, especially the superpowers. But against that it must be recognized that the general attitudes of the two states towards the other's guerrillas persisted even though both countries switched superpowers at different times, as will be seen.

Ethiopia and Somalia

On Ethiopia's eastern flank, its nineteenth-century acquisition of territory brought it into conflict with the claims of Somalia, with the latter's independence from Britain and Italy (on behalf of the UN) in 1960 and unification into a single state. Some Somalis had already questioned the borders, arguing that at the end of the Second World War Britain had permitted Ethiopia to gain additional territory, thus incorporating more Somali pastoralists. Indeed, the Somali constitution explicitly challenged the borders with Ethiopia, Djibouti (formerly French Somaliland) and Kenya (where many in the Northern Frontier District (NFD) were also of Somali stock). These three points of the five-pointed star on the Somali flag became the main targets of Somali foreign policy from 1960, which was seen from Mogadishu less as 'foreign' policy than the policy of completing the independence of Greater Somalia. To this end Somalia began supplying arms to Somalis in Ethiopia, known as the Western Somali Liberation Front (WSLF) from as early as 1961. From then until 1964 there were also localized clashes between Somali and Ethiopian forces. While believing that Ethiopia under Haile Selassie would be intransigent on diplomacy and negotiation as a path to the unification of Somalia, there were higher hopes of Kenya. But these were dashed with the latter's independence, and efforts by Somalia in the NFD were swiftly contained by the experienced Kenyan forces in 1964, though incidents recurred for the rest of the decade. With regard to Djibouti, the initial objective was to pressurize France to keep it out of the hands of Ethiopia; and Ethiopia's was likewise with regard to Somalia.

The appointment of a new prime minister in Somalia in 1967, Mohamed Egal, was followed by a change of policy. Support to the guerrillas was halted, as was their encouragement by radio. Instead, new, more concilliatory relations with neighbours were adopted, partly in the hope that within the context of a proposed expansion of the East African Community – Kenya, Tanzania and Uganda – more chance of a better deal for the Somalis outside Somalia might be achieved. But the hopes of any such community were evaporating by the time of Siad Barre's coup in 1969, though Siad still remained relatively cautious with regard to neighbours, at least initially. His predecessor's 'Africa Policy' was altered somewhat to focus now on the Organization of African Unity (OAU). It led to an endeavour at mediation by presidents Gowon of Nigeria and Nimeiri of Sudan to solve the issue of Somali irredentism, though it failed to produce agreement. Siad then concentrated on relations with the North African states, and even took Somalia into the Arab League in 1974. The newly oil-rich members duly ensured that financial support to Somalia increased.

While Somalia's rulers shifted their approach to Greater Somalia, Ethiopia was remaining firm, and with Haile Selassie still influential in the OAU, it was in a strong position to avoid any danger of being out-manoeuvred on that front. Somalia's Arab involvement was of more concern, reviving as it did ancient Ethiopian perceptions of being squeezed in an Arab-backed pincer: this time in the Ogaden and Eritrea simultaneously. As if to underline the point, Somalia gave support to the Eritreans, at the same time seeking to please its new-found Arab friends.

Ethiopia's suspicions were deepened by Siad's backing from the Soviet Union in the build-up of the Somali armed forces. In the same year that the Treaty of Friendship and Cooperation between Somalia and the Soviet Union was signed, 1974, Ethiopia was being plunged into a domestic turmoil that was to make it appear increasingly vulnerable to its potential enemies, among which Somalia was still high. Siad Barre came under mounting pressure from below to seize the moment and take the Ogaden. Western Somali guerrillas, now aided by regular soldiers out of uniform, were once more making headway in the increasingly chaotic conditions of revolutionary Ethiopia, and the Somali army was keen to exploit the opportunity. But Siad's Soviet backers were threatening to abandon Somalia should he go to war and thereby flout OAU doctrines, and by association damage the USSR's reputation in Africa. Instead, the Soviets promoted their idea of a socialist alliance of Somalia, South Yemen and Ethiopia. However, it was the pressure from below to which Siad bowed, and the WSLF guerrillas were, from July 1977, joined by the regular Somali army. Within weeks they had achieved a series of victories, taking most of the Ogaden and Haud regions. But equally swiftly the Soviet Union abandoned Somalia for Ethiopia.

For Ethiopia the Somali attack was an ancient nightmare of being surrounded by hostile Muslims come true, and a wave of nationalism was encouraged to confront the Muslim invaders. It was a response worthy of another Marxist-Leninist, Joseph Stalin, during the German invasion of Russia in 1940; and it made it all the more appropriate that it was the Soviet Union that came to the rescue with a huge airlift of supplies, and the deployment of a vanguard of Cuban forces to lead the successful counter-attack. But the Soviet Union also insisted that Ethiopia stop at the borders. There was no question of breaking up Somalia when intervention had been to save a sovereign African state.

After the war the boot was on the other foot as far as Ethiopian–Somali relations were concerned. It was Ethiopia that held the initiative and was determined to exploit the situation. Siad had attacked Ethiopia once, but was now weakened and would be further undermined by Ethiopia providing bases and support for Siad's opponents in the Somali National Movement (SNM). There were also reported attempts to promote clan rivalries and clashes, especially attacks on those clans on which Barre was increasingly reliant: the Dulbahante, the Mareehan and Ogaden. This division would at least weaken any resurgent Somali irredentism, and might bring Siad's downfall and the installation of a less anti-Ethiopian regime. In 1983 in particular, there was significant de-stabilization in Somalia which threatened Siad's position.

The situation continued relatively unchanged until 1988 when once more events in one theatre of the Horn rebounded on another. In March of that year, the major EPLF victory at Afabat in Eritrea led to Mengistu needing to deploy troops from his eastern to his northern regions, and that to ensure security in the east a deal should be struck with the old enemy Siad Barre. The two governments agreed to end assistance to insurgents on each others' territory, as well as exchanging prisoners of war from the 1977–78 conflict and facilitating the repatriation of refugees. Opponents of the two regimes likened the agreement to the Hitler–Stalin pact of 1939. The effect was dramatic, for within weeks the SNM, fearful of abandonment by Ethiopia, launched a major assault in northern Somalia, capturing the major town of Burao, and nearly taking all of Hargeisa. The response of the Somali army was equally forceful with massive air and ground attacks leaving wanton destruction and widespread death. From Ethiopia's standpoint, the 1988 agreement was justified in that no significant fresh challenge was felt from the east, though the re-deployed troops were not decisive in the north. However, in spite of the agreement, Ethiopia was to give access once more to certain of Siad's opponents, such as Mohamed Farah Aideed's USC faction. Later, as UNOSOM II wound down in 1994, there were indications that Ethiopia, as well as Eritrea, favoured Aideed's faction in the struggle for power, apparently on the grounds that he represented the best chance for the emergence of a government and the reconstruction of the state, and that almost any government was preferable to bloody anarchy in former Somalia. It was thought that to this end Ethiopia was channelling arms to the USC. From Somalia's point of view it precipitated an explosion of violence which contributed significantly to the prolonged collapse of the regime and decay of the state.

The emergence of the *de facto* government of Somaliland in 1991 added a new twist to relations between neighbours in the Horn. While Somalia no longer had a single voice with which to speak, Somaliland was determined not to be drawn into attempted reconciliation talks under the auspices of neighbouring states simply as another factional party with a part to play in constructing a new Somalia. Having renounced the 1960 union, there was no intention of returning to any possible situation in which the north could once more come under the domination of the south. There may be grounds for thinking that at some stage in the future there could be room for a confederal relationship similar to that mentioned for Eritrea and Ethiopia, but little more appears feasible.

Issues of Somali politics also colour relations with other neighbours, especially Djibouti, which was perceived as trying to mediate apparently to resurrect former Somalia. In any case, relations between the SNM and Djibouti had been somewhat distant, with the latter having for years been cautious not to invite the wrath of Siad's regime in Mogadishu. A comparable caution is shown, too, towards Ethiopia, for though Mengistu had been overthrown, it was nevertheless an Ethiopian government that had entered into the deal with Siad in 1988 which had precipitated the worst of the violence in the north. Beyond the politics, relations have developed with Ethiopia and

Djibouti that have proved advantageous to the re-building of Somali-land's economy. In addition, while not recognizing Somaliland, Ethiopia has begun to use the port of Berbera in order to avoid a number of problems with Djibouti, and has also shown an interest in Zeila.

At one level, Ethiopia's long-running conflict with its two major neighbours in the Horn was a double tit-for-tat relationship reflecting instability within the post-imperial borders. At another level it was an indicator of the impact of the internationally recognized borders on indigenous societies. For Somalis, it concerned a claim to political unity for Somalis under Ethiopian rule; in southern Sudan there appeared little 'indigenous' solidarity with backers in Ethiopia, and conflict pointed instead to divisions with northern Sudan; whereas the case of Eritrea was more ambiguous with limited cross-border ties with eastern Sudan being used by a largely autonomous movement, capable of surviving the shifting sands of Sudanese politics. Yet behind that too, and sometimes revealed, as in Mengistu's call to the nation in 1977–78, lay the ancient conflicts of Christian and Muslim in the Horn of Africa. Above all, it was the longevity of these cross-border conflicts and their significance for developments in each of the three states that make them important. Exceptionally, there were efforts to stop them by agreement, but the central deals – actual and implied – failed to achieve the aims of the parties involved. An implicit Ethiopia–Sudan deal backed the Addis Ababa agreement of 1972, but it was not long in force and it did not negate the conflict in Eritrea; while the explicit 1988 Mengistu–Siad agreement produced the surprise SNM attack in the north of Somalia, as well as later Ethiopian support for Siad's challengers.

Eritrea and Djibouti

The involvement of the two small neighbouring states in the Horn was qualitatively different. They were, for the most part, trying to survive in the face of the turmoil in their neighbours, something that Djibouti had virtually turned into an art-form. With the two major population groups comprising communities with links to Somalia and Ethiopia respectively, it was not surprising that both countries had felt virtually honour bound at different times to lay claim to Djibouti territory, such claims being immediately countered by the other with its own threat of intervention. Djibouti played off the two by trying to retain a semblance of neutrality in the face of the internal instability in its two much larger neighbours, but such a stance was not always easy. The Somali civil war in the 1980s proved particularly difficult. The SNM felt that Djibouti was unhelpful, and gave succour to the

Somali army, while the latter nevertheless accused Djibouti of allowing assistance across its border, and certainly some refugees had taken shelter there. Djibouti later opposed the establishment of the independence of Somaliland in 1991, fearing that it would prove a precedent for others.

Djibouti's relations with Ethiopia proved equally delicate, particularly as movements grew among the Afar. Ethiopia suspected cross-border activity when Afar claims first surfaced there in the confusion of the revolution, and Djibouti claimed later that the FRUD was a result of a reverse intrusion. But in spite of these issues, the overall Djiboutian position was to seek to avoid confrontation with whatever governments it had to deal with in neighbouring states. It also tried to act as a mediator in both disputes between states – notably between Ethiopia and Somalia after the 1977–78 war – as well as over problems within particular neighbours, such as its efforts to promote a Somali peace settlement. That image of reconciliation and construction was also promoted by Djibouti acting as the headquarters for the regional Inter-Governmental Authority for Drought and Development (IGADD), founded in 1986, an organization that was, in turn, to seek to mediate in the war in the southern Sudan. The position of Djibouti with regard to all relations with neighbours was, of course, strengthened enormously by the military support it received from France and the presence of a major French base on Djibouti soil. In addition to Djibouti engaging in political management, there were trade links within the region utilizing both the port and the rail link between it and Addis Ababa.

From 1991 Eritrea also showed comparable skills in trying to manage relations with her new neighbours in the Horn. With the new government in Ethiopia it had a particularly effective relationship from the outset. Indeed, the two were based on back-to-back political relations centred on the Tigre area bordering the two countries. This gave a common ethnic identity to their respective leaderships, and the maintenance of this well-established relationship was important for both new governments. Thus from the outset, the new rulers in Ethiopia were accommodating the Eritreans on their path to formal independence. While Eritrea began by emphasizing the autonomy of its government, especially in the eyes of foreign and international representatives who sought to deal with it from offices in Addis Ababa. Once full independence was achieved in 1993, friendly relations were normalized, including agreements for the joint use of the ports of Massawa and Assab, the return of Ethiopian prisoners of war, and meetings of the Ethiopian–Eritrean joint ministerial commission. Clearly, good relations with Ethiopia are essential, for while in the short run Eritrea is militarily the match of its larger neighbour, in the longer term Ethiopia has greater capacity and is also the world's largest landlocked state with a disposition historically to seek to reach the sea. Eritrea has also to try to keep Sudan's tendency towards Islamic proselytism at arms length, for fear of its possible impact on Eritrea's domestic politics; and at the same time, it has to avoid appearing involved with the FRUD in Djibouti lest that have consequences for the ethnic stability of the young state of Eritrea itself. With regard to Sudan, the breaking of diplomatic relations between the two countries in 1994, and Eritrea's effective hosting of a meeting of Sudanese opposition groups in the following year (including the SPLA, which was receiving arms through Eritrea and Ethiopia), showed the potential dangers to both governments. Ominously, Eritrea accused Sudan of training Islamic militants in the refugee camps in eastern Sudan, while Beja opponents of the Sudanese government set up camps in Eritrea: it led to speculation not only that Sudan has sought to destabilize the regime in Eritrea, but that it may have designs on incorporating the Muslim-occupied territories of Eritrea in the future. In response, by the end of 1995 Eritrean leaders were calling openly for the overthrow of the government in Sudan.

Conclusion

It is hard to exaggerate the significance of neighbours, whether or not neighbouring governments have acted with intent. All the major challenges to regime stability since the 1960s had a significant cross-border dimension. The Eritrean movements needed at least the inefficiency and corruption of the Sudanese state to maintain bases in Sudan and use it as a transit route for materials. Clearly, others involved with the various Sudanese regimes played a part as well, but ultimately those regimes themselves made a contribution ensuring that there was a direct Sudanese–Ethiopian dimension. Similarly, the attitudes of Ethiopia under successive regimes was of significance for the southern Sudanese movements, especially as they generally remained more dependent on external backers than the Eritreans. In particular, the rise of the SPLA under John Garang in the second half of the 1980s owed much to Mengistu's support. Cross-border involvement was no less significant in the case of Somalia and Ethiopia. From the 1960s Ogadeni Somalis received encouragement from Somali governments, and, in spite of a later reduction in support, a rise in such activities preceded the major Somali–Ethiopian war of 1977–78, the largest-scale international conflict in Africa since the Second World War. In the following decade such cross-border support for opposition movements continued, in spite of the 1988 agreement between Siad and Mengistu which proved so short-lived. In the end the civil wars themselves contributed significantly to at least the downfall of regimes in all three countries. Successive regimes in Sudan fell in large part because of civil war in the south, while in Ethiopia and Somalia the various conflicts not only brought down existing rulers but contributed to the experiences of state collapse.

Eritrea was the outstanding example of a new state emerging from the wreckage of a previous government, but it was by no means the only question mark to be raised against the survival of the state system in the Horn: Somaliland, with its unrecognized declaration of independence, and the southern Sudanese, many of whom have sought secession or at least self-determination provided others. As well as challenges to the existing state structure, it was apparent that the success or otherwise of such claims would be influenced in part by the responses of other states. Ethiopia's response was central to the independence of Eritrea, while the reactions of Sudan, and to a lesser extent Djibouti, were also of some significance. However, responses to the independence of Somaliland and the claims of the southern Sudanese have been rather more equivocal. The reluctance of Ethiopia or Djibouti to recognize Somaliland has contributed to the overall sentiment of the international community to seek to preserve some kind of formal identity of the parts of former Somalia, however exiguous. The response of neighbours to Sudan's civil war was more complex, if no less significant. Concern combined fear of the potential of Sudan as an Islamic proselytizer, with residual sympathy for the African cause of the southern Sudanese. By 1994 this had turned into an IGADD initiative to mediate in the conflict, but it was an effort in which a number of the IGADD member states themselves had a stake in the outcome. IGADD's apparent preparedness to include consideration of the possibility of self-determination (and, by implication, the separation of the south from the north) showed the extent to which state re-structuring in the Horn was still an open possibility in the minds of neighbouring states as well as political factions.

The very existence of IGADD is also an indication of the recognition that concern with development issues has regional as well as state dimensions. Whereas the interactions of neighbours have hitherto contributed significantly to conflict, development on all fronts could be helped not just by a reduction in participation in mutually destructive activities, but more positively by combining in a variety of ways which will be discussed later. But though the message may have got across, it is still possible for individual states to seek to project their power across borders for a variety of reasons, and in so doing open the possibility of damaging retaliatory action once more.

7

Superpowers

The emergence of a global international system dominated by two superpowers after the Second World War was increasingly to affect even such poor and peripheral states as those of the Horn. But the processes of superpower involvement were both uneven and sporadic, being driven sometimes by changing perceptions and priorities in Washington and Moscow, including regard for the actions of each other, and at other times by developments within the Horn itself or wider regional circumstances.

The initial rivalry of the USA and the Soviet Union in the 1940s and early 1950s centred primarily on Europe, at least until the Iron Curtain had been effectively lowered across the continent. Africa was still overwhelmingly the preserve of the colonial powers, and in the Middle East there was greater initial concern by the USA at the deterioration of Britain's position than the potential of the Soviet Union. The Suez crisis of 1956 was to jolt that perception severely both because one of the steps towards it was the Soviet-approved Czech arms sale to Egypt, and because the concluding events of the crisis demonstrated the shift in the balance of power in the region away from Britain: Britain's era of power in the Middle East was clearly ending.

In the Horn, US Secretary of State Dulles's intentions of promoting a southern tier of Middle East security, following the collapse of the Baghdad Pact in 1955 (which had aimed at isolating the USSR behind the northern tier of Turkey, Iraq and Pakistan, and possibly Syria, Lebanon and Jordan as well), fitted well with Emperor Haile Selassie's wish for a military strengthening and a counter to the undue influence in the country of the British 'liberators'. The mutual agreement had begun with the discovery of a vital common interest to both: Eritrea. For the USA, Kagnew, a former Italian military facility just outside Asmara, was to become of strategic importance as a vital part of its global communications and intelligence network. For Ethiopia, the acquisition of Eritrea meant the achievement of the longstanding objective of access to the sea, while checking the growing threat of the Red Sea becoming an 'Arab lake'; it also provided the further consolidation of the multi-ethnic empire. From supporting Ethiopia's 'federal' incorporation of Eritrea in 1952 the USA went on to become its main ally militarily. The USA was granted access to facilities for twenty-five years, and Ethiopia received military assistance of all kinds, including arms; indeed, Ethiopia was far and away the major recipient of American military aid in sub-Saharan Africa. It enabled Ethiopia to develop one of the continent's largest armies and it was soon being put to use in Eritrea, with some direct American assistance from 1966. There was also American encouragement of modernization in all areas of Ethiopian society, but this was always accompanied by support for, rather than any intention of undermining, the emperor himself, for stability and security were always foremost in the thinking of successive decision-makers in Washington. Nevertheless, there was some awareness among American officials that the ageing Haile Selassie's grip on power could be slipping, especially after the attempted coup of 1961.

In neighbouring Sudan there was a related, if less well-supported, policy. The emergence of Soviet-backed Egypt in the aftermath of the Suez crisis of 1956 encouraged a US aid package to Sudan which polarized Sudanese parties. The Eisenhower doctrine had been advanced to offer Arab states an alternative source of aid to the USSR, and though Sudan's historically pro-Egyptian 'unionist' parties were unlikely allies for a communist state, the danger remained that they might succumb to the growing strength of Nasserism and allow Soviet-backed Egypt a greater role in their country. This polarization between the blandishments of East and West contributed to the crisis into which General Abboud stepped with his coup of 1958; and subsequently, the aid package from the USA was accepted. While Sudan did not move noticeably closer to America (it was generally inactive in foreign affairs under Abboud), it certainly kept Egypt (and with it possible Soviet influence) at bay as far as domestic political developments were concerned. There was thus broad acceptance by the USA for the military regime which had accepted the highly controversial American aid package.

In Africa more generally the 1960s were perceived as an era of superpower intrusion. Many states were newly independent and both superpowers showed an interest in active involvement, a situation most graphically illustrated in their support for rival sides in the imbroglio in the Congo (later Zaire). But in the Horn the events of the 1950s had largely superceded these developments elsewhere (especially the relationship between the USA and Ethiopia): only Somalia, independent in 1960, and clearly of some strategic significance, was new to the game. The USA's recognition of the unification of British and Italian Somalilands worried Haile Selassie to the point that he paid a surprise visit to the Soviet Union; but the USSR was soon opening contacts with Somalia as well, and arms flowed there from 1963. There was little that was specifically radical about Somalia at that stage but it needed Soviet arms and was beginning to support irredentism, which was disapproved of by the West. The Soviet action was perceived by Ethiopia and the West as opportunistic, especially when it was thought that the Soviet Union was allowing Syria to act as a proxy in giving military aid to the Eritrean Liberation Front (ELF). It thus appeared that Soviet weapons were being supplied to Ethiopia's enemies in two border areas of growing conflict. Moreover, challenges from Somalis and Eritreans re-opened old fears of attacks from Muslim neighbours. Ethiopia could only doubt Soviet reassurances and comfort itself in the continuing flow of US support to sub-Saharan Africa's largest army.

Era of *détente*

The late 1960s and early 1970s brought a change in both the thinking and the fortunes of the two superpowers. The USA was moving from an age of confrontation in Cuba and by proxy in Vietnam, in the direction of *détente*; and as far as Africa, including the Horn, was concerned, a decrease in interest and involvement. Even Ethiopia seemed at least partially disposable: satellite technology had made the Kagnew base at Asmara outdated (while Britain had made the Indian Ocean island of Diego Garcia available as an alternative base) and supplies to the Ethiopian army were reduced. The Middle East fringe argument seemed less significant, since the 1967 war appeared to have contained radical Arab nationalism, whose beacon, Gamal Abdel Nasser, was in any case dead three years later, and the war of October 1973 did little to suggest a major change in the regional balance. Nevertheless, the USA still remained the major backer of Ethiopia.

Similarly, the Soviet Union appeared to have gone through something of a rise and decline. Like its US rival, it too perceived itself as anti-colonial, though instead of the liberal and democratic path to economic and political freedom, it sought the promotion of socialism as the way for progressive new states. Lenin had, after all, proclaimed imperialism to be the highest stage of capitalism, and with its retreat there could, in theory, be gains for socialism in both the declining imperialist powers and the progressive states that had won their new-found independence. The Horn offered strategic possibilities and military facilities were, in practice, the main concern of the Soviets. As early as 1963 the USSR was outbidding by several times Western military aid offers to Somalia, coming up with a package estimated at $35 million. As if to show evenhandedness, there was even an offer to supply a larger amount to Ethiopia, but the latter had no serious intention of abandoning the USA; and in any case, from 1964 to 1967 the USSR was aware that arms it had supplied were going from Syria to Eritrea. The setback for the USSR came, though, with the Arab defeat in 1967, when its arms and training to Egypt in particular seemed of so little avail; and in the Horn, Somalia, under Egal's premiership, appeared to be less concerned to press its irredentist claims (a move encouraged by the USA).

However, by the end of the decade the USSR was re-building its position in the Horn once more. The Brezhnev era may have been noted for its domestic conservatism, but in the Third World it was a time for action. The USSR had built up its nuclear arsenal to achieve approximate parity with the West, from which position of strength it was prepared to move towards *détente*. But *détente* meant in essence the avoidance of nuclear conflict with the USA, not the abandonment of global rivalry which the growth of Soviet power now seemed to make possible. And while the Soviet Union perceived itself as ever stronger, the United States appeared in relative decline. In particular, the Vietnam War seemed to be both humiliating internationally, and debilitating domestically. Now was the time for the USSR to pursue both *détente* and expansionism, and the Horn was an important pawn on the global board. With facilities in South Yemen from 1968, and possibly across the straits as well, the way would be strengthened for the expansion of Soviet naval penetration into the Indian Ocean, a process that was to increase steadily to a highpoint in 1980. It was intended not only as a counterweight to US involvement in the area, but would also contribute to a rise in Soviet influence from the Horn to East Asia, as well as posing a challenge to the West on a number of vital routes, including those used for transporting much of the Gulf oil.

The USSR's opportunity in the Horn came with the coups of Ga'afar Nimeiri in Sudan and Siad Barre in Somalia in 1969 (the latter possibly encouraged by the Soviet Union). Nimeiri's apparent radicalism had the added promise that Sudan was a neighbour of another Soviet-supplied state, Egypt, and that the two countries proposed a union with Libya, which had also experienced a radical pan-Arab coup in 1969. However, the violent leadership convulsions were to lose Sudan to the Soviet Union by 1971, and a year later it was to suffer a similar expulsion from Egypt at the hands of Anwar Sadat. Those setbacks only made Somalia of even greater significance, and by 1974 the Soviet

Union seemed on the way to becoming firmly entrenched. In addition to military and domestic security assistance, there was aid for a number of economic projects, totalling an estimated $285 million. In return the USSR was able to develop naval facilities. The port of Berbera in the Gulf of Aden became a major Soviet facility; in addition the Soviets had use of the southern ports of Mogadishu and Kismayo. The latter was also to become a communications centre, while Berbera in the north was also developed as an air base. In 1974 the two countries signed a full Treaty of Friendship and Cooperation: the first the Soviet Union had concluded with a sub-Saharan African state.

Nineteen-seventy-four was also the year that saw the start of the Ethiopian revolution. Initially it was far from clear that it would produce a major change in international alignments, but then it was not clear where the revolution was going within Ethiopia for some years. As a result, it took time for the superpowers' policies towards Ethiopia to change. The USA was the major foreign presence in the country, and though it had backed the emperor for years, it did not pull out even after his eventual deposition and death. Instead, American arms continued to flow into Ethiopia, even rising in value and sophistication in 1976–77, in an endeavour to balance the seemingly ever-growing supply of Soviet arms to Somalia. Certainly, the volume of American arms was markedly higher than it had been in the years of waning interest from 1969–74, and in the three years from the start of the revolution amounted to some $180 million, including two squadrons of F–5E aircraft. In the world of *realpolitik* inhabited by Henry Kissinger and Gerald Ford, it was thought in the early years of the revolution that it would not necessarily damage America's involvement in the country, and that there could even be some steering of the more moderate new leaders such as Aman Andom. At the same time, continuing US support would also keep the USSR out of Ethiopia. However, Jimmy Carter's election as president in 1977 was followed by an emphasis on human rights as a major criteria for support for states in the Third World, and on this count Mengistu's regime was fast becoming unacceptable. As a result of this dilemma for policy-makers, there were threats to reduce military aid.

Substantial though American military aid to Ethiopia had been, it did not match the Soviet supply to Somalia. Perceiving American resolve to be waning (in spite of the later rise in arms) in the same period (1974–77), the USSR had supplied Somalia with approximately $200 million worth of military equipment, making it the fourth largest army in Africa behind three much larger countries – Nigeria, Zaire and Ethiopia. But developments in the Ethiopian revolution were also making the Soviet Union aware of new possibilities there. In Soviet terms, it appeared that the revolution was becoming more progressive; and the emergence of Mengistu Haile Mariam was also seen as favourable to its interests. By 1976–77 the USSR had decided that the time had come to make a determined move towards Ethiopia, a step that was soon welcomed by Mengistu, who in turn broke dramatically with the USA in the Spring of 1977. Not that the Soviet Union believed that it was abandoning Somalia; on the contrary, it had a new aim, a Pax Sovietica, that would embrace the two countries as well as extending to South Yemen on the other side of the Gulf of Aden. In time, a constellation of Marxist states would develop, controlling an important strategic point.

The ideal card to play to achieve the Pax Sovietica was that beacon of Soviet-style socialism in the Third World, Fidel Castro of Cuba. For his part, Castro did not become involved simply as a Soviet puppet. His hostility to Western imperialism was beyond reproach, and in Ethiopia, as elsewhere in Africa, Cuban involvement fitted naturally with its general foreign policy objectives, as well as a real sense of shared history with the African continent. Furthermore, Castro's importance as a Third World leader would be enhanced in the face of US attempts to contain his influence. However, at Aden in March 1977 not even Castro's warm embrace could reconcile Siad Barre with Mengistu, a message repeated when Siad visited Moscow in August. While the plan for socialist integration was not immediately discarded by the USSR, its chances of success were stopped dead by the intransigence of Siad Barre in particular. For Siad, the issues of the Horn still far transcended international socialist solidarity with his newly Marxist-Leninist neighbour.

In reality, the Soviet Union was now faced with a choice between continuing its relationship with Somalia, or transferring to Ethiopia, and it chose the latter course. Ethiopia was by far the larger country, and had potentially far greater economic capacity. With success in the north against the Eritreans, it could offer attractive naval facilities at Massawa as well as at Asab, and also at the offshore Dahlik islands. (The USSR's floating dock was eventually to be moved from Berbera to Aden and on to the islands.) Moreover, there were doubts about the reliability of Siad Barre. In spite of substantial Soviet aid, he was still something of an unruly client. Indeed, the military aid to Somalia had permitted him to behave in such a way in the Ogaden from early in 1977. On the political front, too, there were doubts about his commitment to the building of socialism, especially with regard to his attitudes to Islam and the private sector of the economy, whereas the eventual creation of a Marxist party had not in practice created the kind of pro-Soviet power centre hoped for by Moscow. In foreign policy he showed disturbing signs of independence, apparently hoping to play off China and the Arab states in some measure against the Soviet Union. In contrast, Ethiopia appeared to be offering a more real appreciation of revolution, having, as it did, certain historical similarities to Russia, while the emergence of Mengistu seemed to offer a safer bet than Siad Barre.

The need for the Soviets to decide conclusively was forced by the Somali invasion of Ethiopia in July 1977. The Soviet Union had already issued warnings about the rising level of conflict in the Ogaden, and it now condemned the invasion unequivocally, halting all arms supplies to Somalia. Meanwhile, Somali forces had captured the Ogaden as far as the mountains and threatened to overrun the whole region. Such a development could be expected to have repercussions elsewhere in Ethiopia that would threaten the whole future of the revolution, and even of the state. Such a development would be the worst of both worlds, for the Soviet Union could find itself pushed out of Somalia and saddled with a collapsing new ally. The only alternative was a rapid and large-scale reinforcement of Ethiopia, which legitimately invited intervention to help a sovereign state under attack in what quickly became the largest supply operation to Africa since the Second World War. By sea and air, arms and supplies worth over $1 billion in total were dispatched to the beleaguered country in an operation that included the biggest airlift since the Anglo-American relief of the Berlin blockade in 1948–49. In addition, Soviet advisers (some of whom had been flown directly from Mogadishu to Addis Ababa) gave assistance, and 15,000 Cuban troops were imported to bolster Ethiopian units on the ground. The tide of war was rapidly reversed and early in 1978 the Somalis were pushed back across the old border, though the Soviet Union was firm in restraining its new ally from any thought of proceeding further.

The Somali–Ethiopian War had served to transform the position of the superpowers in the Horn in a way that neither could have predicted, any more than they had been able to control the outset of the war itself. But the outcome, in terms of the new configuration, was not to be limited to the Horn itself. Rather, it increasingly became part of a wider regional picture. Fears were expressed by some American analysts that the Soviet Union was facing an oil shortage at home, and might have objectives of its own in the Gulf, for which its position in Ethiopia and South Yemen might be useful. Others believed that rivalry in the Horn might be part of an intensifying global confrontation. Zbigniew Brzezinski of the National Security Council in Washington was known as a leading 'globalist' for his view that Soviet adventurism in the Third World had to be checked whenever and wherever it occurred, and in the context of the Horn this meant preventing the Soviet Union from becoming the arbiter of the region and the southern Red Sea. (He was to say later that 'Detente lies buried in the sands of the Ogaden'.)[1] A contrary 'regionalist' viewpoint was put by Secretary of State Cyrus Vance who believed that *détente* and the achievement of a SALT treaty were higher priorities that might be damaged by unnecessary rivalry in less important areas of the world. President Carter seemed somewhat equivocal, but his views appeared to be clarified by other developments in the Middle East. One was the revolution in Iran which brought the downfall of one of America's staunchest allies in the region, the Shah, in 1979, amidst allegations that insufficient had been done to assist him. It was a major blow to US perceptions of security in the Gulf (and the subsequent American hostage crisis was even to contribute to Carter's defeat in the presidential election). The second event, in the same year, was the Soviet decision to send its forces into Afghanistan. To the USA, the eastern flank of the Middle East had weakened. There was therefore new reason to defend friendly regimes on other flanks, a view in which it was encouraged by two of its most important remaining allies, Egypt and Saudi Arabia. The security of 'south-west Asia' was thus central to Carter's thinking in mid-1979, and led to his commitment of the USA to use military power to protect key economic resources in the Third World, especially oil, and promoted the idea of a Rapid Deployment Force for that purpose. As he put it in his State of the Union address of 1980, which became known as the Carter doctrine, 'Any attempt by any outside force to gain control of the Persian Gulf region will be regarded as an assault on the vital interests of the United States of America and such an assault will be repelled by any means necessary, including force.'[2] It also required new basing agreements at the top of the Indian Ocean, and these were made with Oman, Kenya and Somalia. The latter was particularly useful as a counterweight to the USSR in the Horn; it could contribute to rear support for the Rapid Deployment Force in the Middle East and it facilitated the monitoring of Soviet submarines passing through the Bab el-Mandeb. A permanent carrier battle group was also deployed to the Indian Ocean to counter the perceived Soviet naval build-up.

For Somalia, the basing agreement was a ten-year deal. The USA would supply 'defensive' weaponry only, and in limited quantities; Somali forces were not to use the weapons to attack the Ogaden again; nor were they to be supplied to the Western Somali Liberation Front. Critics of the arrangement argued that America's acquisition of facilities at the port of Berbera was not that significant militarily, and that, in return, Somalia would acquire an important supply of arms without having given up its claim to the Ogaden. Moreover, Somalia was still free to seek arms elsewhere, particularly from regional actors.

Second Cold War

Carter's successor, Ronald Reagan, was a ready follower of this conversion to the 'globalist' view. In addition, there was growing concern about Libya. The peace agreement between Egypt and Israel had been the highpoint of Carter's foreign policy and Soviet-supplied Libyan activities in the Horn were part of a broad challenge to America and its allies across north-east Africa. Libya had abandoned the Eritreans for the new radical Ethiopian regime, and then went on to agree a tripartite pact with Libya and South Yemen, signed in Aden in 1981. Its intentions were clearly perceived as hostile with regard to both Somalia and Sudan. To the new US Administration the Aden Treaty was the coping stone in an 'arc of crisis' reaching from Africa to Afghanistan. In addition to support for Sudan and Somalia, new agreements on the use of facilities for military purposes were also concluded with Oman and Kenya, cementing the development of the Rapid Deployment Force begun in Carter's presidency. For Reagan, Qaddafi rapidly became an international *bête noir*. Several attempts to overthrow him were launched, culminating in the unsuccessful raid on Tripoli in 1985.

The 'arc of crisis' was a major area of rivalry in the second Cold War which had succeeded the era of *détente*, and which reached its zenith in the early 1980s. It was a rivalry that was particularly intense in the Third World, focusing on a number of revolutions or potentially revolutionary situations from Central America to Asia, as well as in southern Africa and the Horn (though the rest of Africa was less affected by the second Cold War). In the Horn it meant a continuing and expanding flow of arms. In Ethiopia Soviet arms were to build up over the years to a total of some \$7 billion. The greater part of this was intended for the crushing of opposition in Ethiopia, and thereby the consolidation of the revolution. To this end the Soviet Union was active in supporting the Ethiopian forces in Eritrea and Tigre. But it also provided resources for activities *vis-à-vis* neighbours. As well as supplying anti-Barre elements in Somalia, Ethiopian troops made incursions in 1982, while the Soviets were as ready as the Ethiopians to see the arming of the SPLA in southern Sudan. The American response was on nothing like the same scale as the Soviet's militarily, but it was nevertheless very substantial and important for the regimes involved. Somalia was a major recipient, though not on the scale that Barre kept requesting, which owed much to the exaggerated expectations that he had carried over from the generosity of his earlier patrons in Moscow. The USA was determined to restrict Somalia from invading Ethiopia once more, while at the same time wishing to be seen to be firmly supporting a friend against attacks that were partly sustained from its Soviet-backed neighbour. None the less, the 'defensive' weaponry supplied by the Americans was to be used by Barre to defend his regime by an ever-increasing use of force, and in this way the USA contributed to the proliferation of violence in Somalia. US budget constraints from 1986, coupled with awareness of mounting human rights violations from 1988, led eventually to a fall in American military aid to Somalia, and in 1989 it was halted completely. Indeed, when it came to the time for the renewal of the agreement between the two countries in 1990, the changed situation in both Somalia and the region more widely ensured that it was not even raised in either capital.

Alongside military support, the USA also undertook major assistance for economic development in Somalia. Siad had shown reluctance to move from his socialist policies which had allowed ample opportunity for the state to command resources which he and his trusted associates could deploy largely as they wished. But with US backing the International Monetary Fund and the World Bank intervened to stabilize and liberalize the economy, and other donors such as Italy were generous with aid. In all, some $ 2.5 billion was pumped into the Somali economy between 1980 and 1989. But instead of helping to stabilize the country, the injection of big projects into a weak infrastructure helped weaken the Somali state. One American official was later to write candidly:

> Heavy commodity and cash assistance, instruments chosen by donors to turn Somalia's economy around, opened broad avenues for malversion and structurally undermined Somalia's economy through their inflationary effect. With the best of intentions, donors with large-scale projects and massive assistance inadvertently contributed to the disintegration of the Somali state.[3]

The rise and fall of US support for the regime of Siad Barre in Somalia had been preceded by, and then overlapped with, expanded US support for Sudan. US–Sudanese relations had been improving in much of the 1970s, following the latter's break with the Soviet Union in 1971. In the following year, Sudan had been the first Arab state to resume relations with the USA following the breaks of the Six Day War of 1967; and though the killings by the PLO of two senior American diplomats in Khartoum in 1973 caused embarrassment, it was only a temporary hiccup. Nimeiri came to be regarded in Washington as something of a statesman. Politically, he was seen as the man who made peace in the south in 1972, and sought reconciliation with his northern Sudanese opponents in 1977. In economic policy, he wished to encourage links with Western companies, with Chevron discovering oil, and in 1978 a Sudan–United States Business Council was established. But above all, Nimeiri was regularly welcomed in Washington because of his support for Egypt in the peace process with Israel. For Nimeiri it was not an easy position, since it isolated Sudan in the Arab world (only Somalia in the Arab League gave comparable support) and fuelled his critics at home, but in the last resort he, like Sadat, was seeing the USA as the major force in the Middle East. In 1976 Sudan was made eligible to obtain weapons from the USA, and from 1977 to 1985 it became a major recipient of military aid and training to the value of $1.4 billion. Further development programmes and food aid brought the total to some $2 billion. In addition, as Sudan's economy deteriorated in the early 1980s, the USA used its influence with bodies such as the IMF, the World Bank, and the Paris Club to ease the treatment the country received (as the USA was to do in Somalia as well). Apparently, until well into the decade, American officials still thought that they could not only help to preserve a friendly regime, but also that they could even turn around the deteriorating Sudanese economy. In all, Sudan under Nimeiri was perceived as being increasingly important strategically: with regard to Egypt and the peace with Israel; as a partner in the containment of Libya; and as a counter to the USSR in Ethiopia. In addition, Sudan was seen as capable of becoming something of a show case for Western-backed modernization (with the help of conservative Arab states' money).

It was a situation in which the client was as willing as the patron. Sudan lobbied vigorously and to effect in Washington, so much so that it often appeared that the tail was wagging the dog. However, it left the USA with only limited leverage over the client regime as was seen in the early 1980s when Washington became increasingly alarmed at the twists and turns of Nimeiri, particularly over the redivision of the south and the policy of Islamization. Nimeiri, for his part, appeared confident that America had little option other than to back him, and that it had in any case supplied the means for him to pursue a divisive and repressive policy in the south. (When conflict did break out once more in 1983, both the USA and Egypt moved to dissociate themselves from the closer involvement in the region militarily that Nimeiri tried to extract.)

As well as Somalia and Sudan, US support for Kenya was increased, not only to help stabilize that country, which experienced a serious coup attempt in 1982, but to offset fears in Kenya of Somali rearmament, as well as giving the US Navy access to the port of Mombasa. Total aid to the three countries (Somalia, Sudan and Kenya) over ten years amounted to $2.5 billion. In addition, all three countries were involved in planning and manoeuvres with American Rapid Deployment Forces (RDF) with a view to Gulf security.

The rise of Gorbachev in the Soviet Union was to have a profound effect on East–West relations that brought an end to the Cold War, at the same time as heralding the transformation of Eastern Europe. Both messages were to have an impact on the Horn. The new leadership in Moscow was quick to perceive that Mengistu's regime in Ethiopia was both stubborn and troubled. Its stubbornness was shown in its determined pursuit of the internal wars in the north, together with the reluctance of Mengistu to establish a single party and his domination of it when finally inaugurated. The troubles were shown by the setbacks in the wars and the continuing economic woes, with the famine of 1987–88 following that of 1984–85. Military aid was continued, but it was made clear that the programme would be wound down; a situation that compounded the discontent in the army, precipitated by successive military defeats, as well as encouraging Mengistu into a new agreement with Israel. Mengistu was urged by the Soviets to negotiate with both his main internal enemies, and with Somalia, though it was only the latter that brought success in 1988. Although the collapse of communism throughout Eastern Europe was further undermining the most Stalinist state in Africa, it was not until 1990 that Mengistu unveiled a package of political and economic reforms, and by that time it was too late to have much of an impact.

The USA, meanwhile, was also rethinking its relations with the Horn. In Sudan, Nimeiri's domestic policies were increasingly perceived as self-destructive, especially in the south, while the embracing of Islamic fundamentalism was anathema to a superpower that had been so severely and recently embarrassed in Iran. As a result, there was understanding (and possibly even some connivance) when Nimeiri was overthrown in 1985, but the successor governments were to prove an even more doubtful quantity. The related crisis of civil war and Islamization went unresolved, and contributed to the 1989 coup that ushered in the most hard-line regime since independence, and one which seemed uncooperative with international relief efforts for its suffering people. Sudan's relations with America's major ally in the Middle East, Egypt, became progressively worse, while from 1985 those with Libya improved. Sudan also developed her relations with Iraq, including becoming one of the few Arab states to support Saddam Hussein in the Gulf War, and developed new links with Iran with overtones of Sudan becoming a regional centre for the propagation of

Islamic fundamentalism. In 1993 Sudan was finally placed on America's comparatively short list of states supporting terrorism internationally.

While Sudan was increasingly regarded by the USA as a pariah state from 1989, the position of Somalia was somewhat more ambiguous, not least because Siad Barre clung on to power throughout the 1980s. His actions, however, proved as difficult for the USA to influence as they had been for the Soviet Union in the previous decade. Although American military support was far less in volume and purely 'defensive' in character, in practice arms still found their way to guerrillas in the Ogaden and tension persisted between Ethiopia and Somalia until the 1988 agreement. That agreement, however, permitted Siad Barre to blot his copybook even more by the unleashing of a new wave of repression in the north, at a time when concern for human rights as a central criteria of US foreign policy in the Third World was replacing old superpower rivalry. In such a climate the USA could only suspend aid in 1990 and then stand and watch the violent implosion of the Somali state. In 1991 it was forced to evacuate the new and very expensive embassy complex in Mogadishu in circumstances as humiliating as previous débâcles in Saigon and Tehran, if much less noticed by the media at the time. The decision to return to Somalia through an armed relief operation at the end of 1992 owed more to a new chapter of policy towards the Third World after the Cold War, than to the circumstances that had given rise to the earlier involvement.

While Somalia was being perceived from a different perspective after the end of the Cold War, so too was the more congenial old ally, Kenya. Human rights thinking now became paramount there as well, at the end of a decade in which the presidency of Daniel Arap Moi was seen as having become more paranoid, repressive and corrupt (a perception publicly encouraged by the then US Ambassador Scott Hempstone). Far from being a useful additional port facility, allegedly AIDS-infested Mombasa was more of a liability than a help to the US military. Thus, while there was support for the re-democracy movement and the eventual general election of late 1992, there was overall a decline in concern and commitment for Kenya, the former beacon of Western practice, internally and externally, in East Africa.

That overall perception of change in American thinking was the most important shift of all. The USA had been playing checkers with the Soviet Union on a front that extended from Libya to Kenya, and that superpower dimension to regional politics within the Horn was now dead. And while some strategists had argued the importance of at least some of the acquisitions for broader strategic thinking with regard to the Middle East, that too was in decline. The long Iran–Iraq war had involved greater Western involvement within the Gulf itself, and that penetration was followed up spectacularly by the Gulf War to liberate Kuwait from Iraq's invading army in 1991. The whole role of American access to ports on the southern shores of the Gulf of Aden and the Indian Ocean in either of these Gulf conflicts was minor, and in consequence, the strategic case declined even without the end of the Cold War.

With their interests in sharp decline in the Horn, the two super-powers were left only with the task of extracting themselves with some degree of dignity. As early as 1986 there had been some talks between them on reducing tension in the region (as in other areas of the world), but domestic developments in the USSR later overtook international considerations. For the Soviet Union, soon to become the Russian Federation, the concentration on events at home meant pulling out of Ethiopia (and elsewhere in the Third World), and ceding responsibility to the USA to patch up some kind of settlement on the ground. For the Americans it consisted of recognizing that in the wake of their ignominious failure in Somalia, there was a need to develop their growing relationship with the ever more successful guerrillas in northern Ethiopia, and to seek to broker some kind of deal that would pacify that country at last, and have implications for Somalia and Sudan.

The achievement of these objectives was the major accomplishment of the senior State Department official for Africa at the turn of the decade, Herman Cohen. His success involved working with the grain of events in Ethiopia and forgetting past US positions. It was accepted that the EPLF had, in effect, conquered its own country, and that historically there were no grounds for seeking to perpetuate what had clearly been a failed union. Moreover, the EPRDF, the rising force in Ethiopia, was prepared to accept the EPLF's claim for self-determina-tion. The USA had been improving contacts with the EPLF and the TPLF, a process which had been helped by the end of the Cold War and the fronts' abandonment of Marxism-Leninism in the various guises in which they had espoused it hitherto, though it had to accept that both were committed to the separation of Eritrea. At the same time, the USA had links with the fading regime and was able to broker deals which would facilitate the transfer of power rather than risk a descent into chaos of the kind occurring in Somalia. These included Mengistu's escape to Zimbabwe and Operation Solomon which took some 14,000 of the remaining Falasha to Israel. In the end, the US role in Ethiopia and Eritrea was regarded as a successful clearing up job that was to contrast sharply with Somalia, as well as the loss of influence on developments in Sudan from the early 1980s.

While success in Ethiopia and Eritrea made the USA an important player in those two countries, the overall significance of the Horn for the USA had declined, as had Africa generally. The fact that the USA was to play a leading role on behalf of the UN in Somalia in late 1992 had much less to do with Somalia *per se* than with issues of domestic politics and Bush's reputation for decisive overseas action; as well as demonstrating to the Europeans what decisive military intervention could achieve in the face of their apparent indecision and reluctance in the Balkans. More significant was the irrelevance of the Horn for US intervention in the Gulf crisis of 1990–91: it made any action in Africa look more like an option than an interest as far as the USA was concerned. Africa, always the least important continent for the USA, was of even less concern now that it was the world's only superpower, and voices were raised criticizing both military and development aid to Africa, though humanitarian concerns, for which there was media coverage, aroused greater support. The prospects, then, are for declining economic and military aid, and the aid that is given will in many cases be linked to good governance, re-democratization and human rights, but without necessarily being sufficient to contribute to the stable fulfilment of such conditions. The USA will also increasingly expect that as it withdraws from Africa, the European powers and the European Union will take a greater responsibility for the continent that they did so much to shape historically.

Despite frequent speculation over its long-term policy towards Africa, the power which is likely to continue to provide the lead for Europe, as it has done for the past thirty-five years, is France. In the Horn, its late nineteenth-century rivalry with Britain in particular left it confined to Djibouti. Yet weakness was also strength since it was the coast's strategic opportunities, rather than the interior's confusing responsibilities, of which France was able to make use. As a result, France maintained a significant presence in Djibouti, combining both stability for the territory itself and a capability for projection to the oceans and skies. The former was put to the test with the challenge to President Gouled from the FRUD and his obvious manipulation of the multi-party process. Amidst speculation that France would seek a more consensual alternative ruler, little was done to check Gouled's re-assertion of both his political and coercive dominance. The value of the country was shown during the Gulf War when France was the one country to benefit from its strategic position in the Horn, an importance which is likely to ensure the continuance of French involvement there. Meanwhile, the importance of the region more widely has not been lost on France, and it has been active diplomatically elsewhere as well.

In contrast to France, Britain, for so long the dominant power in the whole Nile basin, effectively retreated with the handover of Eritrea to the 'federation' with Ethiopia; the independence of Sudan; and then the Suez crisis. Its role thereafter was minor, though there was diplomatic involvement, especially in winning Sudan's President Nimeiri for the West in the early 1970s, and supporting Cohen in Ethiopia twenty years later. But perhaps that means that Britain's role was largely negative. Its retreat from its former area of dominance left something of an international vacuum into which other actors, major international powers as well as regional powers, stepped. (No such opportunity was left in much of former French-ruled Africa even had there been greater international pressure on those generally less strategically significant countries.) As in the nineteenth century, the intrusion of outside major powers was largely a product of their rivalry and thus, with the end of the Cold War, is unlikely to be repeated in the foreseeable future. That in turn will leave renewed possibilities for regional powers, but that had been the case, for Egypt in particular, before the European intervention of the late nineteenth century had ever occurred.

Conclusion

Unlike some other parts of Africa, most notably France in West and Equatorial Africa, it was not the former colonial powers that led the way internationally. Nor was there a state in the Horn to compare as a regional actor with South Africa, which played an active part in confronting Soviet-backed movements across the southern African region. The superpowers were unmatched in their injection of armaments into the Horn, and they did so for strategic reasons in which their own rivalry grew, culminating in the Horn's centrality to the 'arc of crisis' in the second Cold War. While the superpowers were developing the strategic possibilities of their clients in the Horn, they were also arming their clients. These weapons were not for use in the strategic issues that attracted the superpowers, but were essentially made available for the regimes to which they were supplied. It was often stated that the weapons were for defensive purposes, rather than intended to encourage attacks on neighbouring states, but that was the problem. The provision of weapons provided client rulers with the means to use force in pursuit of domestic, and sometimes regional, objectives. In the long run the regimes of Siad Barre, Mengistu Haile Mariam and Ga'afar el-Nimeiri all fell, but not before they had themselves been central to the development of large-scale civil conflict that claimed the lives of millions. In addition to their regimes falling, varying degrees of state disintegration occurred as well. The Soviet Union went furthest in trying to support a regime with its backing of Mengistu, but it was ultimately unsuccessful. The USA never went so far, but was no better off for its restraint, for as one official has put it, 'claiming strategic interests where one is not willing to exert force only leads to policy quagmires'.[4] The USA had thus contributed to the Somali quagmire into which it finally took a spectacular leap itself.

8

Regional Politics

While the core of the relations between the three major countries of the Horn lay in their direct contacts with one another, their relations were also influenced not only by the activities of superpowers, but also by the regional relations surrounding them. These comprised primarily, but not exclusively, the activities of those states that bordered on one or more of them. This involved not only the surrounding states as autonomous actors, but also the extent to which their behaviour was a part of some regional system.

The concept of a regional system was particularly relevant to those countries that played a major role in Middle Eastern politics, and the inter-connected events that unfolded there after the Second World War in particular. Arguably, the Horn had been one edge of it for millennia as empires rose and fell (an Afro-Middle Eastern sub-region as it was described earlier), but in the post-Second World War era, the contribution of the last wave of imperialists, the comparatively short-lived formal and informal imperialism of Britain and France in particular, was in rapid decline, and instead the Middle East was emerging as a system of relations between states within the context of the rival superpowers. But it was not just a system of states, it was also a regional system with unique characteristics. It contained in Arabism and Islam not just traits of a broadly homogeneous character, but ones that appeared to proffer ideologies for concerted action. And that sentiment was intensified by the creation of the state of Israel at the heart of the region, both inviting action and taunting its Arab neighbours with their comparative weakness. In this post-war Middle East the Horn remained on the fringe, but none the better for that, for as a fringe it was an area which often appeared to offer room for manoeuvre and manipulation that was lacking in the more contested and tauter core areas, while itself being too marginal to reach either deadlock or significant pursuit of resolution.

Not all the regional players were equal, however, either in ambition or resources. Some Middle Eastern actors in the Horn were involved as neighbours of one or more of the states directly involved. Others were both neighbours and had ambitions to be significant regional actors in Middle Eastern politics, which meant a concern for this fringe area as well. Yet others, that did not border directly on the Horn, perceived it as a peripheral area offering opportunities for significant action of some kind.

African states were in an essentially different position. Post-independence Africa lacked the history, homogeneity and popular ideology for the growth of a major regional system south of the Sahara, and thus, for the most part, African neighbours were just that – neighbours – with their involvement stemming largely from their interests and other alliances. Beyond that, however, lay a generalized suspicion of Arab expansionism that suggested certain sympathies with regard to political developments within the Horn. This inevitably rather crude distinction between the Middle Eastern and African neighbours is one dimension of the approach taken here, while another relates that to major eras of post-Second World War politics.

Radical nationalism

The starting point of significant regional penetration has to be with Egypt under Nasser. Indeed, as a nineteenth-century regional power, Egyptian influence had penetrated widely across the Horn and included thoughts of an East African empire extending well beyond Egypt's territories in Sudan and its Red Sea ports. Others may have intervened to thwart such ambitions, but in the twentieth century the region was still perceived broadly as Egypt's hinterland, not only for historical and cultural reasons, but ever more pressingly because of the Nile basin. Egypt had hoped to regain her 'lost' sovereignty over Sudan, and felt that the latter's decision for full independence in 1956 was as much a product of British manipulation as Sudanese preference. The rising tide of Arab nationalism after the Suez crisis of 1956 led to renewed attempts at the manipulation of Sudanese politics, as usual via the Unionist Party and the Khatmiyya order, and contributed to the political crisis of 1958. Indeed, a number of leading Sudanese figures had been in Cairo holding meetings in the run up to General Abboud's coup, and it was notable, as already seen in Chapter 2, that his intervention had the encouragement of the anti-Egyptian Umma Party. The USA, with its Eisenhower doctrine offering aid to anti-communists (and a specific package on offer to Sudan), was also hovering in the background. But Egypt soon came to terms with the situation, especially as the Aswan dam had top priority, and agreement was reached with Sudan's new rulers on a new division of waters as well as the flooding of much of Nubia.

The downfall of Abboud in 1964 brought little change, for the initial radicalism of Sudan's October Revolution reflected the concerns of the influential Sudanese Communist Party, which was anti-Nasserist. In any case, it was followed rapidly by a period of conservatism. Indeed, that was reflected in the role played by Sudan's prime minister, Mohamed Ahmed Mahjoub, in the historic Khartoum conference which followed the Arab disaster in the Six Day War of 1967, when he, more than anyone else, moved to mend fences in the Arab world. Though in 1969 a further coup brought renewed radicalism of an overtly pro-Nasser character, including the establishment of a union with Egypt and Libya, Nasserism in Sudan was clearly on the wane, even before Nasser's death and then further instability in the country brought an end to it.

In comparison, other Arab activity in the region was small. Egypt was the venue for the founding of the Eritrean resistance movement, and as such it was to be accused by Ethiopia of having nurtured it as a deliberately hostile move. Taking up the theme of Arab nationalism, and now as something of a rival to Egypt following the collapse of the United Arab Republic in 1961, Syria took the lead in assisting the Eritreans, especially before 1967, sending supplies and providing training at the military academy in Aleppo. By so doing, Syria hoped to enhance its radical credentials, especially since Ethiopia was a friend of Israel.

In response, Israel became more active in suppport of Ethiopia. Once more historic links were invoked, as well as the parallel of both as states surrounded by actual or potential Arab and Muslim aggressors. From the late 1950s Israel was developing its 'peripheral doctrine', by which it sought friends on the fringe of the Arab world: Turkey, Iran, and now Ethiopia. In addition, there was the immediate issue of the danger of the Red Sea becoming an 'Arab lake' – especially a radical Arab lake, with Egypt involved in the civil war in North Yemen for much of the 1960s and British rule in Aden being followed by radical nationalism in South Yemen from 1967. Israel therefore trained Ethiopian commandos and security units, and an Israeli communications system in Eritrea provided intelligence for the Ethiopians. In return, Israel was allowed to establish a naval base on the Dahlek islands from which it could contribute to the free flow of Israeli shipping through the Bab el-Mandeb straits.

On the African front in the 1960s the newly independent states of Kenya and Uganda were soon aware of aspects of questions pertaining to their neighbours to the north. Somalia's irredentism contributed to the rise of *shifta* – bandit – activity in Kenya's largely Somali-inhabited north-east region. But direct encouragement by the Somali government remained limited, with greater hostility being directed against Ethiopia, while Kenya stood firm on its colonially created border. By the late 1960s the situation was quietening, and Somalia's new prime minister, Egal, signed a *détente* with Kenya in 1967, helped by the good offices of the Organization of African Unity. Meanwhile, the common threat of Somali irredentism encouraged the links between Kenya and Ethiopia which were to survive the vicissitudes of the latter's domestic instability.

For Uganda, however, the situation was more complex. The rise of conflict in southern Sudan from 1962 was accompanied by an influx of refugees, for whom assistance was soon needed. In addition, there was sympathy initially for the Anya Nya groups in their confrontation with the Arab-Muslim north, and some freelance help was given by Idi Amin and others in the Ugandan armed forces.

From 1967 Israel became involved in supplying and uniting the guerrillas via Uganda (as well as Ethiopia), for, as in Ethiopia, Uganda offered an opportunity that was too good to miss. Following the Six-Day War of 1967, Israel was determined to exploit her military superiority to the utmost, and continue to weaken her Arab enemies as far as possible. At the Khartoum conference after the war Sudan appeared to have emerged as an unlikely player in re-uniting the shattered Arab world, but her civil war was her Achilles heel. Israel's involvement with the Anya Nya gave her an opportunity to tie down Sudanese forces, some of which had been deployed on the Suez Canal, and, at the same time, exacerbate relations between Arabs and Africans more broadly, thus contributing to the international isolation of the former. It was in order to maintain that connection with the Anya Nya in the face of a *rapprochement* between the governments of Uganda and Sudan after 1969 that the Israeli military mission appeared to encourage the Amin coup, only to find itself ejected when he, in turn, executed a *volte face*, forcing an abandonment of the Anya Nya which encouraged the latter to the peace process at Addis Ababa in 1972. (It was ironic that Israel's intervention had been central to the unification of the Anya Nya, without which peace might not have been negotiated.)

The oil era

Nineteen-sixty-nine had been a turning point for the states of north-east Africa. The coups of Qaddafi in Libya and Nimeiri in Sudan were radical and Nasserist, in part to legitimize themselves, but also apparently to be components of what appeared briefly to be a significant bloc linking the new regimes with Egypt. Yet it proved short-lived, particularly as a result of Nasser's death in 1970. Sadat was less concerned with the union with his two weaker neighbours than with consolidation at home. Then came the two surprise moves: first, the ejecting of the Soviet Union and then going on to stage the October war of 1973. After that he swung towards his *rapprochement* with the USA and the development of what has been called 'Sadat's American-centric world'[1] which was to culminate towards the end of the decade in a peace agreement with Israel, at the price of a break with much of the rest of the Arab world.

In contrast, Qaddafi felt deflated by the collapse in 1971 of a union on which he had pinned high hopes, and increasingly threatened by Egypt, a mightier neighbour which had embraced the West shortly after Libya had asserted its independence by the expulsion of foreign military bases. Direct relations between Libya and Egypt deteriorated to the point where, in 1977, they fought a brief border conflict, to the humiliation of the Libyan forces, now supplied with weapons by the Soviet Union. Much has been written about Libya's foreign policy under Qaddafi, ranging from the 'mad dog' syndrome to the rational pursuit of Qaddafi's version of Libya's national interest. This is not the place for such excursions, beyond suggesting that behind most of Qaddafi's moves in north-east Africa generally, it is possible to suggest a situational logic for a small oil-rich state with its own radical ideology and ambitions. In pursuit of these, Libya quite often made an unexpected switch of sides in response to a changing situation and new opportunities. (One has to add, however, that on occasions a less rational thread also appears.)

A regional rivalry with regard to their southern neighbours was to develop between Egypt and Libya after 1971 which contributed to a pattern of involvement that extended across the Horn, even briefly reaching Uganda. Sudan was the first area of rivalry. During the union of 1969–71, Egypt and Libya had both acted significantly in ways that contributed to Nimeiri's survival of the challenges to him, first from the Umma Party in 1970 and then from the communists in 1971. But with the demise of the union, cooperation turned to rivalry. In the early 1970s Nimeiri was wary of being drawn too close to Egypt, not least because of the unpopularity with southern political leaders, with whom peace was so newly established. But as that relationship appeared to grow stronger, and both countries drew closer to the West, so relations with Egypt improved. The need was demonstrated in 1976 when infiltration of the *ansar* (followers of the Mahdi family associated with the Umma Party) almost brought about Nimeiri's downfall. A defence agreement with Egypt was announced; Egyptian troops were sent to Sudan and worked closely with the army and security agencies; and other steps towards integration were announced, including the proposal for the construction of the long-discussed Jonglei Canal in the south. The infiltration of 1976 had been organized from Libya, and had come from there and Ethiopia. The *ansar* had fled originally to Ethiopia following the failed uprising of 1970, but with the Addis Ababa agreement two years later some had decamped to Libya (which opposed Nimeiri's perceived 'betrayal' of the union and drift to the West), where they had been trained before being infiltrated into the capital. Though the leaders of the failed attempt of 1976 made a dramatic about-turn towards Nimeiri a year later, Libya remained an implacable enemy.

The major test was to come in 1979 when, after wavering, Nimeiri endorsed the Egyptian–Israeli peace treaty. He was to overplay this support, and that of the West, in his subsequent attempts to divide and rule the southern Sudan, when his allies, including Egypt, declined to be drawn into any form of military involvement in the face of renewed civil war from 1983. At the same time, Sudan's continuing connection with Egypt, the outcast of the Arab world, gave some legitimacy to Qaddafi's constant hostility, which Nimeiri reciprocated in kind by hosting and encouraging Libyan opposition elements in the early 1980s.

In contrast to the Arabs, the involvement of East African states in Sudan following the Addis Ababa agreement of 1972 was much reduced. With the southern Sudan partially assimilated into the domestic power structure in the country, and northern Uganda, in the shape of Amin and his henchmen, in power in Uganda, the cross-border relations between the two countries quietened substantially until Amin's downfall in 1979. Instead, Uganda, under its new Muslim ruler, itself became an area of interest for Arab outreach with Libya and Saudi Arabia both involved with Amin's regime; the former unavailingly attempting to support Amin to the last, and the latter later providing a refuge in Jeddah.

Meanwhile, another state on the periphery of the evolving system around the Horn was becoming a target for the rivalry of Sudan and Egypt on the one hand, and Libya on the other. Chad had long been one of the weakest states in Africa – the French had spoken only of the south as 'Chad utile' – and after independence conflict between north and south had soon developed along the lines of a reverse image to the civil war in Sudan in the same period. Chad's northern rebels were encouraged by Libya, especially after 1969, partly reflecting the long trans-Saharan links between the two areas. Two main figures emerged during the long conflict of the 1970s, Hissein Habre and Goukouni Oueddi, with the latter regarded as Libya's man. The northerners finally entered government in 1978, but peace was short-lived as the numerous factions struggled for power. In 1980 Libyan troops intervened decisively, installing Goukouni Oueddi at the head of a Government of National Unity (GUNT), while his former ally and later rival, Habre, fled to Sudan.

Libya appeared to have triumphed, but the Francophone states of west and central Africa were alarmed at the outcome of the struggle and the apparent presence of a destabilizing force at their back door, while Egypt, Sudan, and behind them the USA, felt themselves outflanked. The USA in particular used its diplomatic muscle with OAU member states, of which Qaddafi was about to take the chair, to achieve a boycott of it that almost brought the Organization's collapse. But instead Qaddafi agreed to withdraw his troops which were to be replaced by the first ever (and, following its experience, only) OAU peace-keeping force. Meanwhile, the USA, Egypt and Sudan were re-arming Habre's men in western Sudan; and when in 1982 he attacked the GUNT, the OAU force stood aside in disarray and apparent uncertainty as Goukouni Oueddi was swept out of power and off to exile in Libya.

The rise of Saudi Arabia as a regional actor (often with other smaller Gulf states behind it, and formally joined in the Gulf Co-operation Council in 1981) was backed by the rapid expansion of its oil wealth in the 1970s, as well as by the isolation of Egypt in the Arab world at the end of the decade. Prior to that time, Saudi Arabia had been somewhat passive, though none the less concerned at the rising eddies of radicalism, mostly in the form of Nasserist pan-Arabism, communism (whether indigenous or Soviet in form) and, inevitably, Israel. Now as a more active player, primarily through the use of oil money, it was concerned not just with its Sudanese Arab neighbour across the Red Sea, but with the Red Sea itself, with its oil terminals and dangerous pressure points at both ends (the Suez Canal and the Straits of Bab el-Mandeb). Saudi Arabia, like Egypt, sought increased influence in Sudan not only for economic reasons relating to the attempted bread basket strategy, but also as a balance (rather than a direct rival) to Egypt. A distinctive feature of its involvement, and that of the smaller Gulf states, was the support given to Islamist groups, including the Muslim Brotherhood. Saudi Arabia also en-couraged Sudan's laxity, if not complicit attitude, towards the Eritreans operating from its soil.

On the other flank of the Horn, Saudi Arabia was also increasingly active in Somalia, which reciprocated by joining the Arab League in

1974. As well as becoming the major purchaser of Somali exports of livestock, Saudi aid was prominent, especially after the revolution in Ethiopia, and OPEC too was a substantial donor to the country. So close did Somalia come to Saudi Arabia that the latter played a crucial role in encouraging Somalia to risk breaking its links with the Soviet Union and launching its attack on Ethiopia in 1977. However, hopes that Saudi Arabia could persuade the USA swiftly to re-arm Somalia in the face of the massive influx of arms to Ethiopia from the USSR proved in vain, and instead Saudi Arabia, Egypt, Sudan, Kuwait and Iran tried belatedly and unsuccessfully to supply sufficient arms to stem the Ethiopian counterattack. The aim of Somalia's new-found Arab friends after the war was to seek to ensure stability, a pro-Western orientation, and the continuing growth of links with the conservative Arab world. In turn, they were to become increasingly identified with the survival of Siad Barre's regime, at least in the minds of his opponents.

It was predictable in the circumstances that, following the Somali-Ethiopian war of 1977–78 and the shift in Soviet support from one to the other, Libya would appear on the scene. As opposition to Siad Barre developed after the war, Somali dissidents were generously supported by Qaddafi from 1978 to 1985.

In Ethiopia the dramatic events of the revolution in the mid-1970s served to intensify the activities of neighbours. The appeal of Eritrea to Arab nationalism led to Syria's lead being taken up by others in the late 1960s and early 1970s, including Iraq, Algeria, Libya, the PLO and South Yemen (PDRY), while after the revolution Saudi Arabia became involved as well. Until the overthrow of Haile Selassie, Saudi Arabia was quietly content with the situation in Ethiopia, representing as it did pro-Western conservatism. Once it became Marxist, and even worse pro-Soviet, Saudi Arabia became actively involved in trying to unite the Eritreans around the ELF, though in this it was conspicuously unsuccessful. Whether Saudi Arabia really wanted an Eritrean victory, or whether it wished to maintain a conflict that was debilitating for Ethiopia, was open to argument, but its involvement lasted for years.

Much of the Arab support for Eritrea went to the ELF, which was seen as the Muslim faction, and was also due to the success in Arab capitals of its leader, Osman Sabe (though Libya was an early supporter of the EPLF). However, the Ethiopian revolution of 1974 did lead to a switch on the part of two of the more active radical Arab states with close links to the Soviet Union: both Libya and the PDRY switched from assisting the Eritreans to support for Ethiopia. (Libya's change also reflected Ethiopia's willingness to agree to the activities of Nimeiri's Sudanese opponents in the country in the build-up to the attempted coup of 1976, while the PDRY's position sprang from not only the radicalism of the regime, but from a long-felt sense of rivalry with Saudi Arabia.)

Israel, however, was less affected by the transformation in Ethiopia, seeing instead a continuing anti-Arab friend at the foot of the Red Sea. In 1973, under pressure from the OAU in the wake of the Yom Kippur War, Haile Selassie had joined other African leaders in breaking relations with Israel, but still some military and intelligence links were maintained. In 1975 Mengistu called for help once more and Israel responded positively. Training was given to elite units of the armed forces; arms were supplied, including some captured in the 1973 Arab-Israeli War; and when US aid stopped in 1977, Israel supplied help with Ethiopia's US-supplied aircraft. However, when the links became public in 1978 they caused some embarrassment to Israel and the USA, and the level of involvement dropped significantly.

To the south, Ethiopia also had the continuing support of Kenya, perceiving a common threat from Somalia. Despite their links to the USSR and the USA respectively, Kenya still acted as a friend, at least as far as containing Somalia was concerned, and a new defence pact between Kenya and Ethiopia was signed in 1979 after the Somali-Ethiopian war.

Failing autocrats

With the exceptions of Kenya, Djibouti and to some extent Israel, the other regional actors had taken their allotted places within the polarizing Horn that was to characterize the era of the second Cold War from the late 1970s until the middle of the 1980s. Egypt and Saudi Arabia, both aligned with the USA, were active in Sudan and Somalia, while Libya and the PDRY (with the USSR supplying them) were backers of Ethiopia, a situation formalized when those three countries signed the Aden Pact of 1981. And it was not just these countries that neighbours were involved with. Like the superpowers, neighbouring states were also effectively backing regimes and even particular rulers, who in turn accentuated their own personal power by their management of these important and, on occasions, vital external links. Yet as the regimes in the Horn personalized, and thereby centralized, power in their heterogeneous and fragmented societies, so challenges to their own positions were to increase rather than diminish, causing growing concern and confusion to the rulers' friends and allies.

The first to fall was Nimeiri in Sudan. He had overestimated external support from both Egypt and the USA, especially when he sought their help in prosecuting the re-opened civil war in 1983. He depicted the war as being encouraged by the hostile alliance of Libya, Ethiopia and the Soviet Union, in which there was indeed an element of truth. But from the standpoint of his allies, the seeds of conflict lay in his policies, and neither Egypt nor the USA wished to become embroiled in conflict in such a vast and difficult region as the south. It was ironic but perhaps not entirely coincidental that Nimeiri was travelling from Washington and in transit in Cairo when his downfall took place, and stop-over turned into exile.

The years that followed turned once more, as far as Egypt and Libya were concerned, into something of a re-run of the previous decade. Libya's long association with Nimeiri's opponents soon brought links between Qaddafi and the new Transitional Military Council in Sudan. As elections approached, Libya spent freely on a new party it sponsored, though to little avail. However, when Sadiq el-Mahdi was returned as prime minister once more in 1986, Libya knew him not just as an old friend from the early 1970s but as an opponent of Egypt in Sudan, and regular contacts were sustained during his three years in power. There was talk once more of a union, but this time just of the two states and interpreted as an anti-Egyptian move. In addition, Sadiq effectively allowed Libya a free rein in the western region of Darfur from where activities against Qaddafi's old rival in Chad, Hissein Habre, could be mounted, and Libya provided support to Idris Deby as he prepared in Darfur for his successful attack on Habre in 1990. From Sudan's standpoint, the new relationship with Libya also meant the cessation of Libyan support for the SPLA: indeed, Libya switched sides, supplying weapons to the government side and even staging long-range bombing missions.

The military coup of 1989 in Sudan was not, though, a blow to Libyan hopes. There had been past suspicions, for Qaddafi was no friend of militant Islamists in Libya or elsewhere, and Sudan's Muslim Brotherhood had been close to his arch enemy, Nimeiri. This outlook in turn had been fully reciprocated by Hassan el-Turabi and his followers. Nevertheless, in the evolving regional context both regimes were 'radical' and anti-Western, and both were supporters of Iraq in the confrontation in Kuwait in 1990–91. For Sudan, in its growing international isolation, there were hopes of weapons and oil, and by 1994 it was agreeing to a union, though subsequently relations cooled. Qaddafi had domestic problems, and appeared to seek to improve relations with Egypt, by now a leading critic of Sudan. The outcome was a deterioration in Libyan economic and military aid to Sudan, and this soured relations.

With Egypt, the downfall of Nimeiri started a longer decline in relations. There were hopes in Egypt that his going might lead to peace

in the south and the re-starting of the joint Jonglei Canal, but instead
war continued in spite of Egyptian attempts to broker peace (though
Egypt was suspect in the eyes of both protagonists). Sadiq el-Mahdi's
election in 1986, rather than that of its traditional allies, the Unionists,
was a blow to Egypt. There was some brief hope in the coup of 1989,
until the real complexion of the new men was recognized. As the new
regime tightened its grip, many thousands of Sudanese fled to the
north, and eventually Egypt came out openly for the opposition
National Democratic Alliance (NDA) as well as hosting the SPLA
leader, John Garang. Later Nimeiri was allowed to call publicly for a
popular uprising to overthrow Sudan's new oppressors.

Relations worsened during the Gulf War, with Egypt even making
public threats should Sudan seek to aid Iraq, as was being rumoured.
Accusations were also made against Sudan of aiding and abetting the
Islamists engaged in mounting conflict with the regime in Egypt. Then
the old Halayeb dispute erupted once more, with Egypt occupying the
disputed border area between the Nile and the Red Sea. (The re-
opening of the dispute was also due to the interest of both countries
in mineral concessions both on- and offshore.)

Egypt's hostility was matched by Saudi Arabia's in spite of the
latter's earlier encouragement for Sudanese Islamists. The money that
had gone to a number of groups in Sudan soon dried up after the
coup of 1989, especially with Sudan's support for Iraq. In addition to
the cut in financial aid, many Sudanese who had worked in the Gulf
and repatriated significant funds, now found themselves out of work.
Like Egypt, Saudi Arabia began supporting the NDA, the northern
opposition in exile, and was even accused by Sudan of backing
Garang's wing of the SPLA. That was only one of the numerous
charges vehemently directed against the Saudi rulers in a manner
calculated to cause public offence.

But the isolation of Sudan by its Arab neighbours contributed to
its growing links with two more distant Middle East actors, that had
hitherto played little part in the Horn: Iraq and Iran. Iraq had had
some involvement in Eritrea and Sudan in the past, though only of a
minor character, but it became a larger supplier of arms for the war in
the south after the end of the Iran–Iraq War in 1988. This, however,
by no means guaranteed Sudan's decision to support Iraq in the conflict
for Kuwait, a decision which owed more to the regime's perception of
Iraq's radical anti-Westernism. Relations were sustained after the war,
but a crippled Iraq was in no position to show great generosity.

Iran was something of a surprise, for though the home of Islamic
revolution, it had not had particularly close ties with Sudan's Muslim
Brotherhood let alone the many other *Sunni* Muslims in the country.

However, the National Islamic Front (NIF) began to play down the differences and by 1992 Iran had become a new and valued friend, helping in such vital areas as oil supplies and weapons (including financing large arms shipments from China). Immediately there were accusations that Iran was using Sudan to promote the Islamist cause throughout North Africa, and that the two perceived themselves as both a stimulus and a guide to others. (Some, however, felt that such involvement in Sudan was contrary to Iran's more pragmatic foreign policy and might reflect the activities of a radical clique within the country.) However, by 1994 even Iran appeared to have waning enthusiasm for the declining situation within Sudan.

As in the 1960s, the crucial problem for Sudan's African neighbours was the re-opening of civil war, and once more it was Uganda that was most affected. While conflict was growing in southern Sudan and spreading down into Equatoria in the process, Youeri Museveni's victory in Uganda in 1986 meant defeat and alienation for the north. Thus an unstable situation existed on both sides of the border which not only had implications for the two governments, but also gave them opportunities for damaging each other. There were a number of attempts to reach understandings, and Uganda tried to play a role in peace-making; though it was equally clear that Museveni was not ready to see the defeat of the SPLA, especially Garang's faction. The situation became more vital after the downfall of Mengistu in Ethiopia, for then the SPLA had to look to East Africa for help. Initially, some was forthcoming from Kenya, before it decided to play a more neutral and mediatory role. Then the emphasis came once more on Uganda, and such supplies from outside as the SPLA was able to obtain appeared to come mainly via this route (including accusations from Khartoum in 1994 that as in the late 1960s supplies were coming from Israel). Yet Uganda was still looking for a negotiated peace, as its involvement in the mediatory efforts of the Inter Governmental Authority on Drought and Development (IGADD) in 1994 made clear.

The later and more protracted downfall of Siad Barre in Somalia involved something of an extension of the rivalry in Sudan. The Aden Pact of 1981 encouraged not only the support of neighbouring Ethiopia for the SNM and other guerrilla groups (until the Siad–Mengistu agreement of 1988), but also brought the backing of Libya that supplied arms. Simultaneously, Egypt was identified as a supporter of Siad Barre, amidst accusations by his opponents that the Egyptians harboured designs on the region reminiscent of the nineteenth century. Kenya, too, was accused of supplying him with weapons (though it was denied) amidst suggestions of shady links between business and political circles in the two countries.

The Kenya connection was even said to provide the support for Siad to fight back after his overthrow, a counter-attack that nearly reached Mogadishu before USC forces drove him back to Kenya. But by this time there was growing embarrassment for Kenya, as well as the possibility of a sustained spillover of conflict into its north-eastern territory, and in May 1992 Siad Barre was flown off to Nigeria.

The UN intervention in Somalia brought only limited direct involvement of regional powers, not least because in some cases they were perceived as having been partisan in the past. Even the presence of Boutros Boutros-Ghali as UN Secretary General excited hostility from some Somalis, with allegations that it was an Egyptian rather than a UN policy, especially with regard to dealings (or the lack of them) with self-proclaimed Somaliland. Kenya served as something of a jumping-off point for many working in Somalia, especially the NGOs, but it too incited suspicion in some quarters, especially of old links between senior members of the Kenyan security forces and those formerly around Siad Barre.

In Ethiopia the downfall of Mengistu was accompanied by less regional involvement. Lacking Arab friends, in spite of some diplomatic efforts to mend fences, in 1989 Mengistu rather desperately turned to renewed relations with Israel for help. But by that time the situation was getting beyond his control, and the USA warned Israel not to try hard to prop up the falling tyrant. Once he had gone there was broad acceptance of the US-promoted outcome, including the acceptance and later recognition of the new state of Eritrea. The latter, however, brought with it new concern, since there had long been a strategic dimension to the involvement of Arab states in Eritrea. It soon became clear, though, that the new authorities in Eritrea did not regard themselves as behoven to anyone, and that Eritrea would fashion its own relations. (The fact that this could even involve the use of an Israeli hospital for a sick Isayas Afewerki occurred shortly before Saudi Arabia's unexplained expulsion of the interim government's representatives in Jeddah.)

Conclusion

Though it was often possible to interpret the role of regional actors in terms of acting as proxies for superpowers, such assessments were frequently an exaggeration. For all that there has been a superpower dimension to the Horn, there has also long been a real regional dimension, springing from various regional interests, ambitions and rivalries. In this regard the longest running has been the involvement of Egypt, arguably since time immemorial, but more recently since her own imperial involvement in the nineteenth century. More recent still has been the emergence of Libya, whose rivalry with Egypt in particular appears to give some logic to what often appears to be the capricious behaviour of Colonel Qaddafi across north-east Africa.

The extent to which these states and others are real regional actors, and not merely the proxies of outsiders, is emphasized by the fact that though the end of the Cold War has significantly reduced the interest of major international powers in the Horn, that of regional powers continues. Indeed, in the reduction of interest by major international powers and the encouragement of the development of regional organizations to undertake an enhanced role in the affairs of individual states, regional actors may be more, rather than less, important. Egypt's concern will continue, not least because of its vital interest in the Nile basin; Libya's may be reduced if the common challenge of the Islamist movement in North Africa helps to draw it closer to Egypt, its rival for most of the past two decades. Saudi Arabia, as both a state bordering the Red Sea and a rising regional power, will also remain concerned with developments throughout the Horn. Its earlier willingness to support Islamic causes has, however, been moderated by their capacity to unleash forces challenging of its own ambiguity, poised as it is between a presumption to Islamic leadership and a security dependence on the West that was vividly demonstrated during the Gulf War. Also watching, possibly with the opposite outlook in mind, will be the newest regional actor in the Horn – Iran. Here, too, lies at least a degree of ambiguity in terms of its desire for trade with the West and hostility to Iraq; but that has not prevented a new relationship with Sudan, though its maintenance may depend in part at least not only on developments in that country, but also on events elsewhere in North Africa as well.

There is clearly a new era in the Middle East with the end of the Cold War and after the Gulf War of 1991, and it is one that includes the prospect of peace between Israel and her major Arab enemies. However, the possibility remains of a struggle between existing state-based elites and Islamic fundamentalists seeking to utilize the very real social problems, particularly of North African countries. In such a scenario, the Horn remains something of a soft underbelly, and one in which the continuing existence of the regime that has been in power in Sudan since 1989 means that opportunities for the promotion of political Islam internationally may be taken. Iran has not only become Sudan's closest ally since the Gulf War, but has been connected to some Islamist activities in parts of Somalia, while it has even been said to have eyes on possible opportunities in Djibouti. Already, Iran's involvement is causing concern in Egypt, and the possible openings from the Horn to Islamic opposition movements in the Middle East ensures that the old actors in the region will continue to be concerned.

In contrast, the role of African states will still be confined essentially to neighbours which are affected by developments within the Horn. In part this is because of the centrality of their domestic problems, as with Uganda, and in part because of an absence of broad regional ambitions, as with Kenya. Clearly, there is not a potential African regional actor along the lines played by Nigeria in West Africa, or that of South Africa, though individuals and governments may nevertheless harbour their own ambitions.

However varied the degree of involvement of regional actors may have been, there is little doubting their overall importance. Some regional actors have themselves exploited opportunities to attack regimes in the Horn to which they were opposed, while others have come to the aid of beleaguered rulers, and sometimes the same regional actors have done both at different times. Above all, this has reflected the playing out of Middle Eastern rivalries by other means. At the same time, regimes in the Horn have been equally ready to support the opportunities to mobilize regional actors, as have opposition movements. As well as thus encouraging the contributions of regional players to exacerbate more often than they have ameliorated the conflicts of the Horn, regional actors have also made a conspicuous contribution to the means of conflict. Though overwhelmingly the weapons of war have come from industrial powers of West and East, deliveries have often been through a variety of indirect routes involving payment and/or delivery by regional actors.

There is, though, the possibility that if there was to be some reduction in the rivalries and divisions among regional actors, as well as within the Horn, an era of greater cooperation could unfold. One dimension is clearly that of resource development. The Nile basin is already the most developed river system in Africa, yet it could be far greater. With peaceful circumstances within states, this could be undertaken in ways that are cooperative and less damaging to the interests of, and thereby relations with, others. Egypt is the most obvious country that could be adversely affected by uncontrolled upstream exploitation, and in one way conflict has checked the development of the branches of the Upper Nile which might have reduced the waters flowing down to her. But the present flow is not enough with its burgeoning population, and Egypt has long looked to cooperation with others to improve the situation for all (if such is possible). It is ironic that much of the regulation of the Nile took place in the period of British imperialism, and that independence has thus far proved more of a hindrance than a help to the river's greater exploitation. There are other areas too for economic cooperation as well as cooperation on other fronts, including peace-making. The involvement of the East African states, as well as those of the Horn, in IGADD's attempt to broker peace in southern Sudan is an obvious example, and, if successful, could be built on in other areas, as the organization's concern with drought and development indicates.

9

Development, Relief and Mediation

While various states in the international community were contributing to the polarization of politics by enabling both regimes and opponents in the states in the Horn to confront each other militarily, the other major dimension of international involvement was in endeavouring to allay some of the economic, social and political problems of the region. These efforts focused broadly on economic development, relief (especially for refugees and famine victims) and on mediation of conflicts.

All three of the major countries of the Horn are regarded as among the world's poorest, although there may be disagreement about aggregate figures. One estimate put the average income per capita in 1991 in US dollars at: Ethiopia 120, Somalia 170 and Sudan 340.[1] While the media coverage of famine since the 1970s was to highlight the issues of poverty, its existence had been well known to students of the region for many years.

Ethiopia in particular had a well-recorded history of famine, especially in the northern regions of Tigre and Wollo, the historic heartlands of the ancient state. Here overpopulation and erosion, as well as the exactions of landowners, had contributed to intermittent famine for centuries. Most of the highland areas had been limited to crops for subsistence and local markets, notably the staple, *teff*, as well as barley wheat and sorghum. Incorporation of Ethiopia into the global market was limited, consisting mainly of coffee from the south-western areas conquered in the nineteenth century. What little industry there was had been centred on Eritrea until its inclusion into Ethiopia from 1952, when the focus of industry was moved to the central areas. There was only a small amount of mining. How far the very limited incorporation of Ethiopia into the international economy was due to its lack of Western colonization (as the greater involvement of Eritrea might indicate), and how far it was due to the physical impediments and limited resources of the country, is a matter for debate. The involvement with the USA in particular after the Second World War had brought relatively little change to the economy structurally, though there was some modernization in areas such as the transport infrastructure and education, and commercial agriculture had expanded.

Aid was encouraged following the coverage of the 1973–74 famine, with measures to improve peasant production being financed by a number of agencies, including the World Bank and the International Fund for Agricultural Development (IFAD), but the revolution was to lead to tensions with external sources of funding and aid. Politically, a number of Western powers, led by the USA, were to experience growing concern with the pro-Soviet stance of the regime, while nationalization without full compensation of American interests placed a technical obstacle to aid which was not resolved until 1985. Nevertheless, there was still some development aid from the West, notably substantial support from the European Community, as well as a bilateral programme with Italy. Economically, it was the character of Ethiopian agricultural policy in the revolution that caused most concern. The sweeping nationalization of land was followed by the creation of a system of local associations which, in practice, did little to promote overall production levels. Controls to ensure state acquisition of crops for the army and the cities in particular reduced incentives, as did the prohibition of hired labour by more enterprising farmers. Restrictions on population movement, not only to the cities but from poorer to richer agricultural areas, also had the effect of increasing pressure in the poorest areas, especially in the arid north. One trenchant judgement was that, 'What land reform actually did was thus to entrench peasants in their existing mode of production, under conditions that all but guaranteed their progressive impoverishment.'[2] Agriculture came in for further criticism in the West as a result of the villagization policy of the 1980s which grouped scattered peasants, allegedly to provide greater access to services. By 1988 it affected about one-third of the rural population, and was criticized in the West as a step on the way to that old failed path of full agricultural collectivization. The development of fully state-owned farms led to further criticism, especially as it was linked to the resettlement of peoples from the war-torn regions of Tigre and Eritrea. In area and numbers the resettlement programme was far smaller than villagization, but it none the less absorbed a disproportionate amount of government expenditure for little return, and collectivized production in the resettlement areas was abandoned for individual cultivation in 1990. Agricultural policies had alienated the World Bank in particular, which had earlier promoted a small number of projects to help peasants. By the late 1980s both the Bank and the European Community felt that Mengistu's abandonment of various aspects of the earlier socialist programme was not just a political retreat, but the real result of their pressures for a more market-orientated approach to the economy as a whole.

In the meantime, Ethiopia's involvement with the Soviet Union had brought only limited economic assistance. Agricultural policies had even attracted some criticism from Soviet experts, though the Soviets had assisted with transport in the resettlement programme. There was some support for industrialization from Eastern Europe, but the scale remained relatively small, and Ethiopia's main export crop, coffee, continued to be sold on the international market rather than sold or bartered to the country's new-found friends. Clearly, Soviet interest in Ethiopia was primarily strategic, and both Ethiopian policies and economic links with the West were to be tolerated as long as the former interest was not endangered.

Somalia has, like Ethiopia, experienced declining per capita income in recent decades. The colonial period had left it with comparatively little economic development. It was still overwhelmingly a rural economy based on the herding of camels, sheep and goats, with some cattle towards the south, together with some cereal and banana cultivation, also in the south. Exports had historically comprised animals, mainly to Aden and the Arabian peninsula, as well as bananas to Europe. After independence its strategic position helped it to attract considerable foreign aid from a variety of quarters, including both superpowers. A number of projects were concerned with infrastructure, including the ports of Berbera and Kismayu. The USA in particular assisted from 1967, partly to encourage a reduction in irredentist activity with regard to its ally, Ethiopia.

Development aid moved sharply towards the communist bloc once Siad Barre had seized power in 1969 and begun his own socialist project (at which point US aid was cutback). Though less 'revolutionary' than that of Ethiopia – it was far less clear of what it might consist in Somalia's predominantly pastoral society – Siad sought a new direction, though setback by the drought of the mid-1970s. Drought also offered new opportunities, and with Soviet help there were efforts at cooperatives in the south, especially with regard to fishing, but these faded in the 1980s. As in Ethiopia later, the Soviet's main interest was strategic, and particular effort was focused on the port of Berbera. Other aid, though, was not eschewed and Europe and the UN agencies also assisted Somalia.

The situation changed, however, following the Somali defeat in the

Ethiopian war. Siad's turn to the West was successful in attracting new development aid, especially from the USA, with particular emphasis on the improvement of transport infrastructure. However, the aid was far less than Siad sought to cope with the growing political pressures of the post-war period, while Somalia's mounting debt forced it to turn to the IMF and the World Bank. The USA used its influence to help with these institutions, and itself provided much more non-military than military assistance. The plan was to allow Siad only a defensive capability, but to encourage economic and social development. The priority areas were the stabilization of finance; privatization of commerce following the years of socialism; and improvement of economic and governmental institutions. By 1986–87, US aid in particular was becoming vital to the Somali economy, and in official circles there was some belief that progress was being made. It was American politicians who applied the brakes, pointing to the worsening conflict and human rights violations from 1988, leading to the reduction of aid by the end of the decade. The impact of reducing aid itself contributed to the civil war, which was accompanied by an orgy of looting and destruction.

Sudan's experience of the post-independence years was also one of long-term deterioration in per capita income. It was the most integrated of the three into the international economic system, primarily through the vast cotton-growing Gezira scheme established by the British in the 1920s and expanded after independence. But though the backbone of the economy in the imperial era, after independence the falling price of cotton and pressure for wheat consumption led to a partial turning away from cotton, while the scheme aged and needed expensive renovation by the end of the 1970s. Sudan's other major exports, gum arabic and groundnuts, were similarly in the doldrums. Development aid had played a part, including the controversial acceptance of US aid in 1958, but thereafter had not had a major impact.

The coup of 1969, which saw Sudan briefly influenced by the Communist Party, also saw a burst of Soviet aid, but it was halted by the turn to the West after 1971. The 1970s were the era of Arab investment. Oil price rises enriched Arab donors and Sudan was projected as the bread-basket of the Arab world, thus seeking to prevent any retaliatory Western use of the 'food weapon', while Western businessmen were keen to provide the commercial and technical support. However, it appeared by the end of the decade that far from being on the road to development, Sudan had run into a cul-de-sac. It lacked the human and physical infrastructure to assimilate productively all the development efforts: those that succeeded, like the Kenana sugar scheme, were heavily over budget; others, such as the textile factories,

Table 9.1 Aid inflows, 1978–88 (Net disbursements of Official Development Assistance from all sources in $ million at constant prices and exchange rates.)[3]

	1978	1984	1988	1988 per head	1988 % GNP
Ethiopia	238	748	912	20	16
Somalia	313	505	447	63	32
Sudan	570	908	923	39	12

Source: OECD, 1989 Report, *Development Co-operation in the 1990s*

operated significantly under capacity; while others, including the brewery at Wau, never functioned at all. This led to growing indebtedness (compounded by the readiness of corrupt politicians, officials and businessmen to take their capital abroad, allegedly on a scale comparable to Sudan's rising international debt) and by the early 1980s Sudan was deep into arrangements with the IMF and the World Bank.

Relations with the IMF and the World Bank were helped by the 1980s, which became the decade of Western, especially American, aid. Growing superpower rivalry in the Horn in the era of the second Cold War was accompanied by Sudan's rise to become second only to Egypt as a recipient of US aid in the African continent (followed – not coincidentally – by Somalia). Other Western powers followed suit, especially Britain, which put Sudan second globally behind India. But any hopes for the outcome of such largesse were dashed by the political deterioration, especially the re-opening of civil war – which included the cessation of work on the Egyptian–Sudanese project to build the Jonglei Canal in southern Sudan, as well as in the oil field that Chevron had been developing around Bentiu.

Donor disillusionment, as well as the end of the Cold War, was to lead to cutbacks in aid. The rise to power of the National Islamic Front-backed military regime in 1989 was followed by a rapid scaling down in aid from all quarters; and even to the verge of expulsion by the IMF for failure to meet accumulated debts. Where in the previous decades Arab and Western donors had been falling over themselves to give aid, now there was nothing, and the regime sought to make a virtue of it saying, 'We eat what we grow, we wear what we make', though for a growing number of Sudanese there was little food and few new clothes. The decay in years of plentiful aid was simply accelerated in conditions of isolation.

The Horn's ability to attract development assistance is apparently in stark contrast with the outcome in terms of conflict and suffering.

It raises questions of whether aid was none the less insufficient, or inappropriate, or even whether it actually contributed to the problems by distorting economies and encouraging political rivalries? A case for most of these views can be argued; what does appear conclusive from the figures is that all three countries received development assistance largely for reasons of strategic significance and in relation to the ebb and flow of international politics at the global and regional levels.

Disaster relief

While economic 'development' was a part of the setting for political decline, and arguably a contributing factor, there was another totally different dimension from the international community's response to the unfolding situation in the Horn, and this became an area of perceived disasters. Two categories of disaster in particular stood out: refugees and famine. Both are contentious subjects, in terms of definition and conceptualization. That, however, is not the concern here, which has less to do with trying to analyse or re-define the concepts than to survey international perceptions and responses.

In these terms it was refugees that came first in the Horn with the emergence of sustained conflict in southern Sudan in the 1960s. Famine made its entrance internationally in northern Ethiopia in the 1970s. The two disasters seemed discrete and of fundamentally different character. They also seemed capable of solution: peace in Sudan in 1972 appeared to offer an answer for the former, while aid was rushed to combat famine in Ethiopia. From the late 1970s, however, the disasters appeared to become more complicated. First, there appeared to be less of a distinction to be drawn between refugees and famine. In particular, it appeared that both had some connection with conflict (rather than as hitherto primarily the former). Secondly, it seemed that far from either being discrete events for which there was a solution available, they seemed to flow endlessly for over a decade, increasingly reflecting the longer-term and structural problems of the Horn of a political, social and economic character. One participant observer was to call the evolving situation a 'permanent emergency'.[4] Nevertheless, in terms of the international community, operations might have overlapped, but they were still 'operations' and were perceived primarily as responses to particular disasters. Yet while being responses to individual disasters, they were not simply one-off operations. There was a learning curve in terms of the handling of particular disasters and a degree of retrospective analysis (though not always applied next time around). There was also inevitably a context, not just of the immediate disaster but of its international aspects at all levels.

In reviewing the international response to disasters it is necessary to see by whom a disaster is perceived to be imminent or actual; what is done or not done, and why; and what, if any, follow-up takes place.

The Horn in the 1960s

In terms of internationally perceived 'disaster' assistance, the Horn built up only slowly in the 1960s, as a result of the escalation of the wars in southern Sudan and Eritrea, of which the former was by far the main refugee generator. From 1962 onwards the flow of refugees from southern Sudan built up to some 200,000 ten years later, as recognised by the United Nations High Commissioner for Refugees (UNHCR). Of these, by far the largest numbers were in Uganda and Congo (now Zaire) with 71,500 and 59,000 respectively; and there were a further 20,000 in Ethiopia and in the Central African Republic.[5] (The emphasis in Uganda and Congo reflected the extent to which Sudan's first civil war was concentrated in the southernmost region of Equatoria. Refugees also entered Sudan, especially following the unsuccessful Simba revolt in the Congo in 1965.) In comparison, the number of Eritreans seeking refuge in Sudan was far lower with about 45,000 by 1970.[6]

At the outset, the governments involved were inexperienced, but took their lead primarily from the Geneva Convention of 1951, to which they had become signatories, recognizing:

Any person who ... owing to reasons of well-founded fear of being persecuted for reasons of race, religion, nationality, membership of a particular social group or political opinion is outside the country of his nationality and is unable or, owing to such fear, is unwilling to avail himself of the protection of that country ... (Article 1,A(2) of the Statute of the UNHCR, 14.12.1950)

In 1969 these principles were also incorporated into the conventions of the Organization of African Unity (OAU), which added a wider interpretation reflecting African refugee realities as being those fleeing 'external aggression, internal civil strife, or events seriously disturbing public order'.[7]

But it was one thing for poor African states to accept refugees in principle, and quite another to find the resources to support them, and it was thus natural for them to turn to the UNHCR in particular for assistance of all kinds. Founded in 1949, the UNHCR had been established largely in the wake of two major waves of refugees in Europe resulting from the world wars. By the end of the 1960s refugees in Africa were a fast-growing problem, totalling some one million people, and absorbing 70 per cent of UNHCR's budget. The majority was in southern Africa, generated by the colonial wars in the Portuguese territories of Angola and Mozambique, but Eritrea and Sudan ranked high among the remainder. There was also growing recognition that beyond their own humanitarian needs they created problems for the host states, and could also generate tension between host governments and those of the states from which they had fled.

While recognizing its growing responsibilities, UNHCR was aware from the outset of its limited resources, which came mostly from the voluntary contributions of members. Operating in such a poor region, it was probably inevitable that the numbers seeking refugee status would always be larger than that which UNHCR recognized, and that host governments would similarly have an interest in generous estimates and relief assistance. Once it was accepted by all parties – UNHCR, refugees and host governments – that an early settlement of the issues from which the refugees had fled was unlikely, then resettlement became a favoured option. Resettlement might involve the establishment of new agricultural projects, or other enterprises, with the aim of furthering long-term self-sufficiency rather than dependence on international assistance. But such aims had inevitable problems. Local communities might become resentful, and thus account would have to be taken of such sensibilities if resettlement was to succeed. Host governments might also seek to benefit economically and politically from aid to refugees. In Sudan in the 1960s in particular there were such charges of exploitation of Eritreans resettled in the country's eastern regions. While for their part, refugees might react against long-term resettlement by trying to avoid its clutches, as with the Eritreans who moved to Sudan's urban areas, especially those with Western education. Above all, resettlement implied an acceptance of the status quo for the foreseeable future, and the experience of being resettled refugees, far from instigating any such acceptance, generally had a politicizing effect which political groups were eager to capitalize on however much international agencies sought to project their work as 'humanitarian' rather than 'political' in character. Thus by the early 1970s UNHCR in particular was beginning to acquire considerable experience of Sudan and Eritrea as sources of refugees; but it was to be only the start of a much longer involvement of numerous international agencies.

Famine in Ethiopia, 1973–74

The next major 'disaster' of which the international community became aware was the Ethiopian famine of the early 1970s. Unlike the refugee situation from the 1960s, awareness did not build up slowly. In contrast, its apparent suddenness and dramatic revelation made all the more impact. A British television journalist, Jonathan Dimbleby, made a film of the 'unknown' famine in Wollo province that not only shocked the world, but Ethiopian critics of Haile Selassie's regime itself, contributing to his eventual downfall. Two points helped the impact of the report. First, Dimbleby was an influential figure who could command peak viewing; and secondly, famine seemed a much more dramatic event in a world that believed it no longer necessary, whereas refugees were a relatively commonplace consequence of yet another twentieth-century political upheaval.

The famine itself was primarily in Wollo and Tigre in the north in 1973, and there was also a lesser famine in Hararge in the south-east in 1974. It was primarily the result of drought and harvest decline, though nationally the crop failure was limited and need not have precipitated famine. It was the localized shortages, coupled with seeming unconcern on the part of government, especially at the top, to take any ameliorating measures, that led to the conditions that Dimbleby's film so horrifically exposed.

In fact the Ethiopian government was not unaware of the problem and quiet approaches to international agencies had been made, including the World Food Programme (WFP), Unicef and USAID. Discrete aid without publicity was the aim, but it resulted in a lack of urgency, during which there was a rising death rate, eventually to reach an estimated 200,000. The readiness of the agencies involved to cooperate initially on the government's terms was not surprising in the political circumstances. It still appeared to be a stable, if authoritarian, regime with which cooperation was desirable. The emperor was a respected international figure, especially within Africa, and not just a trusted Western ally, though he was that too. That air of compliance, however, turned to one of urgency with the sudden light of publicity and the wheels of the relief juggernaut rolled a little faster. It was still to be criticized nevertheless, for relief food was being delivered to the north when the famine there was waning, and not being diverted to Hararghe when the situation there was still worsening.

In general, however, the famine of 1973–74 did not bring a sense of long-term crisis to the international community. Historians pointed to the 'inevitability' of famine in Ethiopia, though it was still thought that 'development' would bring rectification as it had elsewhere in the world. And while the international agencies had been criticized for their responses, this was down to operational sensitivities and problems rather than any sense that this was an intractable situation that would worsen with the passage of time. It appeared, too, to be a dramatic event in Ethiopia, unconnected with developments elsewhere. In particular, though the famine in Ethiopia coincided with that in the western sahel, and was on the same latitude, the huge intervening area of Sudan did not report a famine. In fact, Sudan's rainfall across the central areas was low in the period, but the long-term processes of agricultural change that were to contribute to the impoverishment and consequent loss of 'entitlement' of many farming families in its western regions had not reached the point of precipitating famine. Meanwhile, in Somalia there appeared to be socialist policies being implemented to improve the lives of the most hard-pressed pastoralists, and thus there, too, famine was not a cause for immediate concern for international agencies.

Permanent emergency 1978–95

The issues of refugees and famine appeared to the international community to have been essentially separate issues to be handled by appropiate different agencies. Refugees were an unfortunate spillover of civil war, but peace in the southern Sudan in 1972, with the assistance of Ethiopia, might be a precedent for the latter, while famine was a calamity of nature that might be better foreseen with improved monitoring, for which the Ethiopian government had set up the Relief and Rehabilitation Commission (RRC). But as the 1980s unfolded, far from disasters seeming to be self-contained 'events', they became instead inter-connected and seemingly endless problems requiring inter-national action. But however inter-connected aspects of the 'permanent emergency' were to be, they were viewed internationally as disasters of particular states, and that inevitably shaped the responses.

Ethiopia

In terms of international impact the greatest disaster of the 1980s was the famine in Ethiopia. Much has been written about its causes, widely perceived at the time as a consequence of drought. Later writing has focused on both the agricultural policies being pursued by the Ethiopian government and the enforced immobility of peasants coupled with low incentives to produce, as well as the effect of civil war in the north, including allegations of a scorched-earth policy amounting to genocide perpetrated by government forces. Whatever the judgements made about the causes, that was to have relatively little impact on the international response in which the dominant factors began as political calculation and later gave way in large measure to popular response to media pressure.

One of the early ironies of the famine of 1983–84 is that its coming was not unforeseen but was calculated by the responsible body in Ethiopia, the Relief and Rehabilitation Commission (RRC). However, it was at a time when that body was perceived as a mouthpiece for an unfriendly regime. RRC estimates and requests were thus questioned. While it was true that FAO/WFP was giving a lower estimate, it was still clearly the case, supported by Western aid agencies, and known to the USA in particular, that a severe food deficit was developing. The Ethiopian government was prepared to receive aid, but was highly suspicious of publicity, and gave the appearance of greater concern with matters at the centre – notably celebrating the tenth anniversary of the revolution – rather than alleviating the suffering (another similarity with the situation under the previous regime a decade earlier). Western governments remained fundamentally hostile to the regime and concerned at 'fungibility' – the opportunity for the regime to be strengthened by relief aid and be more able to pursue the wars to maintain itself in power – as well as what were perceived to be inappropiate agricultural policies. (Cynics suggested that the West hoped instead that famine might prove a trigger for a move to unseat Mengistu as his predecessor had been.) It scarcely requires saying that the regime's Soviet ally was equally unconcerned.

However, as in 1973 the situation was changed dramatically by the Western media, in this case a news film on BBC television in Britain, soon shown around the world, depicting the scenes at a northern camp under government control at the town of Korem. Widespread revulsion at the scenes so vividly depicted and described not only brought instant donations for relief, but put intense pressure on governments and international agencies to react. The UN Secretary General, Perez de Cuellar, appointed an experienced diplomat, Kurt Jansson, as special representative to coordinate the international effort, not least within the UN agencies themselves. Western governments and the European Community were shamed into a rapid expansion of relief efforts that were to assault the logistical problems by sea, land and air. The Ethiopian government was to concede the need for media coverage as well as enhanced relief, and seek to benefit in terms of its own favoured policy of rehabilitation. And even the USSR realized that it would have to be seen to be doing something and contributed mainly to the transport problem.

The highest estimates for those in need rose to 7.7 million, and an armada of agencies were involved in the efforts to supply relief. The major donors of food were the USA and the EC. The former channelled food largely through World Vision, the Catholic Relief Service and CARE; EC food used a variety of agencies including ICRC, Oxfam, SCF and others. The Ethiopian RRC itself handled only a minority of the food and there were some tensions with Western donors and agencies, but these were not widespread, and generally the RRC maintained its reputation as one of the most efficient and least corrupt indigenous agencies of its kind in Africa under its forthright chairman, Dawit Wolde Giorgis.

More questionable than the RRC as a relief agency were the government's aims of rehabilitation and villagization, which it saw as an opportunity to promote within the context of famine relief. The notion that the northern highlands were overpopulated and in consequence agriculturally degraded was not new, and population drift southward had occurred, especially before the revolution impeded such movement. But the plans for resettlement in particular were immediately perceived by critics as having political intentions. More specifically, it was said that it was an attempt to deprive the guerrilla forces of recruits by depopulating the area of able-bodied men: and there were accusations of such selectivity and other maltreatment in the loading of trucks and planes for delivery to the new agricultural schemes, mostly in the south-western lowlands. The USA was determined to have nothing to do with the programme, though some other aid was received for the ill-conceived and ill-equipped schemes that transported some 700,000 people, and may have cost the lives of 50,000 in the process.

While resettlement was the most criticized aspect of the relief operations in the government sector, there was also the question of relief to those in the rebel-held territory in the north. There was the possibility of arrangements with the Ethiopian government that would allow relief convoys across the lines, but on that agreement failed. The other main route was from Sudan, not least because it was from there that the relief arms of the two major movements, the Eritrean Relief Association (ERA) and the Relief Society of Tigre (REST), operated. The problem for donors was that to operate publicly from Sudan was to be seen to be infringing the sovereignty of Ethiopia. In consequence, surreptitious means were devised by which some donor food supplies were delivered using both Western and indigenous agencies, though in total it amounted to only a small proportion of the overall amount delivered.

The conflicts themselves did not stop for famine: instead, relief itself became a further dimension to be manipulated by the parties involved. At different times all parties directed attacks on deliveries to areas held by the other side, but in terms of scale the government aerial attacks were the greatest impediments. However, relief could also be used positively to gain support, and while the government's major response was its disastrous resettlement programme, the EPLF and TPLF were generally far more sensitive and successful in linking the distribution of food aid to extending support in rural areas. Estimates for the loss of life resulting from the 1983–84 famine are of the order of 1 million people.

The 'permanent emergency' meant that drought was to return as soon as 1987, and with it the need for action. Now the situation was reversed. Though the war was much fiercer and with larger areas in rebel hands, the alert from the RRC and international agencies was heeded much more swiftly by donors. Consequently, delivery and distribution by a variety of routes and agencies, including more indigenous agencies, was undertaken and the scenes of mass starvation and death that had so shocked the world before were avoided.

Ethiopia was not just a disaster source in the 1980s. It also became a state within which there were refugees from neighbouring conflicts who required assistance from international sources. The growing conflicts in Somalia and Sudan in the 1980s were reflected in the growth in refugee numbers to reach some 700,000 by the end of the decade, split roughly equally between the two countries of origin. It gave Ethiopia the second largest refugee population in Africa – behind Sudan. The agency most directly involved was once more UNHCR, and with a number of NGOs involved as well. With an expenditure of about US$60 million in 1989, Ethiopia was UNHCR's costliest operation in Africa.

In south-east Ethiopia the largest concentration of Somali refugees was at Hartisheik near Jijiga, while smaller camps were to be found around Aware. In south-west Ethiopia southern Sudanese refugees were centred on Itang and to a lesser extent Panyido and Dima, and again the major agency involved was UNHCR. Though there was drought in northern Somalia, the overwhelming cause of refugees from both Somalia and Sudan was civil war, and understandably the liberation movements were powerful influences in the camps. Itang in particular was central to the operations of the SPLA with the active connivance of Mengistu's government, for whom it served as a local security force, as conflict escalated across Ethiopia in the late 1980s.

Sudan

Sudan's descent into 'disaster' was as dramatic as Ethiopia's as far as the world was concerned, and for the same reason. Drought was once more depicted as the cause, and from the early 1980s until the recognition of famine in 1984 rainfall had certainly been declining. But in Sudan's western regions of Darfur and Kordofan, as in Ethiopia, drought was only the immediate trigger of other factors. In the more arid areas of western Sudan, as in northern Ethiopia, population increase had also contributed to pressure. And as in Ethiopia, economic policy had also played its part: but not the pursuit of immobility in the name of socialist agriculture; rather the rapid commercialization which had marginalized and weakened the capacity of subsistence agriculture to support the population through drought, and which had contributed directly to environmental degradation.

The donor response in Sudan was diametrically opposed to that in Ethiopia, but built on the same premises. The US response in Ethiopia had been distrustful of a socialist government: but Sudan was a close ally, and, providing a degree of discretion was observed to avoid embarrassing a government which had supposedly been building the bread-basket of the Arab world, then the appropiate agency, USAID, was free to act. (An initial response of the government had been to deny the disaster and truck refugees reaching the capital's outskirts back whence they had come.) Having estimated the need quite accurately in 1984, USAID was concerned to make it a show-case operation through a private joint Sudanese–US company, Arkell-Talab. In practice, however, Arkell-Talab's plan to base its operation on a dilapidated railway over hundreds of miles of light sandy soils was to prove a recipe for disaster. As in Ethiopia, the UN entered the scene belatedly, establishing a UN Sudan Emergency Relief Office (UNSERO), but USAID still maintained its dominant role. It did, however, switch its relief strategy from rail to trucks – though no hard road existed west of the Nile – and eventually brought in more trucks to break the local owners' cartel, which had been profiting exorbitantly from disaster. Overall, the relief effort had had to bypass rather than utilize the local infrastructure (the new government-created relief agency played little effective role), and it was criticized for the inital delay; failure to reach out appropriately to the poorest fringes of the relief chain and concentration on food aid when disease was a bigger killer. (In fact, after talk of millions under threat, 60–70,000 was the lowest estimate of those who died from the famine in Darfur, the worst affected region.) Politically, the famine paralleled that in Ethiopia a decade earlier, for the shock of the situation and the government's initial response contributed to the wave of revulsion that brought Numeiri's downfall.

The famine of 1984–85 also had in it a foretaste of the more horrific but far less publicized famine of 1988–89. In southern Darfur, in addition to factors such as those mentioned above, there were inklings of the effect of civil war in the creation of famine, and the expanding conflict was to be central to the famine of 1988–89. This later famine was to be a product of conflict at both local and national level. Locally, the southwards pressures of the Baqqara peoples due to environmental pressures had been putting growing pressures on traditional deals struck between their chiefs and those of the Dinka of northern Bahr el-Ghazal, one of the most heavily populated areas of southern Sudan. Nationally, the government encouraged the arming of Baqqara militias as part of the combatting of the SPLA in the region. Thus the armed conflict of the raiding *murahaliin* (tribal militias) was both military and commercial in character, as the *murahaliin* sought to use force to refurbish their own herds hit by drought further north, and supply the commercial meat market as far away as Omdurman. (As well as northern traders, army officers and local officials were also accused of profiting in the famine.) From 1986 many thousands of Dinka found themselves forced out of their home areas, some further south in the region, others trekked eastward to Ethiopia, while thousands more found their way north to Sudan's main towns, including the capital where they took refuge in pitiable conditions on the outskirts. But the main deaths occurred in camps around southern towns, most notably Abyei and Meiram. Here death rates were to soar as high as anything known in the Horn. In all, it has been estimated that as many as 2 million, about one-third of the population of the south, were displaced either within or outside the region. Estimates for total deaths from famine and disease for 1988 alone have been put as high as 250–500,000.

Getting food aid to the victims of war was daunting. The international operation of 1984–85 in western Sudan, UNSERO, had ended, and in its place was a supposedly strengthened government agency, the Relief and Rehabilitation Commission (RRC), but it proved of limited effectiveness, not least because it was an agency of government. In the far south in Equatoria, meanwhile, a consortium of Western NGOs had been established known as CART (the Combined Agency Relief Team), which sought aid from a number of donors. But CART, with its base in Juba, was to be impeded by the general aim of a government trying to supply aid primarily to the towns, thereby encouraging the depopulation of the countryside, and the SPLA endeavouring to isolate the garrisons in the towns by restricting the safe passage of food to them. The option of sending relief directly into SPLA-held territory via East Africa was adopted by Norwegian Peoples' Aid and World Vision; but not even ICRC's standing could permit it to fulfil its intention to send supplies to both sides (though it did later get relief into SPLA areas). In the event, areas receiving relief were exceptional, which contributed to the scale of the exodus mentioned earlier. In addition, there was the alarming recognition for the agencies that a percentage of food aid was being commandeered by the belligerents and thereby serving to assist the continuance of the conflict itself (as had happened from the mid-1980s in Eritrea and Tigre as well).

Realization of the growing urgency led to the establishment by the UN in 1989 of Operation Lifeline Sudan (OLS), an umbrella organization which involved particularly WPF and Unicef as well as a wide range of other agencies. Begun at a time when there were hopes for peace, such prospects were quickly halted by the takeover of the new regime in Khartoum in June, and as OLS developed, it faced a period of rising conflict in the region. OLS intended to send relief supplies via 'corridors of tranquility' to areas held by both sides and to this effect sought to strengthen both the RRC and its SPLA counterpart, the Sudan Relief and Rehabilitation Association (SRRA). But, in practice, the new government in particular was determined to try to restrict the OLS activities in SPLA-held territory, especially in anything other than basic food supplies, and on occasions the SRRA felt obliged to follow suit. The problems for the UN with regard to OLS were basically two-fold. First, Sudan was a UN-recognized sovereign state and itself a member of the UN so there was a reluctance to take action that could be construed as contrary to the new regime's wishes, even though it soon became unpopular with a number of major international and regional powers. Secondly, WFP and Unicef were both operating other programmes in northern Sudan and were keen that these should not be linked in any way to OLS, so that obstruction by Khartoum of OLS did not endanger development programmes which the UN agencies wished to see sustained in the north. Operation OLS was to be made even more complicated by the split and subsequent conflict within the SPLA. There was an attempt in 1993 to create peace zones for relief free of such conflict, and, indeed, some relief continued to be delivered under OLS auspices, but the problems of operating in a war zone had been by no means overcome.

At the same time as giving rise to its own internally driven disasters, Sudan was also haven to refugees from its neighbours in the 1980s, especially as the wars in northern Ethiopia and Eritrea increased. The government offensives of the late 1970s and early 1980s had driven back the EPLF and the TPLF and many took refuge in Sudan, where the total was to rise to over 600,000, absorbing by far the largest part of the UNHCR budget. The 1985 famine was to lead to a mushrooming of camps and some of the most harrowing pictures to come out of the Horn were from camps like Wad Sherife near the Ethiopian border. But while absorbing much of the UNHCR's money, the camps it ran sheltered less than a third of the refugees, with many more in scattered rural settlements as well as the towns of the eastern Sudan and the capital. The influx, and the life, of some of the camps was also orchestrated, in part at least by the EPLF and the TPLF, with the latter in particular being responsible for an organized evacuation of

Tigrean territory in 1985 and a later return. Even the end of the conflicts in Ethiopia and Eritrea in 1991 did not mean an instant return of the refugees, but rather a lengthy arrangement stretching into the future. Some were tolerably settled in Sudan and understandably cautious about returning to the difficult conditions of their homeland, at least until they had carried out some form of appraisal of their own. And while these refugees from Ethiopia and Eritrea were by far the majority of those that Sudan received, many more were arriving, and sometimes departing, from Chad, Uganda and Zaire with the twists and turns of politics in those countries (though generally without the tit-for-tat element that so characterized the generating of refugees between Sudan, Ethiopia and Somalia). Even after the end of the war in Eritrea, hundreds of thousands of refugees still remained in eastern Sudan, giving rise to the fear that they would once more become pawns in relations between the two countries.

Somalia

Somalia's experience from the end of the war with Ethiopia in 1978 was to turn it into the country in which all the elements of international disaster involvement became intertwined, leading eventually to intervention of an unprecedented character.

The unfolding Somali political instability after the war has already been seen, but the war also unleashed a new refugee problem as hundreds of thousands of refugees, mainly ethnic Somalis, came into the country in a series of waves that continued throughout the 1980s. The main areas for refugees were in the north-west and in the south; and their composition was disproportionately of women and children, as many of the men continued in various activities, including the low-level conflict maintained in the Ogaden, which in turn contributed to the continuing flow of refugees. In the mid-1980s there was a further influx of Oromo and Somali refugees from Ethiopia fleeing the villagization programme. From the outset of the refugee crisis Somalia turned immediately to the international community with the UNHCR in the vanguard, but a number of other agencies were involved as well. From the outset there had to be negotiation over even the number of refugees, with Somalia claiming 2 million and the agencies much less. In 1981 the agreed figure was 650,000 and by the end of the decade there were still 446,000 registered. Even these lower figures, however, put Somalia at the top of the league for the ratio of refugees to indigenous population. It was this situation, coupled with the poverty of the country as a whole, which was to make the refugee situation not just one of relief, but part of the dynamics of the political economy of the decaying state. From the outset of the mass refugee situation the camps became noted for their contributions to the flow of foreign exchange to the country (the total cost was of the order of US$70 million per annum in the 1980s); the employment opportunities they represented, especially for educated Somalis in relief organizations and the unskilled in the transport infrastructure; and the rations distributed, which became a part of the basic food supply through the petty trade that proliferated in and around the camps. While the UNHCR might hope for voluntary repatriation or local integration, as elsewhere in the Horn, the camps were becoming a fact and a way of life. There was a hope in some circles that the agreement between Siad and Mengistu in 1988 might spell the start of a solution, but though there was a sudden flow of refugees back into Ethiopia, the new level of conflict arising from the subsequent SNM attack ensured a worsening situation.

Militarily, Siad sought to gain conscripts from the camps, especially from the Ogadeni in the southern camps. He tried to deploy these against the Isaaq, much to the concern of UNHCR which saw this as a violation of its status. And as the war escalated and moved southwards, Siad and his supporters increasingly looted refugee supplies and extorted protection money in a manner that was to spread to other factions, and indeed encourage the emergence of some groups that were little more than armed racketeers. This parasitic development was by no means confined to refugee camps and foreign agencies but extended to attacks on indigenous Somalis, especially the weaker settled agriculturalists in the southern part of the country.

With Somalia's descent into state collapse and parasitic violence, the issue of relief went way beyond refugees and to a growing perception that many of the country's population were in need of assistance, with figures eventually being announced of 2 million at risk of starvation (in a population of 7.5 million). Somalia appeard to require something more than the past relief actions, which had been seen as just about sufficient in Ethiopia and Sudan. When in December 1991 the UN decided to establish the Department of Humanitarian Affairs, it was Somalia that was cited as a major example of the need for a new body. Yet still political violence appeared to worsen, and with it the possibility of maintaining a flow of relief aid. Towards the end of 1992 it was being reported that up to 80 per cent of aid was being looted by armed gangs, apparently associated with the rival factions (though both this figure and the numbers allegedly facing famine were to be disputed). The response was to be peace enforcement, which has already been discussed in Chapter 3, since it inevitably became interwoven with Somali domestic politics. UNOSOM, sent in 1992, had proved inadequate and the US-led UNITAF force was deployed to enforce the conditions for relief. But after some initial success in improving the flow of aid, the exigencies of Somali politics overtook the delivery of relief. As UNOSOM II engaged the forces of Mohamed Farah Aideed in particular, it was largely left to the relief organizations to operate as best they could amidst the new conflict; and the same conditions were to persist after the eventual withdrawal of UNOSOM II. Some agencies and NGOs continued their work, others withdrew in the face of the continuing operating problems and direct physical danger.

While the heavy hand of the UN was being felt in southern Somalia, in the north, in self-proclaimed Somaliland, the reverse was the case. Instead of active support for Somaliland, the UN and other government agencies displayed suspicion of *de facto* recognition of the new self-proclaimed independent state by doing little. Although UNOSOM had made promises of aid, little was delivered and a senior UN official was quoted as saying that it was 'time to dismantle Somaliland and bring this nonsense to an end'. A number of NGOs, in contrast, saw both a need to act and very real signs of hope in the apparent political reconstruction in the north, and thus some outside relief was delivered, often through local groups springing up on the ground in the new more peaceful conditions than the region had known for a decade.

Mediation

The link between the international involvement to attempt to alleviate famine and the prevalence of conflict in the Horn could hardly be clearer. Thus it is no surprise that growing recognition of the development of conditions amounting to 'permanent emergency' in the 1980s was linked to growing efforts to promote peace between the various belligerents. But while such efforts may have multiplied, they were not new: efforts towards peace had been undertaken in one country or another since the 1960s, and had involved degrees of international involvement throughout.

Sudan had started the peace-making efforts. Just as the conflicts in the south contributed to the downfall of successive governments and regimes, so each change appeared to presage a chance for peace which those newly installed in power in particular could not afford to ignore. The pattern was set with the Round Table conference of 1965, following Abboud's overthrow the previous year, and so too was Sudan's determination to try to resolve matters on its own. There were foreign observers at the conference, but they were there essentially as a piece of international legitimation rather than playing any significant role as mediators. In the event the conference became a very public negotiation which served only to air the manifold differences within the parties in the conflict as well as between them, somewhat to the horror of the foreign observers who could only sit and watch as it ended in apparent disaster, to be followed by the intensification of conflict. (The face-saving committee, that appeared all that was left of the conference, in fact went on to do much of what was to prove the spadework for later successful talks, but it may have been to its advantage that it did so quietly, and without domestic or international limelight.)

The end of the second liberal-democratic period in 1969, which was widely predicted not least because of its manifest inability to address the problem of war realistically, brought another military regime, but this time one determined to try to make peace. Initially, however, it was to be peace on its own terms of a socialist Sudan, but after the break of President Nimeiri and the Communist Party in 1971, the way was open for a less ideological and more pragmatic negotiated settlement centred around the arrangements for regional government worked out within the post-Round Table committee. The Addis Ababa agreement of 1972, which brought an end to the first civil war, was heralded as a triumph not just for Sudan, but potentially for the region more broadly, in particular for Ethiopia as well. The World Council of Churches, and especially the All-Africa Council of Churches, were effective in winning a degree of trust from the government as well as the Anya Nya and doing much of the confidence-building in initial contacts between the two sides. The same 'mediators' also supported the parties, especially the southern representatives, in the initial stages of negotiations, though taking more of a back seat as direct talks finally got under way. Those who negotiated the terms were not so much the military leaders of the respective sides, but more political figures who were aware of the international context as well as the domestic political advantages created by their agreement. The choice of Addis Ababa, home of the OAU, as well as the public blessing of the emperor, was symbolic, but also political: Ethiopia's involvement had potential repercussions for both parties to the conflict as well as possible implications for the host country itself. The wider international community was not directly in evidence in the process, but was undoubtedly active behind the scenes. Western powers in particular saw it as a curtailing of Soviet and potentially Arab national-ist influence in the region, and encouraged both parties discretely. In particular, the potential availability of aid to the new Southern Region and to the north was made clear, and to good effect at least as far as the peace-making was concerned. Once in place, the Addis Ababa agreement was supported by a substantial Western aid package, especi-ally for the repair and development of infrastructure in the south.

The prospect of the Addis Ababa agreement proving any kind of precedent for Ethiopia, however, soon proved illusory. The main advantage as Ethiopia perceived it was not as an example to be followed, but as a weakening for the Eritreans whom Sudan could be pressurized to sacrifice. And for a short while that expectation was rewarded as Sudan restricted Eritrean activities. However, far from delivering the Eritreans to the emperor, it was the latter who was to fail and, as with Sudan's instability, the continuation of conflict within Ethiopia was a contributory factor.

Sudan's renewal of civil war from 1983, and its contribution to the undermining of Nimeiri's regime and his downfall in 1985 brought renewed consideration of peace-making. Initially Sudan sought once more to do it alone, but successive rulers appeared incapable of direct resolution of the conflict. Both the Transitional Military Council and the then prime minister, Sadiq el-Mahdi, had tried the direct path, especially at Koka dam in Ethiopia, but to no effect. The end of the Cold War appeared a particularly opportune moment to address regions of conflict and encouraged efforts in Sudan by a variety of international mediators, especially greater American involvement both by the State Department and former president, Jimmy Carter. The coup of 1989, coming apparently on the verge of a Sudanese settlement, did not deter them and their efforts continued thereafter with Carter, in particular, showing repeated commitment. Norway, too, tried to play a part, but similarly to little effect. These failures encouraged a more active African involvement, particularly after the downfall of Mengistu and the establishment of a period of peace in Eritrea and Ethiopia. Nigeria hosted talks at Abuja in 1992 and 1993, and went out of its way to play the role of honest broker, but by then the SPLA had split, making another option for Khartoum of further weakening its divided enemy at the negotiating table, which it took avidly while stepping up its efforts on the battlefield. A similar situation confronted the neighbouring African countries of the Inter-Governmental Authority on Drought and Development (IGADD) in 1994, though they did endeavour to promote unity once more among the major factions of the SPLA. Others, including the USA, stood back and encouraged IGADD in its efforts, but agreement proved elusive. While the Sudan government resisted pressure for a secular state, it also vetoed the alternative of a self-determination exercise, two southern positions that appeared to have some backing from IGADD, some of whose members had their own interests in the outcome of talks.

The important but unusual conjunction of two parties, which were relatively united internally, prepared to compromise with each other, and in a neutral, if not positively favourable, international environment (which had given rise to the Addis Ababa agreement on Sudan in 1972 but was not repeated thereafter), was similarly absent in Ethiopia. In the early years of the conflict in Eritrea neither side appeared likely to welcome serious attempts at mediation. The emperor clearly had the political capacity in the 1960s, but was far from inclined to negotiate, seeing it as another in the long history of revolts within the country to be crushed, while the Eritreans were weak and divided. The revolution appeared to hold out more hopes, especially in the person of General Andom, but his downfall was associated in part by the harder line on Eritrea being taken by Mengistu. And for their part, the Eritreans, and soon the Tigreans, saw the revolution as an opportunity to intensify the struggle for their goals. Though by the 1980s the situation within the three major parties appeared to have solidified, thus suggesting that one condition for potentially successful negotiations had been met, their relations with each other remained less promising. In fact, there were contacts from 1982–85 but little headway was made. The government's view was essentially that it could present terms and that the unity of Ethiopia in particular was non-negotiable, while the EPLF maintained the right of self-determination and that no agreement could be reached while Mengistu remained in power. Following the failure of contacts, the government went ahead with the presentation of its own new constitution in 1987, in which Eritrea was accorded the status of being one of five Autonomous Regions. However, then, as earlier, the military situation was not such as to encourage the parties towards agreement either. The military balance was to shift totally during the decade, but that shift did not include an appreciable period in which there was a perceived and potentially deadlocked balance of forces that would probably have been necessary for a successful negotiation.

At the same time, the international environment was hostile. At both the regional and broader international levels the second Cold War era of the early 1980s encouraged conflict rather than seeking to promote peace. It was not until the end of the decade, as the reforms in, and then the collapse of, the Soviet Union transformed the international environment, that a more supportive atmosphere emerged. Under strong pressure from the USSR, as well as the USA and the European Community, and following the attempted coup in Ethiopia in 1989, further talks were held, with the mediation of Jimmy Carter. The old problem of national unity soon re-surfaced, but more damning was the continued shift in fortunes on the battlefield, especially with the capture by the EPLF of the port of Massawa in 1990. The USA next tried to play an even more direct part, convening talks in Washington early in 1991, but by then the military situation within the country was changing dramatically as the EPRDF made its unexpectedly successful assault on Addis Ababa. Now the USA was like a midwife attendant at an easy birth, as the earlier cooperation of the EPRDF and the EPLF produced a smooth transition from associated rebel forces into amicable neighbouring interim regimes, with the USA and the international community happy to see an avoidance of an immediate collapse of all forms of authority.

Somalia proved even more infertile for mediation than Ethiopia. Following the war between the two countries and the rise of the SNM, the internal situation was unpromising, and indeed the agreement between Siad and Mengistu in 1988 was widely seen as an alternative to negotiation with the SNM, a position underlined by the bloody confrontation between the two following the agreement with Ethiopia. As the internal situation worsened in 1990, Italy and Egypt made repeated efforts to bring about reconciliation talks between Siad and the factions, but to no avail; and no serious efforts were made until after Siad had fled. Djibouti, long concerned at the situation in its neighbour, hosted two conferences of the fronts that had opposed Siad in June and July of 1991 – excepting the SNM that stayed away, calling for the recognition of the independence of Somaliland, a non-negotiable position. The other fronts (USC, SDM, DFSS, SPM, USF and SDA) did sign a five-point manifesto, but it proved insufficient to prevent the subsequent outbreak of hostilities between Aideed's and Ali Mahdi's factions. The concern then shown by the UN at the start of 1992 brought further talks in New York with help from the Arab League and the Islamic Conference Organization, but fighting continued, contributing to the circumstances in which UNOSOM was launched. The launch of Operation Restore Hope was swiftly followed in January 1993 by talks in Addis Ababa with Ethiopia, the UN, the OAU, the Arab League, the USA, and fourteen Somali factions; and in March fifteen factions announced agreement and elections in two years' time. As the crisis between the USA and Mohamed Farah Aideed deepened, Jimmy Carter intervened, somewhat bizarrely arranging for Eritrea, Ethiopia and Yemen to provide a place of exile for Aideed in exchange for the dropping of the warrant against him. By the end of the year, and with the blessing of the USA and the UN, it was Ethiopia that was taking the lead in initiating another round of talks between the fronts and factions, now including Aideed (flown to Addis Ababa in an American plane).

In retrospect the most notable feature of negotiation and mediation was not that it was tried but that it almost always failed. Only in the Addis Ababa agreement of 1972 which ended Sudan's long civil war did two sides sit down and work out a compromise; and that was to fail in the end, though it lasted a decade. The parties themselves are clearly central to this. To be 'ripe' for resolution requires that the parties individually be sufficiently unified and of coherent positions that talks can take place. It requires a certain balance *vis-à-vis* each other, such as a mutual recognition of military deadlock and some common ground for negotiation. And it also requires an international context that is supportive of agreement rather than offering viable alternative possibilities. Such a combination was rarely achieved. It was a necessary requirement, but not necessarily sufficient, which was where mediation came in. Mediation has come to be seen as a process rather than simply an action, and might involve a variety of parties ranging from NGOs to international agencies. The significant body of writing on the Addis Ababa agreement bears this out, as well as showing how prolonged and multi-faceted the process may be. Mitchell has outlined a range of roles and functions from initial feelers about the outlook for talks at one end of the process to contributions to long-term reconciliation after peace has been made at the other.[8] Yet it is also a list that shows how many stages have to be envisaged in mediatory efforts and at how many points failure is possible. By late 1994 there were those who were feeling that after all the efforts some conflicts at least, such as southern Sudan and southern Somalia, might not be amenable to mediation, and that the outcome might not even be an internationally recognizable form of authority.

Conclusion

Development, relief and mediation, though seemingly separate aspects of international involvement in the Horn, were nevertheless related in complex and intricate ways that defy simple causation, yet contribute to something of a syndrome. The emergence of personalized regimes in all three countries in the 1970s was boosted by the international dimensions of politics, and in turn contributed to differing grandiose approaches to economic development. All failed, indicating less a condemnation of development aid *per se* than the drawbacks of large-scale schemes in fragile African environments, whether supported by capitalist or socialist donors. Furthermore, in their failures lay part at least of the expansion of conflict as schemes were pushed through by unaccountable regimes which contributed both to a range of socio-economic problems and to the upsurge of violence. Violence in turn was multi-dimensional, from surrogate superpower rivalry at one end of the spectrum to the inclusion of localized disputes in broader 'national' conflicts at the other. The complex combination of failed economic development, environmental degradation of all kinds, as well as conflict, in turn produced a pull for international relief efforts, first primarily for refugees, and later for the series of famines that beset the region from Ethiopia from 1974 onwards. These experiences in themselves generated their own review of the character of relief, including discussions of early warning arrangements, medical rather than food aid, coping strategies and implications for long-term development. However, it was increasingly obvious that these discussions amounted in large measure to international sticking plaster as long as major conflicts continued. Mediation had one outstanding success, over the southern Sudan in 1972, and numerous failures, while for one party at least in each conflict war remained perceived as more advantageous than peace. In the end, the central conflicts that had linked the Horn – those in Ethiopia – defied the old nostrum that civil wars in Africa were rarely 'won', by ending in striking victories for the rebels. But the implication of the outcome was that mediation should be less concerned with compromise and holding states together, and recognize that the reverse might need to be the case. It was a conclusion accepted in Eritrea, and also drawn but not recognized internationally in Somaliland, as well as one underpinning the call for self-determination in southern Sudan. The Horn had thus raised, but not answered, two questions of sovereignty: should international relief on occasions undertake intrusions on sovereignty to help those in need; and when should claims to new sovereignty be recognized?

Conclusion

The Horn of Africa has been an area in which indigenous conflict, as well as regional and wider international rivalries, have combined to produce state collapse, widespread social suffering and economic decay. Some of the past conflicts appear to have come to a solution, as in Eritrea and Ethiopia, others continue, as in southern Sudan, and some appear to have lost even enough structure to be regarded as discernible conflicts and appear closer to anarchy (albeit driven by their own perverted logic) as in southern Somalia. But collapse and suffering are not without seeds of change and hope, and there are signs that in the decline of the old post-imperial order new beginnings of various kinds are arising.

One of these signs is the alteration of the old state boundaries of the Horn. In Eritrea independence has already been recognized, and that achievement has contributed to the raising of other claims for recognition (as in Somaliland) or self-determination (southern Sudan). Eritrea's achievement also raises the question of the extent to which its independence was likely to be the exception rather than the rule. It has, of course, been rare for new states to be recognized in Africa, Eritrea is the first since 1960, and while it is easy to cite the Cold War as having frozen borders there as elsewhere, and claim that that era is past, it does not necessarily mean that Eritrea is the first of a number of new states in the Horn.

From the standpoint of making its claim, Eritrea had a very strong position. It had a consistent position, formulated over a number of years, centred on its status as a former UN Trust Territory which had been denied the right of a referendum on self-determination (a right recognized by the UN in other cases such as Western Sahara). It also had a firmly established organization, the EPLF, that had demonstrated its ability to take up the reins of government since 1991. The EPLF had a firm control of the security forces and of the situation, and appeared to have a high degree of popular support, which it insisted on using the two-year delayed referendum to demonstrate. In all, there was little question of its *de facto* control of what had been an inter-

nationally recognized territory. However, one of its greatest assets lay
in the degree of international recognition that it received prior to the
referendum. It had the support in particular of Ethiopia, the state
from which it was seceding, a major and unusual asset for a new
country though not unique. In addition, other immediate neighbours
also concurred in Eritrea's independence. Eritrea was also clearly not
an example of the possible propensity of Africa to move into a new
era of ethnic claims to nationhood. Instead, Eritrea was a state based
on former colonial boundaries every bit as artificial as any other in
Africa, yet was prepared to wage a long and ultimately highly successful
war for those boundaries. As such it represented a form of revolutionary nationalism intending to convert itself thereafter into a form
of civic nationalism which would specifically seek to eschew the politics
of ethnicity (or of religion). Thus, from the standpoint of the new
regime in Ethiopia in particular, Eritrea was not a precedent for ethnic
claims of self-determination once the state had returned to its pre-
1952 borders.

Somaliland, though it proclaimed its full independence in 1991, was
denied similar recognition by the international community. Though it
claimed a former colonial territory status that had been misled in 1960,
there remained the suspicion that it had an Isaaq core, and thereby
posed the threat of other comparable clan claims in the future. Furthermore, there was little enthusiasm internationally for Somaliland since it
lacked any obvious assets (though there were hopes for oil). There has
therefore tended to be the hope in the international community that
Somaliland could, in however loose a manner, return to some form of
re-built Somalia. In addition, as long as there is no recognized indigenous authority in Mogadishu, Somaliland is unable to receive an
agreed farewell which was so helpful to Eritrea. However, time might be
to Somaliland's advantage. In 1991 the SNM which had been at the
core of the new government did not appear to have the solidity or
support which the EPLF had been so successful in building. By 1995
it seemed not only to have survived, but to have evolved at all levels of
government, together with progress on the social and economic fronts.
Furthermore, it was receiving more *de facto* recognition from a variety
of quarters, even grudgingly from the UN. In such circumstances it
may increasingly have a case for recognition, especially since the contrast with the south seems ever more stark, and the prospect of any
stable and effective relationship with Mogadishu seems so remote.

The third main area of the Horn where self-determination has
been raised is in southern Sudan. Here there is not the same 'colonial'
claim as Eritrea or Somaliland, for though administered somewhat
differently, the south was never a completely separate territory from

the north. The south appears to avoid the 'ethnic' tag in its claim to self-determination, but does at times appear to play a race card as an 'African' region confronting 'Arabs'. Indeed, it often seeks to make a virtue of it and particularly of racial reppression (not without reason on occasions at least). In contrast to both the former cases, the southern Sudanese position has appeared weakened by the divisions within the movement, which time has exacerbated rather than healed. Not only is the leadership divided (with accusations of an ethnic element in the splits), but the armed forces seem dangerously fragmented, even at times to the point of localized banditry seeming virtually a way of life. In addition, the degree of popular support for the SPLA factions is hard to discern (in what is any way a massively displaced population), while it has never proved very effective at establishing local administration or services. The position of the south in relation to the north is also complex. It is not entirely clear where the boundary of north and south lies, and even the borders of the Addis Ababa agreement of 1972 would not be unquestioned on both sides of that line. Nor is it altogether clear what the reaction of possible alternative regimes would be to the real prospect of secession. Internationally, there is little enthusiasm for the prospect of an independent southern Sudan, which, though it would have some resources, would clearly also face enormous problems. There are indications that within IGADD there is some support in principle, but this may be as much an attempt at leverage with the Sudanese government in negotiations as a real recognition of, and enthusaism for, the right of self-determination of southern Sudan.

The issue of borders is important because it provides the basic framework within which issues of recovery and development can be addressed. There may be a case for minimal states, but there is as yet no significant case for having no state at all. Nothing better for creating a framework of security has yet been found. The fact that states have not fulfilled a role of providing such security in the past, or that the old borders of the Horn are no longer viable, does not mean that a state-free environment can be envisaged for anything other than a future which is at best undeveloped and at worst violently anarchic.

The search for state structures takes place alongside the search for forms of government. Indeed, the two may be related, as in the case of southern Sudan where it appears that failure to agree upon national government has enhanced the call for self-determination in the south. The end of the Cold War has led to a renewed enthusiasm for liberal democracy as both an expression of human rights and an integral aspect of development. The former is a normative question, but the latter is empirically debatable. The readiness of some in the West to proffer an ideology linking liberalized economies and liberal-democratic

politics seems both over-simplified and at variance with the experience
of many areas. Certainly, the Horn has not been without its attempts
at liberal democracy as a part of the independence settlement which
was a *sine qua non* of imperial departure. The experiences in the cases
of Sudan and Somalia were different but both had significant shortcomings.

Sudan's majoritarian liberal democracy over three periods showed
comparable failing throughout. It permitted successive governments
based on a northern majority to ignore the claims of more deprived
areas, most notably the south, to the point that contributed to civil
war, which was itself, in turn, a major weakener of successive regimes,
whether liberal-democratic or military. In addition, the majority area
of the north was divided primarily along lines of religious affiliation to
Islamic sects in a way that produced weak coalition governments. The
result was weak government at best and civil war at worst, a combination guaranteed to bring questions about the state itself.

Questions about Sudan's experiences of liberal democracy contributed to attempts to find some alternative form. The military regime
of the 1970s established the Sudan Socialist Union as a vehicle for
single-party democracy, though it scarcely forged a clear identity except
as a thin fig leaf for the regime. Its counterpart of the 1990s eschews
single-partyism formally, yet its attempt to build a non-party, federal,
pyramidal structure is perceived by many to be a thin disguise for the
one-party rule of the National Islamic Front. Prior to 1989 its leading
ideologist, Hasan el-Turabi, had appeared to accept liberal democracy.
Later, however, he was to argue the greater appropriateness of more
authentic and, in his view Islamic, approaches to seeking the will of
the people through *shura* (consultation). Between the dominance of
the old parties, and the attempts to control by military-led regimes
there has been comparatively little discussion of alternative forms of
liberal-democratic constitution that might seek to come to terms with
Sudan's size and heterogeneity, beyond calls for federalism. Consociational ideas of all kinds that might have something to contribute
to a more stable form of government have rarely been explored, and
the suspicion remains that political issues remain dominated under
successive regimes by forms of intra-elite rivalry rather than genuine
attempts to seek to build a more viable polity.

Sudan's search for a viable constitution became more complicated
after 1983 when the long rumbling issue of Islamic law surfaced. For
those in power after 1989 in particular, *sharia* became the basic principle of government, around which issues of democracy have to be
formulated. Their claim, though unelected, is that they speak for the
country's Muslim majority and that they aim at the rediscovery of the

authentic Sudanese personality through religious re-assertion. Understandably, many southerners feel that such an objective leaves non-Muslims as a second-class minority in their own country at best, and that the opt out offered to federal regions in the south is inadequate and unsatisfactory. In consequence, government resistance to southerners' demands for a secular state has made a major contribution to the latters' growing call for self-determination.

Somali democracy was equally divisive for constitutional and social reasons. With a system of proportional representation, the emphasis became less a question of majorities and minorities but rather the classic problem of fragmentation. Moreover, it was a fragmentation that appeared as capable of perpetual division as Somali society itself, hence the profusion of parties by 1969 when Siad Barre intervened. Though in discussions with faction leaders in the south constitutional questions pertaining to a democratic future for Somalia are raised (and as seen, Mohamed Farah Aideed at least has paid lip-service to them), in reality the only area where it seems possible to speak of democracy meaningfully is in Somaliland. The extent to which the SNM was a localized organization (to a greater extent than, say, the EPLF in much of Eritrea) suggests that it was relatively open and unhierarchical. The national conference or *guurti* of 1993 did have the appearance of a consensus-seeking form of democracy, utilizing local elders and other leaders. Its lengthy deliberations and its ability to change the leadership without unmanageable acrimony all attested to a form of indigenous, locally backed, decision-making, however far it may have been from a manual of Western liberal democracy. Whether such forms of expression can be linked into wider scales of state structure, or whether they are indicative of an African political version of 'small is beautiful', remains to be seen.

In addition to the systemic problems of Sudan and Somalia as democratic states, there appeared to be a perversion of political culture. Theoretically, the major attraction of liberal democracy is accountability. In any system the danger lies in its transformation into access to the state's resources for the benefit of particular organized interests; in practice there are circumstances in which democracies can be almost as kleptocratic as other forms of government (I say almost because I doubt that many elected politicians have been quite as acquisitive as President Mobutu in Zaire). The practice of parliamentary democracy in both countries became ever more associated in public perception with winning not only direct access to the resources of the state, but also in benefiting indirectly from the allocation of licences, etc. for the pursuit of a slice of international trade. The fact that similar practices on an enhanced scale went on under military regimes led to a subsequent measure of forgetfulness of the behaviour in the democratic eras, but did not imply that a return to liberal democracy would not, in practice, mean a return to the old ways. Little wonder that some theorists of the conditions for the maintenance of liberal democracy have pointed to the desirability of 'a separation of the institutions of rule and of surplus appropriation', while socio-economic analysts would find the Horn generally an unlikely prospect.[1]

Though Ethiopia and Eritrea did not share the same experience of independent liberal democracy as Sudan and Somalia, it is understandable that they show a fundamental suspicion of its propensities to cause division and conflict in society rather than effective accountability of national government. Eritrea's leader, Issayas Afewerki, has been the most outspoken, indicating that the kind of democracy towards which Eritrea is moving will not be one that permits the basing of political parties on ethnic or religious lines, thus suggesting at best the eventual introduction of some form of 'guided' or 'semi-democracy'. The success of this will depend largely on the skill and determination of those in power, for the limitations on free political organization will provoke some critics.

Deviance from the Western model of liberal democracy may be even greater in Ethiopia. Here, the irony lies in the way in which ethnicity has been recognized and not denied by the new rulers. Having an essentially regional and ethnic base in Tigre, the idea of encouraging other ethnic groupings was promoted and brought into an eventual coalition of ethnically based nationalities in the EPRDF. That was to prove not only a vehicle for military victory, but a blueprint for power-holding thereafter. 'Ethnic' parties in alliance with the Tigrean command were encouraged, and with it devolution from past centralized government in Ethiopia towards the federal 'ethnic' regions. There are clearly political questions associated with such an endeavour, most specifically that of the comparability of the 'ethnic' units across the country; but there are also queries about the extent to which a national democracy will be permitted to emerge. And if it does so, is it likely, in practice, to reflect the relative strength and outlook of different ethnic groups, perhaps drawn into rival coalitions, rather than encouraging individual participation in national politics? Under any circumstances other than continued Tigrean control of the centre (which cannot be guaranteed), the promotion of ethnic nationalities could have dangerous consequences for the state as well as for the emergence of a democratic form of government at the level of the whole country. In general, national and ethnic federations have had a poor record in the modern world as experiences from the former Soviet Union to the former Yugoslavia in particular indicate.

Whatever the thinking in the Horn about the nature of democracy, there have been similarities in regard to the process of democratization when compared with other experiences in Africa. All have begun from a seizure of power, whether by insurrection or coup, and the process of an open national conference has nowhere been permitted to decide on the future constitutional shape, with the exception of Somaliland in 1993. As a result, power-sharing governments of national unity, of the kind seen in South Africa and Mozambique in particular, have not emerged, and alienated opposition elements of varying potential are to be found across the Horn. By starting from seizures of power, it is for the most part democratization from above, though with claims that the concentration is on building at the bottom. In principle at least, there is a point in this, for in the situations of collapsed and semi-collapsed states in the heterogeneous circumstances of Africa, building regional and local government foundations are as significant as national government. (British colonial officials in Africa, in particular, long saw democratic local government as a necessary forerunner of national democracies.)

The fact that the regimes in power in the Horn derive mostly from seizures of power by one means or another, means too that the military will remain part of the calculation of political stability in the future. Armies have been involved in change, whether by coups or liberation struggles, and they have also been affected by the changes that they have brought about. Most obviously, Sudan's penchant for military coups led, after 1989, to a new military regime sanctioning the creation of a Popular Defence Force to 'defend' the National Salvation Revolution, as well as elaborate local security and policing. The existence of these new organizations has thus become a novel and untried element with regard to possible future military intervention in Sudanese politics. Eritrea and Ethiopia have been building from liberation movements, but which also have potential political implications. Eritrea has seen some restlessness in the barracks, mainly over local conditions of service, but Ethiopia's present reliance on a Tigrean core to the new evolving national army could have implications for the country's policy of ethnic politics, while the experiences which Somalia has undergone make the military a difficult issue of state reconstruction. In all cases, not only does the military remain part of the equation of stability, but the military itself has to be perceived with regard to issues of composition of an ideological, factional, regional and ethnic character which cannot be avoided or answered simply.

However, the pursuit of liberal democracy in Africa is intended to counter the experiences of military involvement in Africa, even though the latter cannot be discounted. The pursuit of liberal democracy is itself a relatively new aspect of the concern for the improvement of government in Africa. It was preceded by that somewhat coy phrase, 'good governance', which was nebulously defined by the World Bank (with which it was closely associated) as 'the exercise of political power to manage a nation's affairs'. Its concern appeared to be about clean and effective government more than democracy as such. The discussion of 'strong states', initiated by Migdal, is relevant here: strong states need the ability to 'extract, penetrate, regulate, and appropriate'.[2] Concern to reduce the scope of government, did not mean that states should be weakened with regard to basic capacities (indeed, the reverse was the case), but rather that they should seek to do less in areas where it was deemed inappropiate for them to act, particularly in the area of direct involvement in the economy.

With respect to the machinery of government, the traditions of hierarchical rule from a centralized location continued in Ethiopia from the time of Haile Selassie, when there had been some technocratic modernization of the administration, into the revolutionary era in which the new rulers retained, and indeed sought to extend, the powers of central government. A notable example of the relative effectiveness of the bureaucracy was the Relief and Rehabilitation Commission which won a (sometimes grudging) degree of respect from those who worked with it. The downfall of Mengistu's revolutionary regime did not mean the collapse of the old bureaucracy, though new demands arose, especially with the implementation of regionalism.

In contrast, in Eritrea the takeover by the EPLF did mean in large measure the replacement of existing administration, steadily whittled down by the long years of war, and the establishment in its place of the EPLF administration. However, as we have seen, that was already something of a shadow state from both its organization at the centre down to its role in the development of local communities. Thus, while there was much to learn about the running of a state at peace, as opposed to the pursuit of a war of liberation, there was a structure around which to build and a sense of purpose in doing so.

Somaliland appeared to offer a parallel, though perhaps without the roots of experience. It may, in part, have been that lack of experience which contributed to the very limited development of government capacities and led to the change of leadership in 1993, but the SNM had developed a sense of identity and participation that meant that a relatively accountable and localized administration could be built. In spite of early fears to the contrary, a degree of stability was established, and with it rudimentary structures that began to undertake re-building tasks of all kinds in the shattered environment bequeathed by the struggle against Siad Barre. However, in the south the situation was far more ambiguous. Siad's downfall had been accompanied by the total collapse of the state, a situation in which the UN intervened ostensibly to ensure relief and then increasingly to try to re-build order. But there was vacillation between the extent to which this was to be a 'bottom-up' approach, utilizing those perceived as local elders etc., or 'top-down' via accommodation rather than destruction of faction leaders ('warlords'). There may have been hopes of integrating the two levels, though to some observers they were the obverse of each other and the uncertain policy thus doubly doomed.

Sudan saw neither the survival of the old administration, nor the creation of a locally based alternative in areas of civil war. While eager for access to the perquisites of Sudan's declining market-oriented economy, the NIF, in power since 1989, also knew that a state was necessary for the maintenance of power if it was to survive. Its route to power had been via entryism, not only of part of the army's officer corps but in other areas of the state as well. Thus, once in control, NIF members and supporters soon emerged as the real power-holders in a variety of institutions, a move accompanied by widespread purges of thousands of officials, teachers, etc. In effect, this meant a degree of continuity from the old practices, including opportunities for corruption, but carried out by those promoted on ideological or loyalty grounds rather than upon any form of competence. Administration was thus seen as increasingly repressive and arbitrary, and without the concern or resources to provide services which declined rapidly in many areas. The government would proffer at least part of a response in terms of federalism, but reports suggest that this is at best patchy, while in remoter areas of northern Sudan such as Darfur in the west, there has been a substantial breakdown of law and order, notwithstanding the army's success in driving out the SPLA.

Meanwhile, in southern Sudan the kind of social policies associated with the EPLF, or community support apparently given in Somaliland, was conspicuous by its absence. In part, it appeared that the SPLA leadership had for years been relatively unconcerned about development in liberated areas, while the Sudan Relief and Rehabilitation Association never gained the reputation of its counterparts in Eritrea or Tigre. It was ironic that the nearest to an exception in terms of building services, the area of Upper Nile administered by Riach Machar, was also to be the centre of the rise of factionalism from 1991 that was to prove so damaging to the SPLA's cause militarily. Thus, should Sudan's civil war end by separation or in a single state on whatever basis, the state itself at all levels and in all areas is clearly far from being likely to function in ways that amount to good governance, at least without major changes.

Whether speaking of constitutional or administrative aspects of government, concern with good governance in recent years has sought to limit government and in particular to balance it with the promotion of civil society. Defining, identifying and promoting civil society in Africa is itself problematic. It may be the multiplicity of social organizations in the 'weblike' societies of Africa that constitute 'civil society' – including ethnic communities, religious groups and economic networks, all of which abound in Africa. But their activities, while constraining the power of the state in relation to society as a whole, may serve to distort or undermine what many would see as desirable functions of the state. Thus, in seeking what often seems the desired complement to good governance by promoting civil society, what is often being sought are national or nationally compatible institutions that are outside the state, and which reflect actual or potential social values of a broadly integrative character.

In this regard, Sudan had probably the most developed civil society in the Horn with independent bodies of several kinds associated with the professions, and organized labour in particular. Indeed, this civil society was seen as having been at the forefront of the movements which twice led to the overthrow of military regimes in 1964 and 1985. However, though many of the leaders of the NIF, which came effectively to power in 1989, were from the same background, they also recognized the danger, especially since they had chosen to rule through a military clique. In consequence, the existing institutions of civil society were hounded with many of their leaders being detained and imprisoned, and with thousands eventually fleeing the country. In their places there were attempts to establish NIF-sponsored alternatives, but they lacked the credibility of their predecessors, now organized in exile.

Successive regimes in Ethiopia have not allowed similar space for the emergence of civil society hitherto, and there is little indication that it is about to happen. Efforts to create independent national organizations appear to be looked on with suspicion. In particular, there appears to be a fear that such national organizations might become a surrogate 'Ethiopian' force and challenge the desired view of an ethnic federation. It is such suspicions of the actions of what remains a very secretive regime core (*plus ça change, plus ça la même chose*) that have been interpreted as being behind the attacks on university staff in particular.

Eritrea is both similar and different. On the one hand, it appears no more desirous of a potentially critical civil society emerging than does Ethiopia, but on the other, there appears less immediate prospect of one developing. There was some experience in that direction under the British administration after the war, and its repression by Haile Selassie contributed to resistance. But that resistance has gone through much turmoil and conflict in the intervening years, from which has emerged the victorious and now dominant EPLF. Perhaps the seeds of civil society lie among the many Eritreans who left the country, often proving adaptable and successful in other climes. But while many of them remit to their families, few appear in a hurry to risk their rebuilt lives by an early return to Eritrea.

Somalia is in a comparable position as far as educated exiles who might contribute to civil society are concerned. Here the discussion has been less of civil society as institutions outside the state than of local community leaders in regard to the state's bottom-up re-building. In this process such leaders, where they exist, can be resuscitated or perhaps created, retain the problem of linking their activities to a wider administrative and political framework. It appeared that someone or something was needed to hold the ring, with the dilemma of whether the UN should have remained involved as a kind of minimal trustee-ship, pending the greater development and linkage of local authorities, or arrange a deal with self-proclaimed national leaders, and hope that top and bottom could mesh. In the end it was effectively left to the latter to sort it out themselves, but until some measure of national security can be attained, there is not the context in which to speak very meaningfully of civil society in the terms used above.

In the tiny state of Djibouti there is similarly relatively little that can be spoken of as civil society. In the long years of comparative stability there was little attempt to shape society, in the ways attempted elsewhere in the region, but nor was there much encouragement for the kind of political pluralism within which institutions of civil society could grow. And when a challenge did come from FRUD, it was met with violence and repression against the suspect elements of civilian society, as with the dramatic shooting of demonstrators in Djibouti in December 1991.

While civil society is perceived as having an institutional significance of its own in relation to the state, in particular in its supposed role as a form of checks and balances at the national level, the opportunity for it to exist and function is also widely seen as an expression of the rights of individuals to organize and represent themselves. Human rights are expressed largely in terms of political freedoms that go beyond simply rights associated with the exercise of democracy – to form free political parties, vote, etc. – into the ongoing freedoms involved in participating in non-political organizations. Here, the overall situation in the Horn remains uncertain. There are forms of democracy, as I have indicated, but they are constrained in various ways (albeit in constitutional environments which are in most cases still evolving), and thus, in practice, imperfect in terms of human rights. Civil society, for its part, has been both repressed and limited in its development, adding to the picture of a difficult path to the attainment of human rights. Even with the much greater emphasis on international human rights since the end of the Cold War, their attainment remains fraught with difficulty. Within the Horn, Sudan, since 1989, has had a particularly difficult experience: theoretically, the regime has questioned international concepts of human rights against its own interpretation of building an Islamic society; while, practically, the investigations and very critical conclusions of a UN special investigator have been difficult to conduct, and condemned by the government when published.

Reference to the UN's role with regard to human rights in Sudan is one indicator of the involvement of the international community in this field. The UN is one potential source of pressure, but one frequently hedged around with diplomatic constraints since it often involves member states of the organization. Another commonly cited form of pressure is aid conditionality. This is applied to development aid, and the obvious case in the Horn, in practice, has been the drying up of such aid from Western donors to Sudan since 1989; in addition to which, Western powers have an influential voice in the IMF and World Bank. However, the extent of such leverage can be questioned, especially when the scale of aid packages hitherto appeared to be linked to international political priorities. The impact of changing priorities has affected Africa generally, especially against requests from other regions, most notably the former Eastern bloc, and the Horn was once a comparatively favoured area which is unlikely to receive the same flow for the foreseeable future. (Economically, it may be argued that that is no bad thing, but it may have a political impact, in the form of lowered leverage, which rebounds against the agenda of democracy and human rights.) In addition to monitoring by the UN and outside governments, a plethora of human rights groups have sprouted. Some were old and respected, others are much newer and still finding their roles. Most are self-appointed and aim to bring pressure directly or indirectly on governments both within and outside the region, as well as promoting human rights and indigenous NGOs, etc. Their influence can be significant, though it will wax and wane with changing conditions and their own reputations.

Meanwhile, the areas of rights that have engaged the international community throughout the Cold War in the Horn of Africa are still around. As long as war continues, as it does in southern Sudan, refugee issues will remain. By now UNHCR and other agencies are very experienced in operating in the context of the Horn. Responses to new crises, especially the speed and scale of the outpouring of refugees from Rwanda, have led to renewed criticism and discussion of possible measures to improve performance in the future. Peace also brings its own problems, especially with regard to resettlement, a situation clearly evident with regard to the number of Eritrean refugees still in Sudan after 1991. At the same time, war and drought also brought a need for fresh thinking about the delivery of relief within countries. On the theoretical level it contributed to the discussion of a right of intervention to protect civilian populations from the worst ravages of governments and guerrillas; a right increasingly accepted in practice in the Horn, especially since the inauguration of Operation Lifeline Sudan (OLS) in 1989, which was accepted (with restrictions) by the combatants. The UN intervention in southern Somalia in 1992 under Chapter VII was an extension of that into a territory in which there was no effective government with which the UN could negotiate, and in which it was deemed that force might have to be used to ensure the delivery of humanitarian relief. It also contributed to the creation of a new UN Disaster Relief Organization to improve performance. While the experience of Somalia undoubtedly contributed to the need to improve the performance of UN operations, it did little to clarify the circumstances in which intervention would take place in principle. In particular, there were those who felt that in areas of southern Sudan the situation of warring SPLA factions, as well as the attacks of government soldiers, amounted to a situation not so dissimilar to Somalia, though the response in terms of OLS did not involve the use of force where, in parts, that might have assisted delivery (and heightened international awareness of the situation in Sudan).

The emergency relief of famine has itself prompted a growing literature in the past two decades. Malthusian discussion of cases such as Ethiopia have been followed by the issue of drought and long-term climatic changes, as well as the importance of conflict. The solutions raised have included improved early warning, discussion of economic structure and 'entitlement', as well as conflict resolution. The coming of peace to Eritrea and Ethiopia has reduced conflict as a source of food deficit (though in south-east Ethiopia security has still been a problem), yet the problem persists there as elsewhere in the Horn. In Eritrea it is acknowledged that in the wake of years of war and with major issues of reconstruction, food aid is necessary for the indefinite future, while in Ethiopia the long-term rainfall trends have produced increased unpredictability. In both countries recovery from war is proving a long process. Perhaps the most optimistic results are those from Somaliland where regional trade in particular appears to have been something of a stimulus for economic growth since 1991. In the unstable areas of southern Sudan, as well parts of the west of the country, and in southern Somalia, the vicious circle of conflict and food deficit persists.

The choices for governments in the region are limited as far as development is concerned. In addition to their own ideological retreat from variants of socialism, the awareness of conditionality with regard to aid encourages a market orientation. Yet in Eritrea and Ethiopia a residual sense of the significance of government in economic recovery persists. Eritrea rejected a US aid package as over-prescriptive, while in Ethiopia there are signs of an overall wish to manage the economy, as the land policy demonstrates. In Sudan it appears that sectional interest in the form of growing control of the tattered remnants of the economy by the NIF predominates, and the country has sold crops abroad at times of domestic shortage. In the last resort, all appear to feel that the international community has only a limited contribution to make developmentally, while in emergency the right appeal and possible media pressure can ensure the promises and eventually some delivery of food requirements.

The potential significance of both a greater degree of self-help and cooperation at the regional level lay in the establishment of the Inter-Governmental Authority on Drought and Development (IGADD) in 1986. Centred on then stable Djibouti (with its policy of good neigh-bourliness for survival), IGADD drew attention to issues of drought and development as regional rather than simply national questions. The appropriateness of such an approach was obvious, from the possibility of cooperating to develop common resources, such as the rivers of the Horn, to recognition that issues pertaining to such ways of life as pastoralism crossed the generally colonially drawn state borders. Yet while IGADD, from its base in Djibouti, could develop ideas and present plans, it was very short of resources and reliant on hopes from the international community that were only scantily met. With its involvement in peace-making in southern Sudan, IGADD took on a new dimension, though clearly one of relevance in view of the growing recognition of conflict in famine. Welcome though this shouldering of regional responsibility was, IGADD's problems as a mediator were as great as any other in that ultimately it came back to the Sudanese belligerents and their own perceptions and positions. Furthermore, the possible helpfulness of those with regional experience as mediators was offset, in part at least, by the feeling that certain IGADD members had an interest in the outcome that was reflected in their role in the negotiations. (Apart from IGADD there was little chance of a regional body playing a part: the OAU had been comparatively moribund on peace-making, preferring to leave such efforts to IGADD or the Economic Community of West African States (ECOWAS) in Liberia, while the Arab League was generally perceived as partisan where an 'Afro/Arab' issue was involved.)

Yet IGADD's establishment is an indication that the 'greater Horn' has come to stay, conceptually at least. What had led to the expansion of the concept of the Horn – Ethiopia's internal problems and the linkage they had established to conflict in both Somalia and Sudan at the same time – appears to have past, but the need for some attempt at regional political as well as economic management lives on. The USA in particular has shown signs of thinking that IGADD might be a realistic vehicle to promote an economic union in the Horn, and the idea of a federal Horn has been floated in the past. Regional political roles may also be sought by individual member states. Djibouti and Ethiopia both sought a role in reconciliation in Somalia. On a wholly different plane, there is sufficient ambiguity in the foreign policy of the regime in Sudan since 1989 to suspect that there may be endeavours to develop its Islamic project across the Horn, possibly even into countries with whose new regimes it has had good relations, such as Ethiopia and Eritrea (with which alleged involvement by Sudan led to the breaking of relations).

In seeking to undertake regional roles, whether as individual states or within IGADD, there is an awareness that others that have sought to play a regional role in the past are still actual or potential actors. Indeed, with the relations between the states of the Horn having changed so totally, and major international actors having a diminished interest, it is regional actors from the Middle East that make up the theme of continuity. Egypt and Saudi Arabia, in particular, have long felt that they have a role to play, both to protect their interests in the Nile basin and the Red Sea and to project the power which, as the most populous and richest states in the Middle East respectively, they feel is rightly theirs; nor has their activity been without a touch of rivalry on occasions. Nothing that has happened has diminished the Horn's importance for them. Indeed, with the retreat of the super-powers they have ever greater reason to be vigilant. However, the current alignment of regimes in the Horn owes little to them and is, in part, against them. The NIF in Sudan becomes more threatening as tension from political Islam mounts in Egypt and Saudi Arabia (fuelling charges of counter-plots against Sudan), while the Eritrean and Ethiopian regimes were against the grain of Saudi Arabia's policy in particular. Israel is taking advantage of past links with Ethiopia and new ones with Eritrea, and for all its new-found peace-making nearer home, will probably regard these relations as a useful aside. Libya is more preoccupied with domestic problems and the impact of international sanctions, but can never be guaranteed to remain aloof, particularly with regard to Sudan and, by implication, Chad. In addition, there are the more distant participants in the Horn: Iraq has become a lesser force since its setback in the Gulf War, but Iran became a significant backer of Sudan, and has been rumoured to have other possible designs on the Horn.

For the world's sole remaining superpower, the USA, and other major international powers, the significance of the Horn may always have been exaggerated by some 'globalists' and has certainly waned since the end of the Cold War and with the rise to prominence of new problems elsewhere. In terms of US vital interests, it is of much less significance than hitherto. The major strategic concern still lies with the Red Sea, and its possible choke points at Suez in the north, and the straits of Bab el-Mandeb in the south, but there is not the specific threat of the Cold War days. New 'globalists' may be concerned about the spread of Islamic politics in the region, but even should the movement grow, it is far from being turned into a threatening capacity in international terms. The only major power directly protecting a strategic interest remains France and its base at Djibouti, and France is concerned mainly with maintaining that still useful foothold amidst the vicissitudes of the Horn, partly to demonstrate its continuing role in Africa. Under US leadership, and often influenced by levels of NGO campaigning and media coverage, the concerns of major powers centre on general sentiments: alleviation of the grossest manifestations of human suffering; the ending of conflict within states; and support for human rights and the encouragement of liberal democracy. In the longer term, new international interests may arise: the Horn has mineral resources and, as seen in southern Sudan, their extraction in politically unstable conditions may be extremely difficult. Furthermore, continued state collapse may not be contained, but have a wider impact on surrounding states: Somalia's neighbours do not appear sanguine about its current plight. The effects of collapse on population movement may be felt more widely too: European states are increasingly aware of the pressures of migrants from political and economic troublespots, including a growing number from the Horn in recent years.

Realization of this emerging situation prompted the new UN Secretary General, Boutros Boutros-Ghali to publish *An Agenda for Peace* in 1992.[3] In it he argued that with the collapse of the Cold War the era of absolute state sovereignty was past and in its place there should be new roles for the UN to play. No longer divided, the Security Council was now in a position to undertake cooperative action of the kind for which it had originally been intended but which the emergence of superpower rivalry had dashed in a welter of vetoes. With all that now in the past, ways should be sought to identify and address sources of danger before violence can break out (preventive diplomacy and, if necessary, deployment); there should be peace-making and conflict resolution as well as peace-keeping; and more support for peace-building as well as tackling underlying causes, such as poverty. Such tasks should not fall to the UN alone, but combine the efforts of the UN, member states, regional organizations and both international and indigenous NGOs, though with the UN taking a more leading role than hitherto and with the Secretary General himself playing a more active part. It was against the background of such expectations that the UN became more involved in the Horn and more scrutinized.

Somalia was the location for only one of an increasing number of UN operations, but it was nevertheless an important one. By the end of 1992 it had become a situation where it was no longer possible to contemplate seeking to give help to the suffering population by peace-keeping methods, and peace-making was deemed necessary for relief deliveries. However, the motives and intentions of the major protagonists of peace-making intervention, Boutros Boutros-Ghali and George Bush, differed, and the operation itself duly floundered. The failure of UN operations in Somalia in turn affected the credibility of the organization in all aspects and at all levels. The initial uncertainty of purpose, especially in terms of overall objectives of the mission and the means to accomplish them, meant that it appeared to be an operation of drift. Moreover, it was to be for a fixed period, after which the outcome was left uncertain. The UN might have moved towards active peace-making, yet in a context of a state that had experienced collapse on the scale of Somalia's it still appeared that it had to stop short of open-ended trusteeship, while an authoritative structure acceptable to the international community was being nurtured. In this, the UN's performance was equally unsuccessful. Though Boutros-Ghali claimed to have worked over the UN's structure, both his leadership and the agencies involved came in for repeated criticism, from those associated with the UN as well as outsiders, to the point where a senior official, Kurt Janssen, himself resigned.

Perhaps the UN failed in Somalia in part because the exercise was so high profile, and accompanied by all the media coverage imaginable in the circumstances. Its other major operation in the Horn, Operation Lifeline Sudan (OLS), may have had its problems but in a much more inconspicuous way it made some headway year after year. It could be accused of helping prolong war by the extent to which it was manipulated by combatants, but it did save lives. Though needing regular re-negotiation, OLS was not end-stopped, but renewed while conflict and suffering continued. However, it does nothing to end the conflict or the 'permanent emergency' in which it is embedded. The underlying causes to which Boutros-Ghali referred in the *Agenda* are not being addressed in Sudan, but more has been achieved than was managed in Somalia, suggesting that it has been the problems confronted by the Somali involvement rather than necessarily the intervention of the UN as such that require addressing.

The baby does not have to go out with the bath water. In fact, viewed more widely, the UN's intervention on humanitarian grounds is more readily accepted; intervention where the state has effectively collapsed is always likely to be messy and require open-ended if not long-term action, and if the UN is to improve its performance, there needs to be a readiness to learn from the mistakes of the past. But if there is a sufficient nucleus of power which the international community can assist in re-building efforts, then there may be achievements. The World Bank and the IMF have pointed to a measure of economic success in Uganda and Ghana, but it would not have been possible without a concommitant political power sufficient to hold the ring while the economist's medicine was taken (albeit in ways that seemed sometimes to have authoritarian overtones).

The Horn, then, can expect that with regard to humanitarian issues, the UN and other international agencies will be expected to play a leading part in the future. There is not a regional body capable of acting. The existing authorities (including that of Somaliland) have limited governmental capacity and lack the resources. The need remains, at least with parts of the Horn appearing to be in chronic food deficit. And NGOs of all kinds need to cooperate with political authorities and cannot be seen as a substitute for them, as the circumstances leading to the UN's involvement in Somalia in 1992 indicated.

It is commonplace now to suggest that bereft of international inputs, indigenous societies will somehow come to their own solutions – some kind of anthropological and sociological (perhaps also economic and even political) equilibrium. But such a view is fanciful. Self-regulating mechanisms have not been the stuff of many communities in the Horn so much as the waxing and waning of power, including the rise and fall of indigenous states, and with conflict and reformation among societies. Those developments have never been created from outside, but nor have they lacked a significant external influence of varying degrees. The extent of intrusion in the world of international rivalry of varying kinds in the nineteenth and twentieth centuries has been unprecedented and contributed much to the experience of the Horn. It may be that the Horn will be less contested internationally than in the past, but that does not mean that external intrusion will cease, whether from international agencies or major or regional powers. And, of course, whatever the evolving state structure (and there is little sign of the Horn settling for widescale statelessness), the relations between states within the region will also continue to be of significance in the future. What does appear to have decreased is that sense of a combination of indigenous conflicts and international rivals involved in inter-connected conflicts adding up to a region at war with itself. And if that means only a residual concept of the Horn as a group of countries with similar and partly related needs, between which cooperation would be advantageous with a measure of international support, that would be a positive outcome to the generally conflict-laden character of relations and events for decades past.

Notes and Bibliography

Introduction

1. M. Doornboos, L. Cliffe and J. Markakis (eds) *Beyond Conflict in the Horn: Prospects for Peace, Recovery and Development in Ethiopia, Somalia and the Sudan*, Institute of Social Studies, The Hague, and James Currey, The Hague and London, 1992; K. Fukui and J. Markakis (eds) *Ethnicity and Conflict in the Horn of Africa*, James Currey, London, 1994; C. Gurdon (ed.) *The Horn of Africa*, University College London Press, London, 1994; P. B. Henze, *The Horn of Africa, From War to Peace*, Macmillan, Basingstoke, 1991; G. Nzongola-Ntalaja (ed.) *Conflict in the Horn of Africa*, African Studies Association Press, Emory, 1991; P. Woodward and M. Forsyth (eds) *Conflict and Peace in the Horn of Africa: Federalism and its Alternatives*, Dartmouth, Aldershot, 1994.

2. M. Gilbert (ed.) *Historical Essays of Otto Hintze*, Oxford University Press, Oxford, 1975, p. 183.

3. The significance of the longer view in political analysis has been underlined in recent years in works such as: J.-F. Bayart *The State in Africa: The Politics of the Belly*, Longman, London, 1993; and J. Manor (ed.) *Rethinking Third World Politics*, Longman, London, 1991.

4. J. Markakis *National and Class Conflict in the Horn of Africa*, Cambridge University Press, Cambridge, 1987.

5. The classic exposition was S. Huntington *Political Order in Changing Societies*, Yale University Press, New Haven, CT, 1968.

6. R. Jackson *Quasi-states: Sovereignty, International Relations and the Third World*, Cambridge University Press, Cambridge, 1990.

7. J. Migdal *Strong Societies and Weak States*, Princeton University Press, Princeton, NJ, 1988.

8. I. W. Zartman (ed.) *Collapsed States: the Disintegration and Restoration of Legitimate Authority*, Lynne Rienner, Boulder, CO, 1995.

One of the earliest comparative collections on the Horn was I. M. Lewis (ed.) *National Self-determination in the Horn of Africa*, Ithaca, London, 1983. There have since been a number of shorter works than those mentioned above: L. Leatherbee and D. Bricker *Balancing Consensus and Dissent: Prospects for Human Rights and Development in the Horn of Africa*, The Fund for Peace, New York, 1994; Colin Legum 'The Horn of Africa: Prospects for Political Transformation', *Conflict Studies*, 254, 1992; S. Makinda 'Security in the Horn of Africa', *Adelphi Papers*, 269. There is also a more specialized recent collection: J.

Markakis (ed.) *Conflict and the Decline of Pastoralism in the Horn of Africa*, The Institute of Social Studies, and Macmillan, The Hague and Basingstoke, 1993. In addition, there are two journals specializing in the Horn: *Horn of Africa*, and *Northeast African Studies*. *Africa Contemporary Record* provides a useful annual account of developments, while among the newsletters that cover the Horn, *Africa Confidential* and *Indian Ocean Newsletter* stand out. Longstanding journals such as *African Affairs*, *Journal of Modern African Studies*, and *Development and Change* include regular articles on the Horn; and many relevant articles also appear in new journals, to which events such as those in the Horn have given much of their impetus, including *Refugee Studies*, and *Disasters*. Journals such as *International Affairs* have also given growing attention to issues such as international intervention in recent years.

1. The historic Horn

1. D. D. Laitin and Said S. Samatar *Somalia: Nation in Search of a State*, Westview Press, Boulder, CO, 1987, pp. 30–31.
2. Said S. Samatar *Somalia: A Nation in Turmoil*, Minority Rights Group, London, 1991, p. 13.
3. Laitin and Samatar, *Somalia*, p. 42.
4. Ibid.
5. Bahru Zewde *A History of Modern Ethiopia, 1855–1974*, James Currey, London, 1990.
6. Gebru Tareke *Ethiopia: Power and Protest – Peasant Revolts in the Twentieth Century*, Cambridge University Press, Cambridge, 1991, p. 84.
7. Ibid., p. 84.

Other major historical books on Ethiopia include: R. Greenfield *Ethiopia: A New Political History*, Pall Mall, London, 1965; D. N. Levine *Wax and Gold: Tradition and Innovation in Ethiopian Culture*, University of Chicago Press, Chicago, IL, 1965; D. N. Levine *Greater Ethiopia: The Evolution of a Multiethnic Society*, University of Chicago Press, Chicago, IL, 1974; H. G. Marcus *A History of Ethiopia*, University of California Press, Berkeley, CA, 1994; S. Rubenson *Survival of Ethiopian Independence*, Heinemann, London, 1976; E. Ullendorff *The Ethiopians, An Introduction to Country and People*, Oxford University Press, Oxford, 1960; and Bahru Zewde *A History of Modern Ethiopia, 1855–1974*, James Currey, London, 1990. On Haile Selassie and his downfall see: C. Clapham *Haile Selassie's Government*, Longman, London, 1969; P. Gilkes *The Dying Lion: Feudalism and Modernization in Ethiopia*, Julian Friedmann, London, 1974; R. L. Hess *The Modernization of Autocracy*, Cornell University Press, Ithaca, NY, 1972; J. Markakis *Ethiopia: Anatomy of a Traditional Polity*, Oxford University Press, London, 1974; J. Spencer *Ethiopia at Bay*, Reference Publications, Michigan, MI, 1984.

Historical works on Somalia include: L. V. Cassanelli *The Shaping of Somali Society: Reconstructing the History of a Pastoral People*, Pennsylvania University Press, Philadelphia, PA, 1982; I. M. Lewis *A Pastoral Democracy: A Study of Pastoralism and Politics among the Northern Somali of the Horn of Africa*, Oxford

University Press, London, 1982; I. M. Lewis *A Modern History of Somalia: Nation and State in the Horn of Africa*, Longman, London, 1979; Abdi Samatar *The State and Rural Transformation in Northern Somalia*, University of Wisconsin Press, Madison, WI, 1989.

Historical works on Sudan include: M. Abd el-Rahim *Imperialism and Nationalism in the Sudan: A Study in Constitutional and Political Developments, 1899–1956*, Oxford University Press, London, 1969; M. O. Beshir *The Southern Sudan, Background to Conflict*, C Hurst, London, 1968; M. O. Beshir *Revolution and Nationalism in Sudan*, Rex Collings, London, 1974; R. O. Collins *Land Beyond the Rivers: The Southern Sudan, 1898–1919*, Yale University Press, New Haven, CT, 1971; R. O. Collins *Shadows in the Grass: Britain in the Southern Sudan, 1918–1956*, Yale University Press, New Haven, CT, 1983; M. W. Daly *Empire on the Nile: The Anglo-Egyptian Sudan, 1898–1934*, Cambridge University Press, Cambridge, 1985; M. W. Daly *Imperial Sudan: The Anglo-Egyptian Condominium, 1934–1956*, Cambridge University Press, Cambridge, 1991; P. M. Holt and M. W. Daly *A History of the Sudan: From the Coming of Islam to the Present Day*, Longman, London, 1986; Lillian Passmore Sanderson and G. N. Sanderson *Education, Religion and Politics in Southern Sudan, 1899–1964*, Ithaca, London, 1981.

2. Sudan

1. Mansour Khalid *Nimeiri and the Revolution of Dis-May*, KPI, London, 1985, p. 39.

2. R. Jackson and C Rosberg *Personal Rule in Black Africa*, California University Press, Berkeley, CA, 1982.

3. A. El-Affendi *Turabi's Revolution: Islam and Power in Sudan*, Grey Seal Books, London, 1991, p. 163.

4. P. M. Holt 'Holy Families and Islam in the Sudan', *Princeton Near East Papers*, 4, 1967.

Books on Sudanese politics nationally since 1956 include: M. Abd el-Rahim *et al.* (eds) *Sudan Since Independence*, Gower, London, 1986; P. K. Bechtold *Politics in the Sudan*, Praeger, London, 1978; H. Bleuchot, C. Delmet and D. Hopwood (eds) *Sudan: History, Identity and Ideology*, Ithaca, Reading, 1991; M. Khalid *The Government They Deserve: The Role of the Elite in Sudan's Political Evolution*, KPI, London, 1990; B. Malwal *People and Power in the Sudan*, Ithaca, London, 1981; T. Niblock *Class and Power in Sudan*, Macmillan, London, 1987; J. Voll (ed.) *Sudan: State and Society in Crisis*, Indiana University Press, Bloomington, IN, 1990; P. Woodward *Sudan 1898–1989: The Unstable State*, Lynne Rienner, Boulder, CO, 1990; P. Woodward (ed.) *Sudan after Nimeiri*, Routledge, London, 1991. The southern Sudan has generated a substantial literature as well, including: A. Alier *Southern Sudan: Too Many Agreements Dishonoured*, Ithaca, London, 1990; M. O. Beshir *The Southern Sudan, From Conflict to Peace*, C. Hurst, London, 1975; M. W. Daly and A. A. Sikanga (eds) *Civil War in the Sudan*, British Academic Press, London, 1993; M. Khalid (ed.) *John Garang Speaks*, KPI, London, 1987.

3. Somalia

1. D. D. Laitin and Said S. Samatar *Somalia: Nation in Search of a State*, Westview Press, Boulder, CO, 1987, p. 70.
2. I. M. Lewis *A Modern History of Somalia: Nation and State in the Horn of Africa*, Longman, London, 1979, p. 206.
3. I. M. Lewis 'The Ogaden and the fragility of Somali segmentary nationalism', *African Affairs*, 88, 353, 1989, p. 576.
4. Laitin and Samatar *Somalia*, p. 99.
5. Quoted in Said Samatar *Somalia: A Nation in Turmoil*, p. 21.
6. J. Drysdale *Whatever Happened to Somalia: A Tale of Tragic Blunders*, Haan, London, 1994, p. 47.
7. Lewis 'The Ogaden', p. 578.
8. Abdi Samatar 'Destruction of state and society in Somalia: beyond the tribal convention', *Journal of Modern African Studies*, 30. 4. 1992, p. 630.
9. Ibid., p. 641.
10. Said Samatar *Somalia: A Nation in Turmoil*, p. 26.
11. Hussein Adam 'Somalia: Federalism and Self-Determination', in P. Woodward and M. Forsyth (eds) *Conflict and Peace in the Horn of Africa: Federalism and its Alternatives*, Dartmouth, Aldershot, 1994.

The crisis in Somalia rapidly produced a literature of its own, among which are the following books: Mohammed Farah Aideed and Satya Pal Ruhela *The Preferred Future Development in Somalia*, Vikas, New Delhi, 1993; J. L. Hirsch and R. B. Oakley, *Somalia and Operation Restore Hope*, US Institute of Peace, Washington, DC, 1995; I. M. Lewis *Understanding Somalia*, HAAN, London, 1993; S. Makinda *Seeking Peace from Chaos: Humanitarian Intervention in Somalia*, Lynne Rienner, Boulder, CO, 1993; Satya Pal Ruhela (ed.) *Mohammed Farah Aidid and His Vision of Somalia*, Vikas, New Delhi, 1994; Mohamed Sahnoun *Somalia: The Missed Opportunities*, US Institute for Peace, Washington, DC, 1994; Ahmed Samatar (ed.) *The Somali Challenge: From Catastrophe to Renewal?* Lynne Rienner, Boulder, CO, 1994. The crisis has also produced its own bibliography: W. S. Clarke *Humanitarian Intervention in Somalia: Bibliography*, Center for Strategic Leadership, Carlisle, PA, 1995.

4. Ethiopia

The Ethiopian revolution attracted considerable attention including: C. Clapham *Transformation and Continuity in Revolutionary Ethiopia*, Cambridge University Press, Cambridge, 1988; F. Halliday and M. Molyneux *The Ethiopian Revolution*, Verso, London, 1981; J. Harbeson *The Ethiopian Transformation*, Westview Press, Boulder, CO, 1988; Dawit Wolde Giorgis *Red Tears: War, Famine and Revolution in Ethiopia*, Red Sea Press, Trenton, NJ, 1989; E. J. Keller *Revolutionary Ethiopia: From Empire to People's Republic*, Indiana University Press, Bloomington, IN, 1988; C. Lefort *Ethiopia: An Heretical Revolution?*, Zed Books, London, 1983; D. and M. Ottoway *Ethiopia: Empire in Revolution*, African Publishing Company, New York, 1978; Marina Ottoway (ed.) *The Political Economy of*

Ethiopia, Praeger, New York, 1990; Andargachew Tiruneh *The Ethiopian Revolution, 1974–1987: A Transformation From an Aristocratic to a Totalitarian Autocracy*, Cambridge University Press, Cambridge, 1993; M. Wubneh and Y. Abate *Ethiopia: Transition and Development in the Horn of Africa*, Westview Press, Boulder, CO, 1988.

Books focusing especially on resistance began with Eritrea in particular and then attention turned to other areas: D. Connell *Against All Odds: A Chronicle of the Ethiopian Revolution*, Red Sea Press, Trenton, NJ, 1993; B. Davidson, L. Cliffe and B. H .Selassie (eds) *Behind the War in Eritrea*, Russell Press, Nottingham, 1980; A. de Waal *Evil Days: Thirty Years of War and Famine in Ethiopia*, Africa Watch, New York, 1991; H. Erlich *The Struggle over Eritrea, 1962–1978*, Hoover Institute Press, Stanford, CA, 1983; J. Firebrace with S. Holland *Never Kneel Down: Drought, Development and Liberation in Eritrea*, Red Sea Press, Trenton, NJ, 1985; J. Firebrace and G. Smith *The Hidden Revolution: An Analysis of Social Change in Tigray, Northern Ethiopia*, War on Want, London, 1982; Ruth Iyob, *Eritrea: Struggle for Independence*, Cambridge University Press, Cambridge, 1995; Asafa Jalata *Oromia and Ethiopia: State Formation and Ethnological Conflict, 1868–1992*, Lynne Rienner, Boulder, 1993; R. Kaplan *Surrender or Starve: The Wars behind the Famine*, Westview Press, Boulder, CO, 1988; Tesfatsion Medhanie *Eritrea: Dynamics of a National Question*, B. R. Gruner, Amsterdam, 1986; Tesfatsion Medhanie *Peace Dialogue on Eritrea: Prospects and Problems Today*, B. R. Gruner, Amsterdam, 1989; J. Sorenson *Imagining Ethiopia*, Rutgers University Press, Rutgers NJ, 1993; Gebru Tareke *Ethiopia: Power and Protest. Peasant Revolts in the Twentieth Century*, Cambridge University Press, Cambridge, 1991.

5. Eritrea and Djibouti

1. Quoted in L. Leatherbee and D. Bricker *Balancing Consensus and Dissent: Prospects for Human Rights and Development in the Horn of Africa*, The Fund for Peace, New York, 1994.

Neither Djibouti nor Eritrea has yet generated a substantial book on contemporary history and politics in English since their respective attainment of independence.

6. Neighbours and conflict

There are no books specifically dealing with the relations between the three main countries discussed here, though a number of works on the international relations of Africa and the Third World refer to Somalia as a classic case of irredentism. See, for example: N. Chazan *Irredentism and International Politics*, Lynne Rienner, Boulder, CO, 1989.

7. Superpowers

1. Quoted in F. Halliday *The Making of the Second Cold War*, Verso, London, 1988, p. 87.

2. Quoted in G. Lundestad *East, West, North, South: Major Developments in International Politics, 1945–1990*, Norwegian University Press, Oslo, 1991, p. 141.

3. D. Rawson 'Dealing with disintegration: US assistance and the Somali state', in Ahmed Samatar (ed.) *The Somali Challenge: From Catastrophe to Renewal?*, Lynne Rienner, Boulder, CO, 1994, p. 172.

4. Ibid., p. 179.

General works relating to the superpowers and the Horn include: J. W. Harbeson and D. Rothchild (eds) *Africa in World Politics*, Westview Press, Boulder, CO, 1991; D. Korn *Ethiopia, the United States and the Soviet Union*, Croom Helm, London, 1986; D. R. Smock (ed.) *Making War and Waging Peace: Foreign Intervention in Africa*, US Institute for Peace, Washington, DC, 1993; Bereket Habte Selassie *Conflict and Intervention in the Horn of Africa*, Monthly Review Press, New York, 1980; and K. Somerville *Foreign Military Intervention in Africa*, Pinter, London, 1990. For the former Soviet Union, see: R. G. Patman *The Soviet Union in the Horn of Africa*, Cambridge University Press, Cambridge, 1990; and B. D. Porter *The USSR in the Third World Conflicts*, Cambridge University Press, Cambridge, 1984. For the United States, see: Baffour Agyeman-Duah *The United States and Ethiopia: Military Assistance and the Quest for Security, 1953–1993*, University Press of America, London, 1994; J. Lefebvre *Arms for the Horn: US Security Policy in Ethiopia and Somalia, 1953–1991*, University of Pitsburgh, Press, Pittsburgh, PA, 1991; Harold Marcus *Ethiopia, Great Britain and the United States, 1941–1974*, University of California Press, Berkeley, CA, 1983; P. J. Schraeder *Intervention in the 1990s: US Foreign Policy in the Third World*, Lynne Rienner, Boulder, CO, 1992; P. J. Schraeder *US Foreign Policy Towards Africa: Incrementalism, Crisis and Change*, Cambridge University Press, Cambridge, 1994; B. Woodward *Veil: The Secret Wars of the CIA, 1981–1987*, Simon and Schuster, New York, 1987. There has also been a proliferation of writing concerning international relations and the Third World, including: Boutros Boutros-Ghali *An Agenda for Peace*, United Nations, New York, 1992; R. Jackson *Quasi-states: Sovereignty, International Relations and the Third World*, Cambridge University Press, Cambridge, 1990; A. James *Peacekeeping in International Politics*, Macmillan, Basingstoke, 1990; Caroline Thomas *In Search of Security: The Third World in International Relations*, Lynne Rienner, Boulder, CO, 1987.

8. Regional politics

1. Ali Dessouki 'The primacy of economics: the foreign policy of Egypt', in B. Korany and A. Dessouki (eds) *The Foreign Policies of Arab States* (2nd edn), Westview Press, Boulder, CO, 1991, p. 167.

Works on regional politics are overwhelmingly concerned with the Horn in relation to the Middle East rather than to Africa. They include: J. Bearman *Qadhafi's Libya*, Zed Books, London, 1986; F. Halliday *Revolution and Foreign Policy: The Case of South Yemen, 1967–87*, Cambridge University Press,

Cambridge, 1990; Tareq Y. Ismael *International Relations of the Contemporary Middle East*, Syracuse University Press, Syracuse, NY, 1986; R. Lemarchand (ed.) *The Green and the Black: Qadhafi's Policies in Africa*, Indiana University Press, Bloomington, IN, 1988; J. Peters *Israel and Africa*, I.B.Tauris, London, 1992; J. Wright *Libya, Chad and the Central Sahara*, Hurst, London, 1989.

9. Development, relief and mediation

1. G. Loescher *Refugee Movements and International Security*, Adelphi Papers 268, London, 1992, p. 72.
2. C. Clapham *Transformation and Continuity in Revolutionary Ethiopia*, Cambridge University Press, Cambridge, 1988, p. 164.
3. Quoted in A. O'Connor *Poverty in Africa: A Geographical Approach*, Belhaven, London, 1991, p. 144.
4. M. Duffield *War and Famine in Africa*, Oxfam Research Paper 5, Oxfam Publications, Oxford, 1991.
5. A. Zolberg, A. Suhrke and S. Agnaya *Escape from Violence: Conflict and the Refugee Crisis in the Developing World*, Oxford University Press, Oxford, 1985, p. 52.
6. A. Karadawi *Political Refugees: A Case Study from the Sudan, 1964–1976*, unpublished MPhil thesis, University of Reading, 1977, p. 75.
7. Loescher *Refugee Movements*, p. 6.
8. C. Mitchell 'The process and stages of mediation: two Sudanese cases', in D. R. Smock (ed.) *Making War and Waging Peace: Foreign Intervention in Africa*, US Institute for Peace, Washington, DC, 1993, p. 147.

Books on economic development and aid include: T Barnett and A Abd el-Karim (eds) *Sudan: State Capital and Transformation*, Croom Helm, London, 1988; R. P. C. Brown *Public Debt and Private Wealth: Debt and Capital Flight and the IMF in Sudan*, Macmillan, Basingstoke, 1992; S. Browne *Foreign Aid in Practice*, Pinter, London, 1990; K. Griffin (ed.) *The Economy of Ethiopia*, St Martin's Press, New York, 1992; R. Riddell *Foreign Aid Reconsidered*, James Currey, London, 1987. The literature on refugees includes: L. Gordenker *Refugees in International Politics*, Croom Helm, London, 1987; G. Loescher *Refugee Movements and International Security*, Adelphi Papers 268, London, 1992; A. Karadawi *Refugee Policy in the Sudan, 1967–1984*, unpublished DPhil thesis, Oxford University, 1988; D. Keen *Rationing the Right to Life: The Crisis in Refugee Relief*, Zed Books, London, 1992. The famines in Ethiopia and Sudan, in particular, contributed to a substantial literature, including: D. Arnold *Famine: Social Crisis and Historical Change*, Blackwell, Oxford, 1988; J. M. Burr and R. O. Collins *Requiem for the Sudan: War, Drought and Disaster Relief on the Nile*, Westview Press, Boulder, CO, 1995; J. Clay and B. Holcomb *Politics and the Ethiopian Famine*, Cultural Survival, Cambridge, MA, 1985; A. de Waal *Famine That Kills: Darfur, Sudan, 1984–85*, Clarendon Press, Oxford, 1989; F. M. Deng *The Challenges of Famine Relief: Emergency Operations in Sudan*, Brookings, Washington, DC, 1992; F. E. Downs, D. O. Kerner and S. P. Reyna (eds) *The Political Economy of African Famine*, Gordon and Breach, Philadelphia,

PA, 1991; *Ethiopia: The Politics of Famine*, Freedom House, New York, 1990; P. Gill *A Year in the Death of Africa*, Paladin, London, 1986; G. Hancock *Ethiopia: The Challenge of Hunger*, Gollancz, London, 1985; G. Hancock *Lords of Poverty*, Mandarin, London, 1991; International Commission on International Humanitarian Issues *Famine: A Man-made Disaster?*, Pan, London, 1985; K. Jansson, M. Harris and A. Penrose *The Ethiopian Famine*, Zed Books, London, 1990; D. Keen *The Benefits of Famine: A Political Economy of Famine Relief in South-western Sudan, 1983–1989*, Princeton University Press, Princeton, NJ, 1994; P. King *An African Winter*, Penguin, Harmondsworth, 1986; S. Maxwell (ed.) *To Cure All Hunger: Food Policy and Security in Sudan*, International Technical Publications, London, 1991; L. Minear *Humanitarianism Under Siege: A Critical Review of Operation Lifeline Sudan*, Red Sea Press, Trenton, NJ, 1991; P. Raikes *Modernising Hunger: Famine, Food Supplies and Farm Policy in the EEC and Africa*, James Currey, London, 1988; A. Sen *Poverty and Famine*, Clarendon Press, Oxford, 1981. Mediation in the Horn has produced far fewer books: H. Assefa *Mediation of Civil Wars: Approaches and Strategies in the Sudan Conflict*, Westview Press, Boulder, CO, 1987; and F. M. Deng and I. W. Zartman (eds) *Conflict Resolution in Africa*, Brookings, London, 1991.

Conclusion

1. S. Bromley *Rethinking Middle East Politics*, Polity Press, Cambridge, 1994, p. 166.

2. J. Migdal *Strong Societies and Weak States*, Princeton University Press, Princeton, NJ, 1988, p. 15.

3. Boutros Boutros-Ghali *An Agenda for Peace*, United Nations, New York, 1992.

Other relevant books for these themes include: A. Adedeji (ed.) *Africa Within the World*, Zed Books, London, 1993; M. R. Berdal *Whither UN Peacekeeping*, Adelphi Paper 281, London, 1993; J. Harbeson, D. Rothchild and N. Chazan *Civil Society and the State in Africa*, Lynne Rienner, Boulder, CO, 1994; B. Neuberger *National Self-determination in Post-colonial Africa*, Lynne Rienner, Boulder, CO, 1986; and J. Wiseman *Democracy in Black Africa*, Paragon, New York, 1990. Human rights issues have generated regular and detailed publications, including those from: Africa Rights; Africa Watch; and Amnesty International.

Index

Abboud, Ibrahim, 38, 40, 120, 134, 151, 152, 184
Abdullahi, Khalifa, 16, 19
Abyssinia, 101
Adam, Hussein, 84
Addis Ababa, 29, 32, 185; agreement, 186, 187, 188, 189, 193
Aden, 15, 152; provision of meat, 26
Aden Treaty, 122, 141, 158, 161
Adowa, battle of, 15, 17
Afar Liberation Front, 113
Afar people, 111, 112, 130
Afewerki, Issayas, 108, 110, 162
Afghanistan, invasion of, 140
Agricultural Marketing Corporation (Ethiopia), 94
agriculture, 32, 98, 100, 109, 168, 175; mechanization of, 48
Ahmed Gran, Imam, 12
aid, 167, 185; agencies, 174, 176, 179, 202
Aideed, Mohamed Farah, 72, 74, 77, 78, 85, 128, 184, 188, 195
AIDS, 145
Akol, Lam, 58
Albania, 96, 101
Algeria, 120, 157
Alier, Abel, 44, 45
All-Africa Council of Churches, 185
Amhara people, 29
Amin, Idi, 153, 155
Andom, Aman, 90, 95, 137, 187; death of, 122
Angola, 173
Ansar Sunna movement (Sudan), 57
Anya Nya guerrillas, 40, 44, 46, 121, 123, 153, 185
Anya Nya II, 50, 51, 53

Aptidon, Hassan Gouled, 111
Arab League, 126, 143, 156, 188
Arab nationalism, 185
Arabism, 120, 150, 151
Arabization, 21, 39, 56, 134
Arap Moi, Daniel, 145
Arkell-Talab company, 179
Asmara, 32
Aswan Dam, 38, 152
el-Atta, Hashim, 43
Axum trading empire, 12, 14
el-Azhari, Ismail, 36–7

Ba'athism, 37, 43
Bab el-Mandeb, 140, 152, 156
Baghdad Pact, 133
Bale revolt, 32
el-Banna, Hassan, 55
Baqqara peoples, 19, 179, 180
Baraawe, 25
BBC film of Ethiopian famine, 176
Beja Congress (Sudan), 37
Beja people, 120
Beni Amer people, 120
Berbera, port of, 25, 26, 138, 140, 168
el-Beshir, Omer, 54
borders: issues of, 82; permeability of, 61
Bosnia, 76
Boutros-Ghali, Boutros, 75, 76, 77, 80, 87, 162, 206, 207, 208
Brezhnev, Leonid, 136
British Somaliland, 27, 33, 35
Brzezinski, Zbigniew, 139
Bush, George, 75, 76, 77, 207

CARE, 176
Carter, Jimmy, 137, 140, 141, 186,

218